Spiegel & Grau

New York

2009

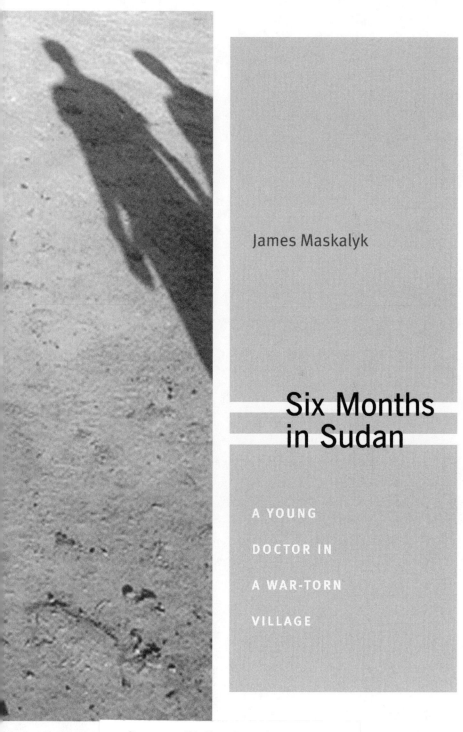

James Maskalyk

Six Months
in Sudan

A YOUNG

DOCTOR IN

A WAR-TORN

VILLAGE

Published in the United States by Spiegel & Grau,
an imprint of The Random House Publishing Group,
a division of Random House, Inc., New York.

The SPIEGEL & GRAU Design is a registered
trademark of Random House, Inc.

Originally published in Canada by Doubleday of Canada,
a division of Random House of Canada Limited.
This edition published by arrangement with Doubleday Canada,
a division of Random House of Canada Limited.

ISBN 978-0-385-52651-7

Printed in the United States of America on acid-free paper

www.spiegelandgrau.com

9 8 7 6 5 4 3 2 1

FIRST U.S. EDITION

Book design by Barbara M. Bachman

FOR AYEN

"I'm not telling you to make the world better, because I don't think that progress is necessarily part of the package. I'm just telling you to live in it. Not just to endure it, not just to suffer it, not just to pass through it, but to live in it. To look at it. To try to get the picture. To live recklessly. To take chances. To make your own work and take pride in it. To seize the moment. And if you ask me why you should bother to do that, I could tell you that the grave's a fine and private place, but none I think do there embrace. Nor do they sing there, or write, or argue, or see the tidal bore on the Amazon, or touch their children. And that's what there is to do and get it while you can and good luck at it."

— Joan Didion
Commencement address at the University of California, Riverside, 1975

Three Areas

Kilometres
0   100   200   300   400   500

These maps were adapted from those supplied by UNEF/GRID-Europe.

SUDAN OIL INDUSTRY

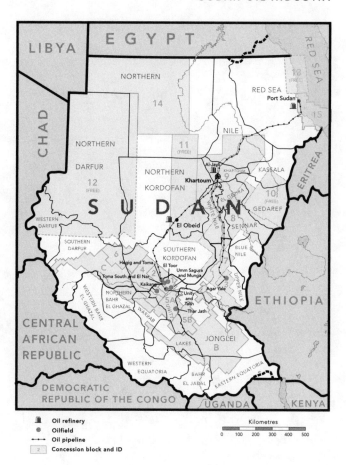

🏭	Oil refinery
●	Oilfield
←•→	Oil pipeline
2	Concession block and ID

Kilometres

0   100   200   300   400   500

AUTHOR'S NOTE

THIS BOOK, AS MUCH AS I can recollect the details, is true. I have attempted to be accurate chronologically with the scenes I have placed between the blog posts, but may be off by as much as a few days. They did, however, occur. The conversations are from my memory, and though their words are conjured, the content is not.

I have changed the names of people in my mission and of the patients I describe. Where patients' details may have made them recognizable, I changed these too: maybe from man to woman, malaria to pneumonia, three years old to seven. Many situations I describe in Abyei are too common to be identifying. Being shot or dying from diarrhea, for instance. Even less so, that these people are now scattered somewhere in Sudan's wide desert.

While I was living my days there, I could not identify what drew so much air out of the place, why everything was imbued with such seriousness. I understand now. Everyone was hushed, listening for war's shaking knock. It came.

Though a current of war runs through each chapter, so does one of home. As it would be for me and you to be driven from the place where we had our first child, or fell into our first love, the thought of return sits heavy in the minds of the people who left Abyei. May they return, may their streets be safe. I dedicate this book to that hope.

There was an online life to this book. There still is. In our growing labyrinthine library, my blog sits somewhere. It makes me glad. It is real in a different way. If you look for it, you can find it. Try sixmonthsinsudan.com.

During my six months in Sudan a young woman on her first MSF mission, Elsa Serfass, was killed by a "random" act of violence in the

Central African Republic, a country suffering from the same lawlessness and surplus of guns as Sudan. I never got a chance to meet her. Many who choose to do this work go wherever they are needed. Most of them come home, but some don't. This is even more true of national staff than it is of expatriates. May we remember and honor their names.

I will give some of my proceeds from this book to Médecins Sans Frontières (also known as Doctors Without Borders) and some towards a fund that will help students from Abyei, if the schools are rebuilt there, to access further education in Sudan.

My time in Abyei was not easy to live through, though worthwhile, nor has it been easy to recount. I am, however, grateful for both opportunities. They have allowed me to stay firm in the world, to make peace with things I may otherwise have tried to ignore.

SIX MONTHS IN SUDAN

THE END

I DECIDED THAT THIS BOOK should start at the end. It is the place I am trying most to understand.

This is it. I am standing in a field watching sparks from a huge bonfire float so high on hot drafts of air that they become stars. It is autumn in upstate New York, and the night is dark and cool. Wedding guests huddle together, white blankets loose over their shoulders. They murmur, point at the fire, then at the sparks.

I am standing by myself, swirling warming wine. A man to whom I had been introduced that night, a friend of the bride, rekindles our conversation. He is talking about an acquaintance, a nurse, who worked during an Ebola outbreak in the Congo years before. He recounts her story of how, after days of watching people die of the incurable virus, she and her team decided that if there was nothing to offer those infected, no treatment, no respite, they would give them a bath. They put on goggles and masks, taped their gloves to their gowns, and cleaned their sick patients.

Before he can go on, I stop him. I can't talk about this.

"I'm sorry. No, no, it's okay. It's nothing you did. I'm going to go inside. Glad to have met you."

I had been back from Sudan for a month. I had worked there as a physician in a small overwhelmed hospital run by the NGO Médecins Sans Frontières. I returned to Toronto sick and exhausted but convinced I was going to make the great escape. I was working in emergency rooms again, surrounded by friends. Things would be like always.

In this field of cold grass, where hours before my friends had been married, I heard ten seconds of a story, and during them realized there were things I had not reckoned on.

It was the taping of the gloves. The whine of the white tape as it stretched around their wrists, forming a seal between their world and the bleeding one in front of them. I could imagine the grimness with which it was done, could see the flat faces of the doctors and nurses as they stepped into the room.

As he was talking, I cast back to the measles outbreak that was just starting as I arrived in Abyei. One day we had two patients with measles in the hospital, the next day four, the next nine, the next fifteen. The rising tide of the epidemic soon swept over us.

I rewound to a film loop of me kneeling on the dirt floor of the long hut we had built out of wood and grass to accommodate the surge of infected people. I was kneeling beside the bed of an infant who was feverish and had stopped drinking. I was trying, with another doctor, to find a vein. The baby's mother sat helpless on the bed as we poked holes in her child. She was crying. She wanted us to stop. Small pearls of blood dotted his neck, his groin. We failed, his breathing worsened, and he died. I stood up, threw the needles in the sharps container, and walked away to attend someone else. Behind me his mother wailed. I can see my flat face.

Who was that person? I am not sure if I know him, not sure that I want to.

People who do this type of work talk about the rupture we feel on our return, an irreconcilable invisible distance between us and others. We talk about how difficult it is to assimilate, to assume routine, to sample familiar pleasures. Though I could convince myself that the fissure was narrow enough to be ignored, it only took a glance to see how dizzyingly deep it was.

The rift, of course, is not in the world: it is within us. And the distance is not only ours. We return from the field, from an Ebola outbreak or violent clashes in Sudan, with no mistake about how the world is. It is a hard place—a beautiful place, but so too an urgent one. And we realize that all of us, through our actions or inactions, make it what it is. The people I left behind in Sudan don't need us to help them towards a health system that can offer immunizations—they need the vaccine. Fucking yesterday. Once that urgency takes hold, it never completely lets go.

Just as our friends wonder at our distance from their familiar world, we marvel at theirs from the real one. We feel inhabited by it. We plan our return.

I have done this work before, but I have never looked back. Now I will. I am going to wear that flat face again, toss and turn in a tangled bed. But I also will feel, for the second time, the cool relief when a child I had bet everything on started to recover, to stand close to the young soldier who volunteered to give blood to a woman he didn't know, to visit again the members of my small team. Some of the work in repairing the world is grim; much of it is not. Hope not only meets despair in equal measure, it drowns it.

This book started as a blog that I wrote from my hut in Sudan. It was my attempt to communicate with my family and friends, to help bring them closer to my hot, hot days. It was also a chance to tell the story of Abyei, Sudan, a torn, tiny place straddling a contested border in a difficult country. Mostly, though, it was where I told a story about humans: the people from Abyei who suffered its hardships because it was their home, and those of us who left ours with tools to make it easier for them to endure. It is a story that could be told about many places.

The blog became popular. Part of me wants to believe it was because of my writing, but that's not it. It is because people are hungry to be brought closer to the world, even its hard parts. I went to Sudan, and am writing about it again, because I believe that which separates action from inaction is the same thing that separates my friends from Sudan. It is not indifference. It is distance. May it fall away.

So, this is where I stand, at the end. In the dewy grass, sparks stretching to the sky. It is cold away from the fire, and I shiver. In the distance I can see light bursting from the farmhouse door. Inside, people are dancing. I thrust my hands into my pockets and walk across the field, away from the end, towards the beginning.

THE BEGINNING

I T WAS MY MISTAKE. The beginning was not that clear. It fooled me again and again. It was like preparing for a marathon. You think it starts on the day you decide to do it, when you lace up your shoes for the first time, step outside, and look at your watch. But soon it is the day of the race, and that is the beginning. But no, here you are shuffling to the starting line with a thousand others, high with anticipation. This must be it. Then, the shot.

The real beginning of Sudan, for me, was when I dropped my bags into the dust of compound 1, looked around me, and saw no one. That was the moment, that was the starter's pistol. Go.

The larger story, the soft bookends to my time in Sudan, began when I was twenty-three years old, a medical student between my first and second year. Most of my friends were taking vacations or were busy in Canadian hospitals, trying to add lines to their CVs, when I stepped onto a flight to Santiago, Chile. I had received money to support a six-week international rotation and was looking to impress my older girlfriend. It was my first time anywhere that was somewhere else.

On my first day of work there, I hung off the back of a bus headed towards a public hospital and reluctantly handed my fare to the person next to me. Minutes later, my change and ticket were returned, passed hand to hand through the crowd. It was at that hospital that I saw a man whose fingers were so heavy with gout, so knotted, that he couldn't pick up a coffee cup. I was working with a cardiologist who spent his days employed in a public system where families tried to find someone with a credit card to finance their grandfather's angioplasty. At nights, he traveled to private hospitals to consult on the health of the wealthy so he could send his children to university. I went home convinced that if I was being trained to take care of the sickest, they surely were in other places.

For my residency, I chose emergency medicine because it would give me the widest set of skills and wouldn't require me to have a patient practice. I would leave no one in a lurch when I left Canada for weeks at a time.

The story started in rural Cambodia four years after Chile, when I spent a month alone, as a new medical resident, conducting medical clinics in the morning and a needs assessment in the afternoon, trying to understand the health needs in a group of recently surrendered Khmer Rouge. I arrived at the Phnom Penh airport with a backpack full of donated pills, and a letter from the commander of the valley guaranteeing my safety. I drove south with a borrowed translator in a borrowed Land Cruiser and found fourteen thousand people who had exchanged one struggle for another. Instead of fighting the government, they were fighting to carve rice fields from the jungle. It was there I ate my first meal surrounded by starving people, there I saw a woman whose breast cancer had pushed through her skin and to whom I had nothing to give but acetaminophen, there that I walked out of my guest house to find food and stumbled over the feverish body of a woman nearly dead from HIV left at my door, like a cat would a mouse. Overwhelmed and alone, I first discovered my helplessness in a world beyond my control.

I returned to Cambodia two years later to set up a university project that would introduce new doctors to the medicine of poverty. I looked at a heaving shelf stacked with reports on reports of how Cambodians should address their own health and realized that as the one with the resources, it was my privilege to waste them. I set up a meeting with a Cambodian health official and asked what he would have me do.

After I graduated from my specialty training, I heeded the advice of a teacher who told me not to let my lifestyle expand to accommodate my potential income. I rented a small apartment in Toronto and rode my bicycle to the emergency room. I made it six months before leaving for Bolivia, then to southern Africa, to write about the neglected diseases Médecins Sans Frontières was treating. I found a community of people carrying dusty bags with whom I shared sympathies and space. I learned that the larger question of these diseases, whether HIV or Chagas, was not how best the world could help those affected but whether we would appreciate our capacity to do so. No matter how many hollow zeros were added to the death toll, my family and neighbors could not understand what the numbers measured because they could not feel the consequences. The response to the tsunami was profound because the size of the wave could be measured by the height of the boat in the tree. If I presumed to work on distant problems, and to write about them, that's what I had to show.

The story started when I was standing in a customs line, waiting to board the plane to Germany for pre-departure training with MSF, when my friend Matt called and asked why I had decided to go. I told him I wanted to see who I was when everything was taken away, when all the insulation between the world and me was removed.

It started when I arrived in Germany and shared my room with three African men. We stayed up late and talked about what we looked for in women and laughed at how different our tastes were. Later that week, we sat and calculated how much plastic sheeting we would need if our team found a hundred thousand refugees on our doorstep. And in a classroom in Bonn, with thirty others bound for different places, I was told for the first time that I could expect to come back different, that my friends wouldn't want to talk about the things that I would, that I would have less in common with them than ever before.

I was sitting on the hard plastic chair outside my friend's office in Toronto, waiting for him to get off the phone. My cellphone buzzed in my pocket and I looked at the display. It read "MSF Toronto." On the other end was the human resources officer asking if I would accept a mission in Darfur, a mission with only men, a mobile one with security risks. I left the building, got on my bicycle, rode through leaf-filled alleys, and asked myself what I was willing to lose. I got home, read the Joan Didion quote that appears at the front of this book, and decided that I might as well risk it all.

Two months after the Darfur mission fell through because of security concerns, deep in the Canadian winter, about to make other plans, I checked my email during a lull in an evening emergency shift and saw a subject line that said only, "Sudan?"

I read the profile:

MEDICAL DOCTOR
ABYEI project-MSF-SWITZERLAND
Southern Kordofan-SUDAN

Requirements
- Special knowledge:
  -Reproductive health and minor surgery highly
   recommended.
  -Tropical Medicine
- Special qualities:
  -Psychological strength
  -Interest to work in remote environments

It started when I sent back the message "yes."

I stood on the porch of the house where I had been allowed to quietly come and go over my last few uncertain months in Toronto waiting for a mission, and shared an uncomfortable hug with Steve. He was leaving on a vacation, and we wouldn't see each other until I returned. He walked towards the fence and, before he reached it, spun around and took a few steps back. "It's like the last days of disco," he said, turned, and clattered the gate shut.

My final night in Canada, I walked through a skiff of new snow, my arm laced with Sarah's. Though I'd been home the last few months, my heart was not. I wanted no ties. My departure seemed like a convenient breaking point for us, at least to me. We arrived at a bar full with my friends gathered for a birthday party. "So when are you going?" one of them asked, as uncertain as I was from my flightless holding pattern. "Soon," I said. I lingered by the bar, sipping a beer, and after a few minutes caught Sarah's eye. We spent a last night together in my borrowed home.

I woke up alone. I could hear Sarah. In the shower now, now on the stairs. The door creaked open, paused. Creaked shut. Gate clattered. I swung my feet onto the cold hardwood floor. The house was silent. I got dressed and walked downstairs. My packed bags were by the door, and I moved them to the snowy porch. I turned the lock for a final time, then dropped the keys in the mailbox. I had no home. I was free.

The story started when I was sitting on the plane, flying from snowy Canada to snowy Switzerland, my backpack wedged in the luggage hold below me, writing a letter.

12/02: jet plane.

in the airport, finally on my way. i have been waiting for a beginning for some time, not knowing where or when it would come. it's here.

of the many lessons i thought i might learn with this, i knew one would be: "be careful what you wish. you might get it."

i said i would go anywhere, that i wasn't afraid of being isolated, that i had a wide complement of medical skills and could do a little of everything. i could work in a small team with little backup, improvise if necessary. if there was a time in my life where i could go to a place that required close attention to security, it was now. no wife, no kids, no house, no debt, no one waiting for me to get back.

so, i wished, then got it. i am off to sudan. a small town in the middle of the country, right on the border between north and south. for those with a grander memory of the struggle there, you will know that it has been at war for decades. much of it is between the south and the north. it is a conflict about resources. and allegiances. and history.

darfur has become a media story, particularly in the past three years. there the war rages on, and the fighting is vicious. but sudan has rarely been at peace since its independence in 1956. it has more people displaced from their homes, because of conflict, than any other place in the world. most of them are from southern sudan where war still smolders. the people there feel deeply the effects of chronic conflict. for a nation, it is like a chronic disease. one wastes away from thousands of tiny insults.

the place that i am going is called abyei. you can check it out on google earth. it looks like a smudge in the sand. it sits in an area claimed by both sides but owned by neither. tensions, i have been told, are high.

i will be working in a small hospital with a small team. the patients will be regular size. the mission is a new one, and there isn't much infrastructure. aside from that, i know little else. i will find out more in geneva.

boarding now. i learned something else these past few months: one shouldn't think with certainty about the future. it has helped see me through.

that's it for me. boarded. wine service. better take it while i can get it. soon, suddenly, sudan.

ARRIVED IN GENEVA on an overnight flight and stood sleepless, blinking under bright lights. I hefted my two bags from the circular parade of black cases and looked at the clock. I was overdue at the MSF office with still a train to catch.

This is the way it works in MSF as a volunteer: you are either in or you're not, you buy it or you don't. You take public transit and stay in hostels. You brief sleepless and fly economy. An unnecessary dollar spent on you is one less for the field.

I put my backpack on and tightened the straps until it felt snug and weightless, then stopped at a kiosk to get a train schedule. Minutes later, the Swiss countryside was blurring beside me.

I walked from the train station, with my backpack on and my suitcase rolling behind. The office was twenty minutes away by foot. Geneva was temperate, its streets bare of snow. Taxicabs slowed beside me and honked. I waved them on.

On a final corner sat a building draped in scaffolding, and behind bright metal bones a banner shouted: "Malaria!" I pushed through the glass doors and into a hallway lined with posters. One showed a pill set like a jewel into a gold ring; another decried rape in the Congo. People walked past them, talking loudly, papers under their arms. A woman with a large backpack on edged past me and out the door. I walked to the front desk. The woman behind it hung up the phone to have it ring again. I smiled and waited.

On a whiteboard beside her was written a list of names and countries: people leaving on mission, people coming home. Mine sat misspelled in the "Out" column and, beside it in brackets, "MD North Sudan." When she was done, I pointed at it.

"That's me."

She looked down at her busy desk. On it was a piece of paper with names and times: my briefing schedule. She handed it to me. At the top was: "James Maskalyk MD (Sudan) Stay in Geneva: 12.02.07 to ????"

She showed me to a room where I could store my things. It was full of luggage. People leaving, people coming home. The walls were lined with rows and rows of gray plastic boxes, on their mouths written "DRC" or "Mozambique" or "Myanmar." Inside some were letters, or small bound parcels making their way to the field. They were grouped together geographically. I traced my finger from Asia to Africa, from South to North, and next to "Tschad" sat a box labeled "Northern Sudan." I shook it. It was empty. I stepped from the room and closed the door.

I sat in meeting after meeting, sleep headache bunched behind my eyes, and tried to concentrate. Facts that were meant to illuminate my days, the course of my months, were laid out before me. I was told about life on mission, how one should behave around alcohol, around drugs, about the perils of sleeping with one's team members. I was given the layout of the hospital, the pattern of pathology, the hierarchy of responsibility. I was told about the diseases I would see, ones that my medical training rarely touched, ones I had encountered mostly in textbooks. Malaria, tuberculosis, guinea worm. In my satchel was a sheaf of papers I had already printed off, some on leishmaniasis, some on leprosy.

I would have no access to x-rays in Abyei, no basic lab tests. The nearest surgeon was three hours away, and the road to him was not always safe. I would be expected to birth babies and handle trauma. I was asked if I would perform an abortion if it was medically necessary. I said that I would.

I was responsible for the Sudanese people in the hospital, but so too the expatriates on my team. I was told that the doctor I was replacing was leaving after only three months to pursue a master's. I wondered how many master's started in March.

During my last meeting of the day, I learned more about Abyei. The project was the crucible where North meets South. In a peace agreement signed two years before, the one that ended Africa's longest, bloodiest war, it was agreed that the Abyei question would be settled later. Soldiers from each side faced each other across an invisible divide and between them sat the hospital. And our compound. And soon, me.

Everything around Abyei was a vacuum built by twenty years of guns. One that both sides, South and North, were trying to get people from all over Sudan to fill in preparation for a referendum that was to determine Abyei's fate, and with it the destiny of Sudan.

There were a few other NGOs in the area, and a large UN mission. Together we were in the middle of nowhere. Us and thousands of Sudanese people returning to make a home where there was none; canaries in a coal mine.

I shook my head clear. I was in the security briefing with the operational director. This was important. I should write this down.

Where's a pen?

"All right. Well, I guess the biggest risk is full-scale war. Not very likely at the moment, but it can change quickly. Okay?"

"Okay."

"Things in that area are very tense. It is a very important area for both sides. Historically, but mostly because that is where most of the oil fields are, okay?"

"Okay."

"I haven't been there. Not yet. It's still pretty new. So far there has been no real fighting. A few small skirmishes, some gunfire, nothing too hectic. The North and the South take this place very seriously, and are very much in control of the militia. Not like Darfur. You'll be given more specific details in Khartoum."

"Okay."

I looked at what I had written. "War" and "oil." That should be helpful.

In Germany during my pre-departure training, I had watched colleagues get phone calls or emails ("I'm going to Sri Lanka!" or "They offered me Myanmar!"), and silently crossed my fingers for a place at war. I took French lessons so that I might end up in Congo, or Chad. I read books about Sudan.

The country was at war, and had been for years. The conflict had not ended, it had shifted fronts. Currently it was Sudan's western province of Darfur that was on fire. In Abyei, for now, the fighting had stopped, and in its place was a shaky truce. I was going to where I wanted to be. Close to war and its consequences.

Pushed by the sharp thrill of being somewhere new and rare and exciting, pushed towards that free feeling where anything can happen. Pulled because I wanted to understand. I understood the blind actions of large companies because they were a multiplication, a millionfold, of a greed I knew, stripped of accountability. I appreciated the wisdom of the Red Cross's silence because I have, at least briefly, known patience. I valued MSF's vigor and indignation because I understood outrage at injustice. But war, I didn't know it. Not yet. Not well. But it's in me somewhere.

I think there is at least one other reason I wanted to be in its way. As a new medical student, I was in the hospital one afternoon, sitting in a small, windowless room with a man and a woman, my teacher behind me. We had discovered a tiny tumor in the woman's brain. It had spread from a cancer in her lung she didn't know she had. It was incurable. I was going to tell her. Minutes before, my teacher and I had sat at an Arborite desk in the nursing lounge as he explained how best to deliver bad news.

"I have some serious news. You have an aggressive form of cancer," I said. "It is very advanced. It must have spread quickly. We'll do everything we can, but at this point there seems little chance of cure. I'm so sorry."

I watched the color wash from her face. Her husband sat beside her like a stone. And I, for the first time, understood that though I was living, I was also dying. I have never forgotten it.

Because of that, part of me wants to walk towards it.

AFTER TWO DAYS OF BRIEFINGS, they were nearly done. My last meeting was with a woman in the communications department. I explained to her my intention to write a blog, and my hope that it would allow a different exposition of life in the field. It would be insistent, rough, and fresh. It would fit our mandate of *témoignage*, of bearing witness. MSF Canada was fully supportive, had set up space on their web page that could be updated by text email, even by SMS. I was going to be the first to try it out.

The communications liaison was reluctant. She explained to me that an MSF worker, the year before, had kept a blog in Sudan. In it, she had come out heavily in favor of the Darfurians, and labeled the Khartoum government complicit in the tragedy playing out there. It was an unwise public declaration when our presence depended on the permission of the northern Sudanese government. All of our visas, all of our supplies, most of our national staff were passed under Khartoum's watchful eye. It was an administration known for its attention to details.

Anything I posted would be read not only by my family and friends but by Khartoum. That was certain. And if they perceived we were interfering in their activities, they might begin to interfere with ours.

I said I would take great care. I had been briefed in Canada by the communications department, and was aware of the risks for my team as well as for MSF in a country known for its resistance to outsiders. My interest was not in telling the political story, not exactly. It was detailing the medicine of poverty. Readers could draw what conclusions they wanted. I passed to her the URL of the few posts I had written so far. She promised to read them.

"I haven't been to Abyei yet," she said. "Hope to get there. It's difficult, though. Good luck."

I stood up from her desk and walked upstairs to my last order of business. The administration desk for Sudan was on the wide second floor, in the middle of a cubicle maze. It was covered in papers and passports and its phone rang incessantly.

Behind it sat Catherine; beside her, a map of eastern Africa. Thick black strokes carried out from its different countries, each ending in a flower of passport-size photographs. From Darfur, three lines arrived at a field of pictures and names. From the center of Sudan, a lonely mark arced out past the edge of the paper and stopped at a label that read "Abyei." Surrounding it were five small faces. The team. A field coordinator, a logistician, an administrator, a nurse, and the doctor I was due to replace. I leaned closer.

Catherine hung up the phone. I smiled and handed her my photo. She took a piece of tape, doubled it over, fixed it to the back, and pushed me into Abyei's orbit.

"Your visa's still not ready. We can never tell with the Sudan embassy. Especially Abyei. People have waited for weeks. Keep checking back."

I left her to a ringing phone and went downstairs to the library. I grabbed a book on meningitis from the shelf and sat down on one of the rough couches in the middle of the room. A woman sat down beside me and folded her arms unhappily. She was short, her blond hair pulled back in a loose ponytail.

By this point, after even my few days in and out of the MSF office, it was obvious who was on their way to the field and who was coming from it. Those who were leaving were well dressed and curious, their eyes full of questions. Those coming home wore their months on drawn faces, curiosity stamped out.

"Where are you going?" I asked.

"Sorry?"

"What country are you going to?"

"Sudan. I'm a midwife."

"Yeah, I'm going to Sudan too. Doctor. Darfur?"

"No, I was supposed to go to a place called Abyei. But they just refused my visa. Khartoum said they don't need any more midwives. I'm going back to Italy."

"Oh. Shit. I'm supposed to go to Abyei too."

"Do you deliver babies?" she asked.

"Not if I can help it."

"Well, you'll have to. It's a mess there. They have no midwives at all, not at all. But what can I do?"

"Sorry."

"Yes."

She stood up.

"Hey, my name's James."

"Antonia."

"Well, I hope I see you down there soon," I said.

"Maybe. Who knows. And I hope you're not wasting your time. Ciao."

One day passed, then two, then three. I would walk to the office and stand meekly in front of Catherine's desk until she acknowledged me with a shake of her head that meant "not yet." I would give her my email address again, or remind her of the phone number of the guest house. The rest of the time I wandered Geneva's streets or sat in my small room, reading about tuberculosis and staring at the blank brick wall.

It became Friday. No word. The embassy closed at noon, and if my passport wasn't returned by then, I would be in Geneva at least another weekend.

I looked at my watch. Ten to twelve. I steeled myself for Catherine's frustration at my insistence, and picked up the phone.

16/02: visa.

my visa has come through. i am going to pick it up at 5 o'clock, the end of the day. i leave tomorrow at 5 a.m. for khartoum. the midwife had her visa refused. apparently sudan is happy with the quality of deliveries in abyei and feels that there is no need for further expertise. wait until they get a load of me. the red carpet will stretch all the way to europe.

i do have a few tricks up my sleeve. one of them is that one with the fake hand, where you greet the woman and say "hi, i'm dr. maskalyk" then turn away leaving her holding the hand. i use it to scare them out of labor.

this morning, half asleep, i stumbled into the hallway of my tiny hotel and ran headlong into a man my age holding a toothbrush. "dentifrice?" he asked. i returned to my room and found him some toothpaste. we chatted. he was with msf too. most of us in this place are. it's like a halfway house. we are either halfway gone, or halfway home.

he is a logistician. he was on his first mission in guinea-conakry, but was evacuated a few days ago, after only two months in the country. guinea is at war with itself. the government has recently imposed a 20-hour curfew to deal with increasingly violent protests. msf treated 275 wounded in the capital over the weekend. neither of us knows what has happened since.

"what now for you?" i asked.

"no plans. no idea. good luck," he said and turned away.

FIVE O'CLOCK. CATHERINE was gone but on her desk was an envelope with my name on it. In it were my passport and ticket. I walked down the stairs and out the sliding doors of the MSF office.

On my way back to my hostel, I stopped at a pharmacy to pick up tablets for malaria, and next door purchased a package of Gauloises. I had decided to start smoking. Restart. I knew I would have company in Sudan. Cigarettes were tools. They marked minutes. The downside is that they're not easy to like. I needed practice.

My passport felt heavy in my pocket as I climbed the steps to my room and let myself in. My suitcase was laid wide on the floor. In it were many of the things I had been carrying around with me for the last two months, from place to place, from Germany to Brazil to Toronto to here. I had been through it, packing and unpacking, then again, trying to pare down what I needed even further. The flight to the field, from Khartoum to Abyei, I would be allowed only 15 kilograms of luggage. I grabbed my stack of books, hefted them up and down. About 5 kilograms. My computer was 2. Halfway.

I took a cigarette from my pocket, lit it, and sat down in the middle of my scattered belongings.

There was no way to tell what would start tomorrow. I could not see Khartoum, could not make that place real. Tomorrow it would fall up at me from the ground, and once I landed, I would be met at the airport and the work would begin. I stood and picked from the wastebasket a map of Geneva given to me on my arrival, and smoothed it flat. I put my jacket on, slipped the Gauloises in my pocket, and went down to the street.

Hours later, back beside my bags, I started to put things back in, layer on layer. I stacked my books at the bottom of my backpack, and on them my camera, a set of small speakers, and the balance of my clothes. I set my running shoes on top.

It was nearly 2 a.m. I was to be picked up in three hours. I undressed and lay in bed. My mind swam in circles. I looked at the clock: 3 a.m. I imagined blackness.

My alarm went off. I dressed, put my backpack on, and clunked my suitcase down the stairs. A car was waiting for me, and in the back seat was a tall black man. He stepped from it and offered me his hand.

"Ajak. Just ended my mission as field coordinator in Congo. Going home to Nairobi," he said.

"James. From Canada," I said as I loaded my luggage into the trunk. "I'll be in Sudan tomorrow. I'm on my way to Abyei."

"Oh?" he said, brightening. "My family is from there. Ajak Deng. Mention my name. People will know me."

I took a pen from my pocket and wrote it down.

"Are they all as tall as you?"

"Yes," he said, and opened the car door for me.

"Just a minute. I'll be right back."

I ran upstairs, took my coat off, and left it hanging on the back of a kitchen chair for someone halfway home. I vaulted back down the stairs, stepped into the open car door, and the vehicle rolled away.

THE OVERHEAD announcement woke me.

"Ladies and gentlemen, we have begun our descent into Khartoum. In preparation for arrival please ensure that your cabin luggage is stowed in the overhead bins or under the seat in front of you and your chairs and table trays are returned to their upright and locked position. The local time is 9 p.m. The temperature in Khartoum tonight is 95 degrees Fahrenheit."

I looked around me. The plane was full. It would continue on to Ethiopia after a stop in Sudan, and I tried, with a glance, to guess who would be stepping off the gangplank with me.

Some were obvious. Men dressed in long tunics and white kufi hats glanced at their watches and set the time. Others were less clear. Two Europeans sat in the row in front of me. I tried to catch their eyes a few times, but could not.

The plane slowed to a halt and I stood up. Few others did. In total, eleven of us, in a plane of a hundred, pushed past the other passengers towards the door. Whatever business was being done in this country, it was largely closed to the world.

The door opened, and with it, desert air blew in as from a bellows. For a cold-loving Canadian who, when he was a child, would clear a pond and fire pucks at his little brother in below-zero temperatures and return red and exhilarated only when they had lost all the pucks in the snow, it was an unavoidable embrace.

We stepped down the stairs and onto the tarmac. Row on row of white planes, bare except for the black UN stencil, sat silent: a plane graveyard. It would not be the last time I marveled at the immense resources the United Nations poured into Sudan, nor at its rows of idle machines.

On a bus to the airport terminal, the Europeans chatted with one another, or on their phones, old hands.

We stood silently by the luggage carousel and waited for it to turn. I pulled my MSF shirt from my satchel and put it on. Bags rolled onto the rubber conveyor belt, and one by one, people grabbed theirs and walked towards the exit, mobile phones to their ear. Mine came and I followed. I took my sheaf of documents from my bag and presented them to the uniformed man behind the customs counter. He barely acknowledged me. Midway through his bored inspection of my papers, a man walked past, stood in front of me, and clapped the customs guard on the shoulder. The guard broke into a smile and rose to give him an embrace. They spoke brightly in Arabic for a few minutes, laughing and gesturing. I was forgotten. Any importance to my arrival was in my own mind.

Their exchange finished, the guard cast a flat glance at me and waved me through with a flick of his fingers. Next. Next person trying to save the world.

Past the swinging door, a Sudanese man held an MSF sign. I walked up to him and smiled. He smiled back, gestured for my suitcase.

"MSF Swiss?" I asked.

"Oh. No. MSF Spain," he answered, looking over my shoulder. He waved at someone, stepped past, and grabbed a blue duffel bag from a man behind me. They walked out of the airport, duffel swinging between them.

I sat in the airport hall for half an hour, backpack and suitcase at my feet, and watched it empty. Soon I was alone. I wondered if I had misunderstood my instructions. I slung my satchel to the front and put my backpack on. Rolling my suitcase behind me, I walked out of the airport, past its single shop selling fragrances and chocolates labeled with looping Arabic script, and into the warm Khartoum night.

On the step of the airport, leaning on a signpost, a man with an MSF shirt was smoking and talking to a friend.

"MSF Swiss?" I asked.

"Yes. Dr. James?"

"Yes."

He grabbed my suitcase and hefted it into the box of a nearby pickup truck. I threw my backpack beside it and climbed into the passenger seat.

"Where do we go?" I asked.

"Guest house."

We pulled out of the parking lot, past rows and rows of white cars and onto the street.

"Where are we?" I asked. "In the city, I mean."

He smiled at me, then made the "small small" sign with his thumb and finger. No English. I rolled down my window and lit a cigarette.

We turned onto a road several lanes wide, separated by a broken and crumbling median. Traffic was dense and moving slowly. We edged through it towards a dark laneway. A final corner and the truck lights swept across an empty lot. At one end, a pile of garbage smoldered beside the steel skeleton of an abandoned car. The truck rolled to a halt.

I pulled my bags from the truck and set them on the ground. The driver handed me an envelope. Inside it were a thick bundle of Sudanese dinars, a form letter explaining which room I was to sleep in, and a briefing schedule for the following day. I thanked the driver with my only Arabic word, and stepped into the black guest house. It was mine alone. I dropped my bags in my room and lay down on a foam mattress, pressed flat from all of the backs before me.

—

I WAS PICKED UP the next morning and taken to the MSF office. The sun, at 8 a.m., was already intense. I tried to memorize the route the car took so I could walk it alone.

The sky was cloudless. Above the low buildings in all directions were slender minarets. We ground slowly past an empty dirt lot, broken bits of concrete mounded at each end to form football nets. Sand gusted across it, billowing plastic bags in whirling circles. We turned right and continued straight on our dirt path until it crossed a tarmac one. Just beyond it was a school, a type of university. Women wearing fine headscarves sat together fanning themselves with their textbooks; men walked arm in arm, talking and smiling. No one looked at us. The car stopped.

On a white metal gate was the MSF emblem. In front of it were two cars, each marked with the same red dashes. I got out and opened the metal door to a courtyard, and past it was the Khartoum office of MSF Switzerland.

I was greeted at the front desk by the Sudanese receptionist. She asked for the papers I carried from home and handed them to another woman who quickly left the office. There were several iterations of travel permission in Sudan. I needed a visa to enter the country, another to travel to specific places within it, and a third to leave. There were stories of people waiting in Khartoum for weeks both on their way to the field and coming from it. I was told in Geneva that because of political sensitivities, a travel permit for Abyei was very difficult to get, and to expect delays.

The office was large, and on two floors. At the entrance, row on row of boxes sat, the names of projects written on their rims. Of the projects administered by this office, mine was the only one not in Darfur. In the box for Abyei sat three manila envelopes. I put them in my bag.

I waited in the foyer for my first meeting, with Brian, the head of mission. I picked up a month-old newspaper, its headlines shouting at the mistruths contained in a recent NGO report detailing violence in Darfur. Propaganda. I set it down.

On the wall behind me was a corkboard of faces, everyone who had been through these doors, sat in this chair, read these papers, and headed off to the field. There were about forty, some yellowed from the heat, some smiling, others stern. I recognized one of them. Someone I went to medical school with? I wasn't sure. I couldn't place the name. Perhaps she was married now. As I studied her face, she grew less familiar.

"Dr. James? Brian will see you now."

I was pointed upstairs. There was a broad door with "Head of Mission" stenciled on it in black. I knocked. A tall man, my age and with curly hair, opened the door and gestured me in. He was talking on a cellphone, his accent Australian. He smiled and held up a finger.

As head of mission, he was the person most responsible for MSF activities in the country. It was his job to liaise with the coordination center in Geneva and the field to ensure that the mission was fulfilling its mandate and adhering to humanitarian principles. As the most prominent face of the organization in the country, the position required political skill and experience. Particularly in Sudan.

His analogue in the field was the field coordinator, Bev. Her function was to see that the objectives were carried out on the ground, her attention to security one objective lens closer. She had less interest in the larger political tableau, and instead had a closer relationship with local military commanders and community leaders. If violence flared in Abyei, the discussion about whether to evacuate would be between the two of them.

Brian finished on the phone and offered me his hand.

"Glad to meet you, James. And that you could come on such short notice."

"No problem. Glad to be on my way somewhere."

"Have a seat. So. What brings you to Sudan?"

I sat down and told him my story.

In turn, he told me his. He was a general practitioner, trained in

Australia. He had worked in Sudan for several years, first in the field as a physician in the South, during the long war. He knew it well and had worked closely with the population of people I would be working most with, the Dinka.

"You'll know the Dinka. Dark skin, tall. Like six feet at least. Even the women. Some of them have ritual scars on their foreheads and faces."

Until the war came, the severe geography of Sudan isolated them from the rest of the world. A desert in the summer, in the winter full of swamps, mosquitoes, malaria. Many were nomads, and traveled with the seasons.

Abyei was home to another group, the Misseriya. They were Muslim, had lighter skin, spoke and wrote Arabic. They too moved with the rains. They came to Abyei in November or December and stayed until the wet season that started in June. We tried, as MSF, to employ people evenly from both groups.

The two tribes had lived in the area for generations. They would trade with each other, sometimes even marry. Occasionally a fight would erupt over grazing land, or the theft of cattle, and some men would go to war. Since it was in neither side's interest to perpetuate conflict, tribal leaders would mediate a solution.

The British, in their flight from colonialism in the fifties, left a Sudan united in name only. Khartoum, in the North, with greater ties to northern Africa and the Middle East, remained the focus of power, and it soon became clear that it had no intention of sharing with the South. A civil war began shortly after the British left, and ended with the Addis Ababa agreement in 1972, and with hundreds of thousands dead or displaced. It was a short respite. In 1983, in response to an edict that the Khartoum government intended to make Sudan an Islamic Arab state, fighting started again. It was much heavier this time because the SPLA was formed, uniting southern resistance.

"You know the SPLA?" Brian asked.

"Yeah. Sudan People's Liberation Army. John Garang and all that."

"Exactly. And the SPLM is their political arm."

Now war was brought to even more of the South, but in a different way. Tribal militias were used, particularly around Abyei, and exploited traditional differences. Groups like the Dinka and Misseriya, used to occasional conflicts, now found themselves part of a greater one, one with planes and guns, one with no end in sight. And this time, civilians were targeted. Villages were burned to the ground, hundreds of thousands of people fled, took nothing. Many went to Ethiopia, or Kenya. Many, even the Dinka, went north to Khartoum. It was safer there, right next to the enemy, than it was in their own homes.

"Anyway, the North didn't care. It just wanted fewer soldiers in the South. Got it?"

"Uh-huh."

"So, basically, the South doesn't have much of anything. Never really did. That's what they were fighting about. They have land, but no infrastructure. Whatever there was the war knocked out. The rest of it has been built piecemeal by NGOs and the UN. So they're hungry."

"Right."

"Okay, last piece. When you fly to Abyei, you will pass over two straight things on the ground. One will be the road to El Obeid. The other will be an oil pipeline, built by the Chinese, running from the oil fields around Abyei to the Port of Sudan. Full of oil around there."

"Oh."

In 2005, a peace agreement was signed, and both sides agreed to stop fighting and establish an administrative border that would allow the South to function autonomously. Except. Three areas were not delineated as belonging to either North or South: the Nuba mountains, the Blue Nile State, and Abyei. Abyei was the most contentious. There was to be a referendum in 2011 that would decide whether it would belong to the South or to the North. In anticipation of it, people were being encouraged to return. By both sides. They were being told they would find schools, a hospital, that they should build a tukul—a hut— for themselves and one for another family. When they arrived, they saw that there wasn't much of anything.

Both sides have their armies in town and militias in the surrounding countryside. There were soldiers from the North, SAF—Sudan Alliance Forces—and the SPLA. There were also some from the JIU, the

Joint Integration Unit, a combination of forces from both sides, intended to allow the SPLA and SAF to withdraw.

"They're not, though. Neither side seems ready to back down."

"Right."

"When we did our exploratory mission there, we thought there might be as many as a hundred thousand civilians coming this year, but there haven't been that many. But we'll see. Maybe people are afraid to come back. We don't quite know. Anyway, that's why we're there. Any questions?"

Yes . . . what? Holy shit.

"Um. What is the compound like?"

"Pretty basic. Everyone has their own tukul. No cellphone, no Internet, no electricity. Power is from a generator. There is a sat phone, satellite email. You'll see. Anything else?"

His phone started to ring. I shook my head.

"All right. Well, I'm around." He stood up. "You'll get more details in the field from Bev. She's good. She's non-medical so she'll need your help with the hospital and stuff, but she really knows what's happening on the ground."

"All right."

"You're meeting with Marc next, right? He's our medical coordinator. He's across the hall."

I shook Brian's hand, walked to the facing door. I knocked. It was answered by a thin man wearing wire glasses, in his hand a cigarette.

"Come in, James. Come in, come in. Please. Take a seat," he said in a round French accent, gesturing towards a chair.

"Thank you."

"Sorry. The air conditioner is not working."

"It's all right."

"Well, let's get to business."

This meeting was longer. We sat and smoked at his broad wooden desk, fan spinning lazily above us, as he outlined the main areas of my medical responsibility. First, I would be responsible for all of the inpatients in the hospital, and all emergencies. I would be supervising one Sudanese MD, newly graduated, and two Sudanese medical technicians, both of whom had done a short training course and could diagnose and treat simple things, like dehydration and malaria. Second, there was the therapeutic feeding center, the TFC.

"Have you worked with malnourished children before?"

"Um. Not really."

"First mission?"

"Yes."

"Ah. Well. We are approaching the hot season. You'll have more and more starvation, mostly children. The youngest ones. There are guidelines."

"Yeah. I've seen them."

"Okay. What do you know about TB?"

"A little bit. Diagnosed a few cases. Never treated anyone for it."

He paused. "Well, MSF is having its first ever TB workshop in March. All sections, people from all over the world. It's just around the corner in Ethiopia. I think you should go."

I told him I did too. Today was my first full day in Sudan, and already I was thinking about when I would next be out of it.

We weren't done. I would be responsible for collecting statistics and monitoring epidemics. There had been some deaths from meningitis in a nearby military camp, and Abyei was cinched, with much of Sudan, by Africa's meningitis belt. Further, a couple of cases of measles had been diagnosed nearby. The last vaccination campaign in the area had been years before. Finally, I should be prepared to handle several wounded at one time. There wasn't just the threat of multiple casualties from an outbreak of war, but a week ago a vehicle collision had sent thirty people to the hospital.

I would be given more specific instructions by the MD I was replacing. Marc handed me a stack of medical articles to take to the field, and showed me to his door. I shook his hand.

"Good luck. I'm sorry to say tomorrow is my last day. After that, you will ask your questions to Brian. He'll be acting as head of mission and medco."

"You're leaving?"

"Yes."

"Oh. Well, good luck."

"And you."

His door closed. I went downstairs and received my per diem for my next days in Khartoum, and was told that if my travel permit was approved, I would be leaving Wednesday on a World Food Programme plane, which traveled twice a week to Abyei.

I stepped out from the office and onto the street. The doors to the university were closed, the students gone home. It was near dusk, the sun shadowed and fading. Somewhere behind me, a muezzin took up the call to prayer. It was the first time I had heard it.

I couldn't make out his words, only long-drawn syllables. I turned past the university, crossed the tarmac road, and walked towards the guest house.

19/02: sudan.

it is dusty here. and windy. not a cloud. i am having trouble sleeping. not just from the heat, but because my head is full and my mind too active. i wonder about things i cannot know, like how i am going to recognize my first case of kala azar, or how i might manage the dozen injured patients i may never see. i have gone from not thinking about the future to completely inhabiting it.

My travel permit came through on time and I was due to leave the next morning. I had spent my two days in Khartoum wandering back and forth to the office. The first day I walked back, I got lost. Went too far. Ended up walking around in smaller circles until I recognized the dry, empty lot and its stone football nets. Through practice, I established a direct route.

I had a new roommate, a Darfurian driver waiting to return to the field. We chatted on occasion, and smoked together. I asked him once to join me for dinner, but he declined. The per diem we were given was too small for the Turkish restaurant I liked, and it was the only place I knew. I left him watching one of the dozens of Arabic channels on the television, and when I returned, he was in bed.

On my last night, I packed my final list of things. My pack already weighed 20 kilograms, but I could pare it down no further. I was reminded of when I traveled to Cambodia, my backpack full of unlabeled white pills and a letter I wrote for myself giving me permission to "import" them in my pocket. When I confessed my nervousness to the physician who was helping me plan, he shrugged and said, "Just try to look important."

In Khartoum's domestic airport, I received my printed paper ticket, and my backpack was weighed, then hauled off behind the desk. My driver queued behind me, pretending to be a passenger, holding my carry-on full of books. I grabbed my bag from him, clapped him on the shoulder, and walked through the empty security gate to the departure lounge.

I sat on one of its hard plastic chairs and waited for the flight to be called. I would be taken from Khartoum to El Obeid, from there to Abyei. I was told that the last person who had waited for her flight hadn't understood the Arabic announcement and missed it. She had to be driven the distance by car. It took three days. I strained to hear the flight numbers.

The call came. I queued up with six other passengers. Our tickets were checked, and we were led out onto the hot tarmac, between UN planes, to a small aircraft with WORLD FOOD PROGRAMME written in UN blue on the side. Much of the NGO work in Sudan, however little we liked to admit it, was entirely dependent on the United Nations.

The WFP plane was small, enough room for twelve passengers. We boarded it and climbed into separate rows. No one spoke. The South African pilot turned around in the small cabin, a few feet ahead, and greeted us. He described our route and apologized in advance for the bumps. It was the hot desert air, he explained, a reliable pleasure of being in Sudan.

Flying was not my thing. In Cambodia, I was sitting with a friend in a small restaurant when the upright barrel of the AK-47 of a customer next to us slid along the edge of his table and landed with a thwack at our feet. Its owner smiled sheepishly at us and picked it up. In Malawi, I shivered with a fever in the back of a truck on its way to the nearest hospital. Still, when I questioned my choice of career, it was never because of the guns or the diseases that might find my living body as good as the one behind me. It was because the job put me on plane after goddamn plane, multiplying the statistical chance that an engine would fail and I would fall out of the sky, a fool who ignored the equation.

The plane stuttered to a start, and after a quick run, we were in the air. As we climbed, the plane's tail wagged back and forth. I looked at the other passengers. They seemed unconcerned. I buckled my seat belt, whatever good it would do when we smashed into the sand at three hundred miles an hour and caught fire.

We banked over Khartoum. For the first time, I saw the Niles. One of them, the White, pours out of Lake Victoria, Africa's largest lake, its water swimming with cichlid fish and Nile perch. It passes through Uganda, then over Sudan's border until, a thousand feet below, it meets with the Blue carrying water from the cool highlands of Ethiopia. United they stretch from Khartoum across the desert and empty into the Mediterranean Sea.

Around us, the sky was cloudless. The shadow of our small plane followed us on the ground. As we moved higher, it grew smaller, and finally disappeared.

We were soon far from the city. Over the flat, dry landscape below, camel paths crossed one another, their trajectories slightly different. Towns organized in right angles, like a hedge maze, appeared on the sand. Slowly, the settlements became smaller, rounder, until they were only lone huts circled with a large fence. Soon even these were gone. No paths, and no people. The earth was a huge red circle rimmed with blue.

The rest of the passengers were asleep, save me and the woman behind. I turned and squeezed my face between my seat and the rattling hull. I could see her bright print dress. She leaned forward and smiled.

"Where are you going?" I asked.

"Sorry?"

"To which part of Sudan are you going? Kadugli? Abyei?"

"Oh, I'm going to Abyei. You?"

"Same. MSF. I'm the new doctor. James is my name. What about you?"

"Nyala. I'm working with a Sudanese NGO. I'm only going to Abyei for a few days."

"What for?"

"I am meeting with local groups, you know, community leaders and such, to talk about public ownership of resources."

"Like what? Oil?"

She laughed. "No. No one in the community will ever own those ones. Though they should. I'll talk with them about water, for instance, or electricity. Public goods, public ownership. In the case of Abyei, it's a bit premature. But you can't really have the dialogue too early. Only too late. How long are you going for?"

"Six months. Well, I guess closer to five from today's date. Is it nice, Abyei?" I asked.

"Well. I don't know. Nice enough. Where are you from?"

"Canada."

"Oh! I was born in Khartoum but I lived in Saskatchewan for many years. My daughter was born there. We live in Khartoum now. I liked Canada very much."

"I grew up in Alberta. We were neighbors."

"Is this your first time in Sudan?" she asked.

"Yeah."

"What do you think so far?"

"Well . . . it's kinda early to say."

"Well, James, I always tell people, you will either love it or hate it. Me, I love it. My life in Canada was very nice, peaceful. But there is something about Sudan. It becomes a part of you."

"I hope it does. I like hearing that."

"It's not an easy place to love. It's complicated. I guess everywhere is, but maybe this place more than others. Most people here are good. Too many of us suffer, though. Too many resources in the hands of too few."

"It's a common story."

"Yes. Too common. But here . . . Well, you'll see. People are so poor. Many can't read. The government is something that happened to them, not because of them."

The plane made a slow descent towards El Obeid and landed. The other male passenger got off, black attaché case under his arm. Nyala and I continued to talk about our different countries on the tarmac. We were exchanging places. This time, I was the immigrant. We took to the sky again, five of us now, and over the drone of the propellers, she talked about her home.

She explained that most people in Sudan weren't rebels, or military. Many were nomads. For centuries, people walked for hundreds of kilometers, some farther; some would walk all the way from Eritrea through Chad, or the Central African Republic. They knew the land only to use it for their cattle, to pass over it.

That life was dying throughout Sudan. There was no room for it any more. Too many farms, too many borders to cross, all these new invisible lines. Tensions grew high between them and the landowners, and soon between one another.

Then the war came. People were told that the last of their land was at stake, their livelihood, that their ancient enemies were at their doorstep ready to take it away; if they didn't strike first, they would lose. They were given weapons, and they struck. With the odds so heavily in their favor, they razed.

People fled, and now no one marched to the capital demanding electricity, or oil, or hospitals. They were too busy trying to find their brother, or their child. More guns poured into Sudan, and with them more fighting. Banditry took the place of trade, militia groups the place of schools.

And the people were left eating dust. Not even the land is theirs any more. After twenty years, one was left with places like Abyei.

"In the end, that's what we've lost—our way of life. Our memory of it, and of our home, is all we have. No matter how long we are away, we feel we must come back to it."

"Is that why you're on the plane to Abyei?" I asked.

She smiled. "It's because in my heart, I am a nomad."

She turned towards the window. We were both tired from yelling over the wind. The plane buzzed on. Below, ghostly green trees waited by the banks of dry riverbeds for a gush of water still months away. On the sand, a few patches of scrub. The horizon was flat and unending.

I was glad to be quiet. Everything was heavy. Every instance, every encounter, every conversation. Each moment assumed an exact weight. I put my head against the window. It rattled. I took it away. My understanding of the world had gone up by an exponent.

All of the passengers had fallen asleep except me. The pilots were silent, not even talking to each other. I wondered how many times they had done this run, how many good intentions they had ferried across the sand compared to how few they had brought back.

The plane starts to descend. It bumps against hotter layers of dry air, shakes and clatters. I glance at the women. They're cool with it.

I place my face against the crack of my seat.

"This must be it."

"You're probably right," Nyala says.

We are now only a hundred meters from the ground. I can see, through the bare trees, the grass roof of an occasional hut. As we drop lower, a goat runs on one of a hundred paths, its owner chasing behind.

In an instant Abyei flies into sight. In the middle of a dry patch of earth, a colony of huts and people and movement and then, gone. We are buzzing again over the thin forest.

"I think we missed the landing strip," a passenger shouts.

"I think they were checking for goats," I answer.

We loop around, turning neatly on our side (and, in my opinion, nearly completely over). The plane rights and, with aplomb, lowers onto a cracked, rumbling strip of land.

We stop in a cloud of dust. It swirls around us, then disappears on the wind. To our side, underneath a large leafless tree, sit three Land Cruisers. Their drivers wave to the plane. Smiling, the other passengers wave back.

"Welcome to Abyei," the pilot announces in a South African drawl as he opens the door. "The weather on the ground is hot and dusty and forecast is . . . what was the forecast again, Mike? Right. Hotter with more dust. We hope you enjoy your stay. Oh, and for the record, you're both wrong. We were looking for donkeys."

Our bags are unloaded on the ground. I grab my backpack and walk towards the tree. It offers little shade.

Fuck, it's hot.

I can't see an MSF vehicle. They must have been able to see the plane. I put my backpack on the ground and sit on it. The villagers who have come to watch us land are now straggling back home. I fumble for my camera.

Click.

Two of the Land Cruisers pull away. Nyala sits in the passenger seat of the third. She leans out the window.

"I can give you a ride, if you want," she says.

"I don't know where I'm going," I answer.

She laughs. "Abyei's not that big."

There is no sign of another car.

"All right. MSF compound. Thank you." I throw my bags through the rear door.

We bump across the landing strip and enter Abyei. There appears to be one red dirt road. After a few hundred meters on it, we stop. On a grass fence is a red and white door, and in the middle of it, a small MSF sticker.

"Here you are," Nyala says. "Welcome home."

"Thank you. I don't know what I would have done."

"No problem, James. I'll be seeing you."

I take my bags, and her Land Cruiser drives off. I knock on the gate. It creaks open. A tall, thin Sudanese man steps out to greet me. He's holding a radio.

"I'm James. The new doctor."

"Welcome, welcome." He gestures me in, closes the door, then turns and sits down on a wooden chair, perched in the shade of a grass awning.

I walk past him. To my left and right are two huts with grass roofs. I can see no one in either of them. I continue on. The ground is dust. I pass a large white canvas tent full of tires. Beyond it is a square brick building, and inside, an African woman is making food. I wave. She waves back, turns towards her pot, stirs it.

In the middle of the compound, flanked on all sides by half a dozen huts, is a tin-roofed house with no walls, a gazebo. Chairs are scattered around on its floor and a makeshift couch sits at one end.

I walk to it, to get out of the sun. I take my bag from my back and throw it on the floor. It lands in a puff of dust. I look around.

Where is everyone?

Bang.

CHAPTER I

(Blink.)

What?

(Blink.)

knockknockknockknock.

"Yes . . ."

"James? Sorry to wake you. There's been an accident. We need you at the hospital. James?"

"Yeah. Okay."

Whatthefuck.

I open my eyes. Mosquito net. Grass roof. Right. Abyei. Made it.

I lift off the corner of the mosquito net and a fine cloud of dust descends. I swing my feet to the cement floor and stand up. My back is wet. My mouth tastes like ashes. I'm dizzy, just for a second. Then, a headache. I sit back down, lean my head on my hand.

What happened last night? Oh yeah. Party. Someone was going away. Or a birthday. I can't remember. Nyala was there. Who else. Some of the team. Tim. Smoked a hundred cigarettes. And then what. Sick. Diarrhea. I lay by the latrine until dawn. What time is it now? Ten. Whoa. Ugh.

Hospital. Right. Accident. Cotton. My head's cotton.

I look around the hut. Tim, my Swiss tukulmate, is gone. I reach underneath the bed for my stethoscope, searching. There it is. I stand, take the MSF shirt dangling from a rope strung between sticks in the grass roof, look around for my shoes, then slide into them.

I open the low door, bend underneath its frame, and clip my head on the beam of the awning.

"Motherfuck."

I rub my head. Paola, the Italian nurse, is standing right outside.

"Sorry, James, but we need you at the hospital. Car accident. Sandrine is already there. So's Bev. I think there's quite a crowd," she says.

"Okay. No sweat. I gotta get some water."

"They need you right now."

"I'll drink it on the way."

Paola leads. She and I met two days ago, on my arrival. Young, cute. Boyfriend. I walk into the small brick kitchen and grab a plastic Coke bottle filled with warm water, then jog into step behind her.

Glug-glug.

I am having a tough time drinking water and keeping up. I'm spilling some of it on my shirt. We walk out of our gate, turn right, then right again at the tire half buried in the red dirt.

Okay, this is our compound to the right, behind the grass wall. Glug. Compound, compound, compound. On the left, another grass wall, huts behind it. Sixty paces and the grass walls end on both sides. To the right, a football field–sized flood plain, and at each side, football goals. Empty. Too hot.

Coming up on my left is a military compound surrounded by barbed wire. Which faction? Government, I think. SAF. Bev told me on my second day. Yesterday. Wow. Seems longer. Difficult to keep it all straight.

We sat for an hour in a hot hut. As the rest of the team talked in the gazebo, we hunched over maps as I recorded a list of names and acronyms. She told me who I should watch out for, who was best to avoid, and ended with, "Just leave it to me." That sounded fine. When the time came for Sandrine, the departing doctor, to show me the patients she was leaving me, Bev suggested that my time would be better spent going on an early-evening tour of Abyei. We bumped across untracked ground, past half-built huts until we had done one large circle. It took about fifteen minutes. I was to meet with Jean, the logistician, to get a technical and communications briefing. When I poked my head into the logistics tukul, he was deep in conversation with one of the mechanics, both their hands black with grease. "Tomorrow?" he said. "Or the next day? Oh, one thing. Handset. We use channel 5. Don't be without one." I took it from him and put it in my tukul.

Shit. It's under my bed.

Paola and I pass the military compound. Inside, some soldiers are washing their camouflage uniforms. A goat has climbed to the top of a mound of rubble, and another circles him, waiting for his turn to be king. In the corner of the compound, facing the juncture of the road I'm on and the approach to the hospital, sits a howitzer. I duck underneath its barrel, which appears to be aimed towards the great nothingness that surrounds Abyei, and turn left onto the hospital's driveway.

In it sit three cars. One of them, a white Land Cruiser, is ours. The other two are military green. A crowd is gathered at the small entrance.

Paola pushes past and I follow. Inside the hospital, people are milling, pushing, yelling, straining to see what they can of the action. A little girl sits on the ground between angles of legs, crying.

I don't know the hospital yet. It seems huge. I don't know where I am supposed to be. There's Bev. Her eyes are wide, her thin frame tight with stress. She is hurrying towards me.

"What's going on?" I ask.

"Bloody rollover. Military truck ran into a car, then turned on its side. Six soldiers in the back. They're mostly just banged up, but one of 'em's got a big gash on his arm. Sandrine is in the tent with a civilian who got run over. I'm crowd control." She turns away.

I edge through a group of women, babies on their hips, and walk towards the tent. On my way, I glance into the tiny emergency room. It is filled with soldiers.

In the tent, a man is lying on a cholera bed, grimacing. Sandrine is bent over him, listening to his lungs.

"What's up?"

"Oh, James. Sorry to get you, but there's just too many people. Mohamed is in the emergency room with one of the others, and this guy, I don't know. I think he got run over. I started an IV and I'm giving him a bolus. Pressure's okay."

His shirt is off, but his pants are still on. Coarse tread marks march over his thighs.

"His lungs are good? What about his belly?" I ask.

"Seems okay."

I feel his abdomen. It is soft. I put one hand on each side of his pelvis and push down. He screams.

"He's probably got a pelvis fracture. We should cut his pants off. You log-rolled him?"

"Not yet," Sandrine answers.

"Let's do that. We should give him some morphine first."

We turn him on his side, one person holding his neck steady, two others pulling him over. I feel along his spine. As I get down lower, he shouts in pain.

"Maybe a lumbar fracture too," I say. "Seems to be moving his feet okay. That's good."

"Transfer?" she asks.

"I don't know. What do you think?"

"We can."

"Maybe it's all from his pelvis, I don't know. It feels stable, but if not, the guy needs to be in traction or have surgery. Is there an orthopod at that other hospital, whateverit'scalled?"

"Heglig," Sandrine says. "Don't think so."

"X-ray?"

"Yes."

"Well, it's probably worth a transfer, then," I say.

"Okay. We'll do it."

"Are you cool here, Sandrine? Should I go help Mohamed?"

"Yeah. That's a good idea."

She leaves tomorrow. She is an infectious-disease specialist and has been here three months. Today she is on call. Yesterday we were both pulled in so many different directions, we had little chance to speak.

On a nearby veranda, two of the rollover victims are lying on the ground, each attended to by soldiers in green fatigues. They are moving. I consider that a positive sign and walk past them to the emergency room.

It is full. I can barely squeeze myself inside. On each of the two beds lies a soldier. One of them has a clean piece of gauze on his head. I pull it aside. An abrasion. I turn to the other bed and see Mohamed holding a cloth firmly down on the upper arm of the second patient. He and I met briefly during my whirlwind day. He is the other doctor in the mission, recently graduated from a medical university in Khartoum. He is young, brown skinned, with a smile full of bright, white teeth.

"Mohamed, you okay?"

"Oh, James. How are you, man?" he says, grinning.

"Good. What's up with this guy?"

He takes the cloth away, and blood starts shooting from a large gash in the patient's upper arm in a thin, red stream.

"Okay, okay. Got it."

"I think it was the glass from the windshield," Mohamed says.

I feel the pulse in his wrist. It's strong. "Hey, can you ask him to wiggle his fingers."

A flicker.

"Make a fist."

A bit.

"Thumbs up."

Nothing.

"Ask him if he can feel me touch his hand."

No.

"Radial nerve. His arm is fractured?"

"Seems so."

"Any other injuries?"

"No, I don't think so," Mohamed replies.

"Well, I guess we'll have to wash it out and sew it up. Splint it. I'll look for the nerve, I guess. We have ketamine, right?"

"Yes."

"If you get me some, I'll start. It's going to take a long time."

It does. Over an hour. His arm is broken in half. Thin spicules of bone keep snagging my glove, ripping it. I can't find the nerve, can't see enough of the bone to trace its route. I am reluctant to cut any farther. Sweat drips down my forehead and into my eyes. My stomach cramps, and it makes me feel nauseated. I wash out the wound, cut away the black pieces of crushed tissue, sew his triceps together, then close the skin. Lastly, with Mohamed's help, I put him in a long arm-cast.

I finish wrapping it and open the door. A man in military fatigues pushes quickly past.

"Doctor. Tell us what is wrong."

"Well, sir, this man has some scratches on his head. He is going to be fine."

"Good."

"The other soldier has broken his arm, and has a large cut in it, at the break. I have cleaned it out and sewn it up. It's possible he cut the nerve as well. Right now, he can't move his hand. That might recover, but possibly not. Time will tell."

"You must take him to Khartoum."

These guys must be SAF.

"Sorry?"

"You have to fly him to Khartoum. He is one of our soldiers. He needs an x-ray."

"He doesn't need an x-ray. The bone's broken. I can see it. The rest of his arm is okay. These fractures usually heal very well."

"You said he can't move his hand."

"I know. The nerve has been bruised or cut. He could use a neuro-surgeon. But not urgently, not today. He can wait a few days."

The patient starts to groan behind me, his anesthetic worn off.

"You must fly him to Khartoum."

Another soldier enters the room.

"Listen. We don't have a plane. We have a Land Cruiser. We can take people as far as three hours from here, to a bigger hospital, but only if it is going to save their life. And there is no neurosurgeon there. And we can't take people to Khartoum. We simply can't."

"Why are you refusing? I know you are going to take the civilian who was run over. Why won't you help us?"

I need to get out of the emergency room. I need some air.

"Excuse me, excuse me."

I push past and step into the courtyard. The scene has settled. Bev has done her work well and only a few mothers of children in the feeding center remain. One of the injured men on the veranda is gone, and the other is sitting there, his leg bandaged, sipping tea.

The soldiers follow me out.

"Doctor, I don't understand . . ."

"I've explained things as clearly as I can."

"I think it would be best if you took our man somewhere he could get better help."

"I agree," says a man who has come to join us from the veranda. His hair is gray, and he is wearing a large white tunic. "I think you should listen to this soldier here. You're new. I understand that, and you don't know me yet, but I am one of the leaders around here, and . . ."

Bev turns the corner.

"Bev. Can you help me out over here?"

I take her by the shoulder, lead her a few steps away.

"I mean the guy needs a neurosurgeon or an orthopod I'm not sure maybe a general surgeon can handle it but he would have to dissect the triceps away look for the nerve sew it up but it's not that straightforward maybe in Khartoum I don't know and these guys they're all—"

"James. I'll take care of it. Gentlemen, come with me."

And with that, she leaves. The soldiers follow. My anxiety quiets. I walk back to the tent. Sandrine is scribbling out a referral note.

"You okay?" I ask.

"Yeah. You?"

"Yeah, I guess. Some drama. Is it always like this?"

"Not always."

"Wow. Anyway. I think Mohamed has taken care of the rest of the patients. I'll make sure. If there's nothing else, I'm going back to the compound. I feel kinda shitty. I'll write orders for the guys in the emergency room."

"See you back there."

I stop in the nursing room and find an empty chart. I am not certain what drugs we have, or how best to order them. I grab a chart on the desk. It looks like the system is to make a full circle, or half-circle, depending on the dose, and draw them on a line that marks the time of day when I want them given. I turn to the cupboards, find some antibiotics and some morphine, and hand the rest of the orders to one of the nurses whose name I don't remember.

I leave down the hospital road, and the hot wind blows across the open field. I turn right at the corner, duck at the cannon, left at the tire, and I'm back to the gate. I knock. The door opens, and I step past the guard. I walk through the compound and past the kitchen. Tim is sitting in the gazebo, smoking, the sat phone in his lap. He sees me and stands up.

"How's the hospital?" he asks. "Bev said someone pulled a knife?"

"I didn't see that. I was in the emergency room forever. I'm going to lie down. I ate something bad, I think."

"Right. See you later."

I duck inside the tukul. It's like an oven. I poke my head outside the door.

"Dude, are there any fans?"

"Nope. Not enough power."

" 'Kay."

I lie down on the mattress. My hips dig into the metal frame. I look up at the mosquito net, orange because of the copper dust. Beyond it is the peaked grass roof, and between its narrow strands, small lizards rustle around, trying to shake out an insect. I turn on my side and wrap the pillow around my head. It smells like sweat.

22/02: made it.

the luggage restriction proved not to be a problem. i had a fleeting fear that my undeclared kilos might send us hurtling towards the ground in a thin metal airplane shell, gasless, just because i wanted to haul ulysses around the world for the fifth time. it didn't. the book now sits proudly on the windowsill of my tukul, fully confident that it will leave it as it came, its spine strong and unbroken.

a dirty, dusty, rumbling landing later, and i was there. here. for those who don't know exactly where abyei, sudan, is, i will draw a map. the X marks it.

no   X   where

right in the middle.

i will spend some more time later talking about my hut, its 3-x-3-meter blank cement walls and its straw roof, how it captures heat so well, and . . . actually, i don't think i will spend any more time on it. that's pretty much it.

i will talk more about the hospital, more about the team here, and how they seem the best kind of people.

and more about abyei, the town. its braying goddamn middle of the night donkeys and barking middle of the night damn dogs, its people, and its dustdustdust.

I AM SITTING IN THE GAZEBO, waiting for the morning meeting to begin, the one where we discuss the day's activities. Tim is leaning on its low cement wall sipping from a coffee cup, his face to the morning sun. I can hear the soft voices of the people who live on the other side of our compound's thin grass fence, murmurs I can't understand. Shadows are long and the air is still.

The medical team from compound 2, our national staff, are due to arrive soon. Like in most MSF missions, national staff make up the vast majority of employees. Nurses, cleaners, cooks, drivers, guards. Of the forty or so people who work for MSF in Abyei, only five of us are expats.

Sandrine has gone to the hospital already to say her goodbyes. Her flight to Khartoum, and from there to Geneva, is due in a few hours. The plane will land just over . . . there. Just behind the hospital. Right where I landed, four days ago.

She and I spent yesterday afternoon together. As we walked the hospital grounds, she introduced me to the patients that were now mine. They were difficult to keep straight, scattered as they were, some inside wards, others lying on the ground in the open air.

The hospital is a collection of disconnected rooms. As you enter, from the hot hospital road, you walk along a corridor that is filled with patients fanning themselves with registration cards, waiting to be seen. Off to the side, to the right of the corridor, is the nursing room, a small room with a drug cabinet, a single patient bed, and a crowded desk full of patient charts and open bottles of pills. Past this is the small, dark emergency room.

There are a half-dozen other patient suites. Most of the patients seem to pay no attention to our hospital structure. Their order of preference appears to be: veranda, hallway, courtyard, and, lastly, hospital ward. The rooms are hot, stagnant places. Little air gets through them and the light is poor. Contrast this with the veranda, which yesterday was packed with family members, breeze blowing through, people laughing like they were on the deck of a cruise ship.

I remember, as a medical student, working in the emergency room for the first time, trying to make sense of what it contained. It seemed so large, so complicated; it was not a world, it was a separate universe. With time, it shrank. This place will too. Right now, its rooms and hallways form a maze full of people I cannot talk to, nor properly help.

Yesterday, as we turned towards the back of the hospital, towards the two rooms reserved for patients with contagious tuberculosis, Sandrine pointed out a broken section of the skirting cement wall. An orange plastic barrier had been put into the gap. She explained that when MSF started working here, about nine months ago, government soldiers were living in the hospital. They had removed part of the fence that their military compound shared with the hospital and, with that, claimed Abyei's most valuable resource as their own.

One of the first things MSF did was declare that our presence in the hospital was conditional on their armed absence. We put up the orange plastic barrier, and it has stood since. The hospital was returned to Abyei. I thought that of all the good MSF might do here over the years, that would be the single greatest act.

Sandrine pointed at a humming generator in the corner.

"This gives us power for some of the day. It's mainly used to cool the drugs in the storage room and the vaccine fridge. If you need it at other hours, for the oxygen concentrator or whatever, ask the guard to turn it on."

We passed a group of patients gathered around barrels set on a high wall.

"There is no running water. Each day the UN trucks it in for us and we pump it into these blue barrels here. The orange ones are for washing hands. Lots of chlorine."

A room near the front held two small refrigerators and a shelf lined with reagents. A tall man in a lab coat was peering through a microscope.

"Okay, here's the lab. Hi, Ismael." Ismael lifted his head, raised his hand. "Ismael is great, but there is only so much he can do with the tools. He can test for malaria, meningitis, TB, hepatitis, HIV . . .

um . . . blood groups too. Oh, and urine and stool. I think that's it. No electrolytes, no blood counts."

"Cultures? Blood, stool, sputum?"

"No."

We turned the corner and stopped at a patient's bed. The boy on it looked like bones glued to bones. Sandrine told me he had measles last month and showed up on the hospital's door several days after. She handed me his chart. His fever hadn't broken for four days. He glanced up at me as she told me his story, then looked back at the wall.

"Where are his parents?" I asked.

"Haven't seen them," she said. "He came alone."

She pointed to her right. "Almost forgot. In that room, the one that looks like a storage closet, is Mansood. He came in with a cellulitis, around his knee, about a month ago. He hasn't been able to walk since. Mohamed will tell you more. He should know pretty much everyone too."

Next were the patients with measles. There were two of them, on the veranda, near the female ward, their mothers fanning them with pieces of cardboard. We moved on.

"And this is the TFC. The malnourished kids are kind of mixed in with the general pediatric patients, but we try to keep them separate so we can organize feeds better. Paola is working on that."

The children in the feeding center drooped in their mothers' arms. One or two had their hands wrapped in gauze so they couldn't pull at the tubes in their noses, or at their intravenous lines.

"It's a struggle with the mothers. They wait until the last minute, when their kid is almost dead, to bring them to the hospital. Then, after a few days, when he's no better, they want to leave."

She asked if I had any questions. Yes, I said. What am I supposed to do? Where do I start?

She said it was up to me. There were no rules. She told me that once she left, I could talk to Marc. I told her he was gone. She seemed surprised. She promised to write me a full handover from London.

We walked down the hospital's hot, hot road towards the compound. Wind gusted sand across the empty football field. I asked Sandrine if she was happy to be going home. She said she wasn't sure, that there were things she would miss. For the rest of the day, I watched her buzz around the compound excitedly, scarcely able to conceal her delight.

As sad as I am to see her go, as much as I don't look forward to being alone with this hospital to take care of, trying to figure out how to start or when to stop, I can't disguise my interest in her tukul. Today I woke up early to pack up my few things and move them from Tim's to the front of hers. It is not an elegant gesture, claiming someone's tukul before it cools, but I want it. I want a place.

I hear the buzz of voices. Here comes compound 2. It's almost eight, time for the meeting. After it, I want to do some teaching. There's Mohamed. I like him already. The night before, at Sandrine's farewell dinner, he shyly showed me some pictures he was taking. One of a bird, a falcon, sitting statue-still on the top of a tukul. Another the fragile sliver of a new moon.

"Good morning," I say, standing up, and juggle my coffee into my left hand.

"Good morning . . ." "Good morning . . ." They shake my hand, walk past me, and sit down to continue their conversation in Arabic.

Bev comes from her tukul, cigarette in her fingers. "Morning, everybody. We'll start soon. We'll wait a minute for Jean. There was a problem with the electricity in the hospital last night. We'll see if he turns up." She walks to the kitchen to grab a piece of bread.

I sit on the makeshift couch, its back a futon mattress doubled on itself, Tim beside me. He has been an excellent tukulmate to this point. He said the same of me. Both were compliments to the other for not snoring. The only time we are in the tukul is when we try to sleep. It is too hot otherwise.

More people filter in, men dressed in long-sleeved shirts, the women in traditional gowns, scarves wrapped around their faces. I take a mouthful of coffee and taste cardamom.

Jean shows up, his hands covered with dirt. Sandrine is beside him. "Sorry, everybody. Fuse went in the hospital." He sits down.

"Okay, everybody. We're late, so let's get this started."

The first few chugs of our generator, then clackclackclackclackclack. Bev raises her voice above it.

"First, today is Sandrine's last day. She flies out in an hour, so if you haven't already said goodbye, now's your chance."

Bev continues, reciting the schedule for the week ahead. Mobile clinics, measles monitoring, car repair, changes in military activity. My presence is not given a mention. It seems, after three days, I am a fixture. The machine, and its exchangeable parts, keeps moving forward.

The meeting finishes. Bev asks for questions. There are none.

"Now, why does no one ever have any questions? Am I that good? I guess so. Mohamed, question? No? All right, then. Off you go." She stands up.

There is no movement. Now, a little shuffling. Someone puts his hands on his knees, pushes himself up. Slowly, the rest of the group, about ten in total, does the same. Sandrine suggests a photo, and everyone starts to queue. I leave them and go to the kitchen.

I put my dirty coffee cup down in the sink. On the small propane burner, a large pot of water boils beside three metal water filters. There are a few pieces of fresh bread left on the counter, their outer edges black from the newspaper they were wrapped in. I take one. From the small fridge in the corner, I grab a warm bottle of water, then reach around to plug the fridge in. It begins to strain. I step back outside.

Everyone is still taking photographs. I will defer teaching until tomorrow.

I leave compound 1 on my own. I know the route. Right, tire, cannon, duck, left. The sun is already hot. Children pass me on donkeys; soldiers walk by with guns drooping over their shoulders and their caps pulled firmly down. A teenager on a bicycle talking to his friend sees me at the last second and swerves.

At the hospital the dusty MSF flag dangles from its short pole outside of the gates. Patients already line the hallway, waiting to be seen. I walk past them and into the nursing room, gather up all the paper patient charts, and start to go through them one at a time.

23/02: r&r.

friday was the traditional muslim day of rest and the day off for this msf project. however, there is little distinction between the work and any life outside of it. at 7 p.m., we are still talking about the day that passed, at 8 p.m., our plans for tomorrow. it is our last word before sleep, and our first on awakening.

of the patients that i saw on my first day, the ones thrown like match-sticks from the back of the truck, we transferred one to another hospital for an x-ray, and i have since been told his pelvis was fractured. i saw another, his arm casted, driving away from the hospital, his loose camouflaged sleeve flapping behind him like a flag.

the thing that has worried me the most so far is not the political situation, nor the risk of getting ill, nor the remoteness, nor the lack of hospital resources. it is that, on fridays, our kitchen staff has the day off, and we must cook for ourselves. cooking is easy in kensington market. you can barely find the jamaican allspice for all of the organic lemon-grass. here in the local souk, well, there are tomatoes. onions. goat. um . . . i'll let you know.

MOHAMED AND I ARE making our rounds. Two families, both from Abyei, both with young boys infected with measles, occupy the same veranda. They are the two sickest children in the hospital. We must keep them separated from the rest of the patients and hope that the hot wind scatters their virus into the empty sand rather than into the feeding center.

I've seen measles a few times. The rash is particularly hard to recognize on black skin. You have to let the light hit the fine bumps tangentially to appreciate the random pattern the virus draws over the torso. If you close your eyes and run your fingers over the child's back, you can feel it, a million soft points.

The other signs are more obvious. Red eyes rimmed with yellow glue, the shaking cough, the high fever you can feel before your hand reaches the forehead.

"Why is it," I am saying to Mohamed, "that they are all getting antibiotics?"

"Because of their cough."

"Yeah, but measles is a virus. Everyone gets a cough. You know, 'cough, coryza, conjunctivitis.' Measles."

He is silent. When I sat with my team the first time, I said that they had more to tell me about medicine in Sudan than I could teach them. Our job would be to learn from each other. Sandrine has been gone for one day, and already I am doing things differently, repeating discussions from a week ago.

"I don't think it's a good idea. At home, I only treat bacteria when I know where they are. Otherwise they develop resistance, right?"

He nods. We cross amoxicillin off the list of medicines, increase the dose of paracetamol. The mothers sit on separate beds and ask no questions. Underneath the beds are two empty bowls wiped clean of beans. I take my hand from the boy's back and stand. Beside him is his little sister, about nine months old. She wasn't there yesterday. I shake my head. We have only a few doses of measles vaccine.

"Mohamed, can you tell them again that no children are supposed to come visit unless they have had measles? They'll get sick, like him. And the little girl should stay here now too." A little boy comes barrelling around the corner, wearing only a T-shirt, and runs into my leg. "And who's . . . ? Shit." This isn't going to go well.

Two more patients left to see.

We walk to the back of the hospital, to the only private room in the place, an empty closet. A wheelchair with one of its front wheels missing sits propped outside of it.

Mohamed greets Mansood in Arabic. He is an old man for Abyei, perhaps in his fifties. He is Dinka, tall and thin, his feet callused from years and miles. On his left knee is a thick bandage soiled with pus. Beside his bed is a long walking stick. He takes it and pushes himself into a sitting position.

How is he feeling? All right. Weak. Still not hungry.

"He used to be a strong man," Mohamed says. "Even when he came in. Now he's like a baby."

We unwrap his knee. It is swollen and warm. Below the kneecap is a small area of broken skin and from it leaks a pale brown fluid.

"Has anyone stuck a needle in his knee?" I ask Mohamed.

"No. We were treating him for skin cellulitis."

"I think we should stick a needle into the joint. If there is pus, we'll try to take out as much as we can, then irrigate it. Have you aspirated a knee before?"

"No."

"I'll show you. You put some local anesthetic in, then put your needle in an 18-gauge here." I point at a spot two o'clock to his kneecap, just under its lip. "Direct it this way, pull back on the syringe. Easy. We'll do it after lunch."

"Okay."

I tuck Mansood's chart under my arm. One left, the boy whose fever remains unbroken. I changed his antibiotics the day before to target different bacteria, to expand the coverage. On my arrival at the hospital, the first thing I did was check his temperature: 101.3 Fahrenheit.

He is lying on his side in the same position Mohamed and I left him in yesterday, his thin chest moving quickly up and down. I put a hand over his ribs. He's hot. I turn to the nurse.

"Has he been getting his paracetamol?"

"Yes."

"What about his antibiotics? Were they given?"

"Yes."

"Is he eating?"

"Not much."

The boy starts a staccato cough.

"He's malaria-negative . . . maybe TB? But this all started post-measles. That's a pretty big coincidence."

Beneath my hand, his ribs feel like a wooden accordion, pulling apart, coming together. I motion for him to sit, mime listening to his lungs. He pushes himself up and leans forward.

"Sounds are way down on the right. Could be an abscess or empyema. We should stick a needle in. Or a chest tube. He needs an x-ray. And some parents."

Mohamed says nothing. Yesterday we confirmed that the boy had no family, that he lived in the market, begging.

I look at my watch. "Maybe we should do this now. If you take these charts to the nursing room, I'll get set up."

Mohamed nods.

In the operating theater I find a syringe, a couple of needles, antiseptic, and local anesthetic. Mohamed returns with some sterile gloves. Together, we carry the boy into the operating theater and sit him on its table.

"Mohamed, explain that we have to put a needle in his back." What is he, ten years old? "Tell him it won't hurt that much. He'll feel just a pinch at first. And tell him that when we ask, he has to breathe out slowly, okay? That's when I'll take the needle out. We do that so he doesn't take a big gasp as the needle is pulling out, right? He could suck in a bunch of air through the hole, and collapse his lung and all that."

We clean his back. The white gauze comes away black with dirt. I listen to his back again, thump one of my fingers with the other until the sounds goes from hollow to dull, then make a mark with the hub of the needle. I inject a few cc's of anesthetic into his back. It raises his skin up in a wheal.

"You always have to go above the rib, right? Not below. That's where the neurovascular bundle runs. You can hit an intercostal artery."

I take a large syringe and put on its tip an 18-gauge needle.

"So landmark like this, just over the top. Is he doing okay? He's okay? All right, he's thin so we don't have to go very far . . . You can kind of feel the lining of the lung pop as the needle enters it, then pull back on the syringe, and . . ."

Blood.

Shit.

"Okay, tell him to breathe out."

I landmark one rib below, put in some anesthetic, get another needle, push it through, pop, pull.

Blood.

Damn.

"Tell him to breathe out."

I'm sweating now.

Why the blood? No way I hit a vessel twice. Maybe he bled into his abscess, or has an infected hemothorax . . . I don't know. TB?

"Okay. Tell him one more time. One more. Good. Great. And . . ."

Blood. Dark blood.

"Breathe out."

I empty the syringe into the garbage in a thin red stream. It hisses as it hits the plastic.

"All right. I can't find any pus. I don't know. I think we should probably put in a chest tube. Basically, he's going to get septic and die if he's got pus in his chest and we can't get it out. But we've got to try to find someone. A friend, an uncle. If it doesn't work, we can't transfer a ten-year-old to a hospital alone."

The boy sits stoically, three raised targets on his back, dried blood at their center. We wipe him clean, put on a dressing, then carry him back to his bed. He rolls over and faces the wall.

Mohamed and I agree to meet in the afternoon to aspirate Mansood's knee and try the chest tube. As he leaves to find lunch at compound 2, I return to the veranda that holds the measles patients. I smile at the families, and motion for the charts that are tucked again under their plastic mattresses. They give them to me. Beside "Amoxicillin," where two hours before I wrote "Stop," I write "Restart."

26/02: today.

today, i woke early, determined to run out of town and find a bit of space in the flatness that surrounds abyei. at 6:30 a.m., the sky was still dark. as i ran, past the trucks and buses leaving for el obeid or khartoum or juba, full upon full of beds and blankets on top of beds and blankets, dawn happened. but the sun never rose. not past the meniscus of dust along the horizon. a windstorm had lifted the sudan sand, and it covered not only my tukul and abyei, but the wide sky. by 8 a.m., the sun was only a gauzy ghostly hole, the color of beeswax.

today, when i was doing rounds, and i was figuring out what to do with a young boy who developed a fever after a run with measles, a boy in whom i had already stuck a chest tube and three needles to try and drain a large collection of bacteria, as i was deciding whether to stick more things into his chest or send him to another hospital or if he was going to die, and heard from my translator that this boy, already ghostly, had refused food that morning, i looked down and beneath his bed was a butterfly struggling to right itself on the floor but instead, spinning in circlescirclescircles, its wings tracing round grooves in the dust.

today, a whole rash of measles. i had it as a child. so did my brother. i have no memory of it. all i have are pictures showing how miserable we both were. i doubt they are in memoriam of this special time; more likely we just sat still for 30 seconds. people sit still with measles because they don't want to move. their eyes get infected, their skin flakes, their fevers are severe. measled. miserabled.

today, a baby died about ten minutes after coming into the hospital. she was dirty and covered in grass. the family came from far away, and asked if i knew somewhere nearby where they could bury her. i said i did not. they thanked me and left.

when i ask people in the hospital where they are from, they answer in days. "three days away," some say.

i admitted a girl from two days away. her mother had died in the hospital two months before, and she was her only child. her father was a soldier with other wives. a neighbor found her lying on the ground and hitchhiked to abyei to deliver her to our door, an orphan. she was so severely dehydrated that when i listened to her heart, she tried to suck on my stethoscope. she could drink, but no one gave her any water. today she is better. she gained a kilogram in 24 hours. from 5 to 6. the man who brought her said he can't stay, doesn't know her relatives. her problems are ours now.

there is a little boy here who the staff is so fond of that i think they are delaying discharging him because they would miss him too much. he is always between your legs, and crawling onto your lap. if it comes to me, i am never discharging him either.

I AM SITTING ON A PLASTIC STOOL. Kneeling beside me, a young girl heaps spoonful after spoonful of sugar into my tea. My two new Arabic words, to bring the ringing total to three, are "sugar" and "separate." I said them when she showed up with the tea, but must have mispronounced them. I am too shy to say them again.

Tim sits beside me, smoking. It is just dusk, a little late for us to be in the market. We've been told to avoid it after dark. Though alcohol is not sold openly here, it exists. I'm not sure if its visible absence is because of expense or a remnant of sharia law. Either way, as the day winds on, one can watch the soldiers' eyes become glassier.

My days, so far, all seven of them, have been of the compound-right-tire-straight-cannon-left-hospital variety. I got home late this afternoon. The gazebo was full with a meeting. I tried to lie down on my dusty bed, but the heat was stifling. I ducked into the administration tukul to find Tim, and a few minutes later we were walking on the rutted road towards the market.

Beside us a group of Dinka men sit talking, resting their long arms on their knees. A donkey ambles past. The air is hot and still and on it, the smell of burning garbage. The girl leaves my side and puts her hot tin can back onto the coals.

"So, it looks like they are going to send in the emergency team from Geneva," Tim says.

"Yeah, I heard," I say, and stir my tea, swirling the thick layer of sugar.

There are about twenty patients with measles now. One day there were two, the next day four, then seven. I have been keeping track of them, where they are from, when they started to get sick. Whenever there are more, I tell Bev and she talks to Brian. We were waiting to see if the numbers would cross the threshold to qualify as an epidemic. They do.

Tim lights a cigarette.

"Those things are killers. Seriously, dude," I tell him. "Killers."

He holds out his package. I take one.

"I thought doctors didn't smoke."

"I don't smoke. If I did, I would have cigarettes of my own."

"Oh, right. Sorry."

He hands me his lighter.

"That's okay. So . . ." I take a long drag from my cigarette. "How's life in the admin tukul?"

"I can't complain," he says.

"Bev seems stressed."

"Yeah. Seems that way. She's off, or on. Mostly on."

"Does she sleep?"

"Can't say. Not much."

I pick up the small glass of tea by its rim and take a sip. Ow. Too hot.

"When did you get here again?" I ask.

"A few weeks before you. When was that?"

"A week ago."

"Jesus. Seems longer."

"Tell me about it."

I lean back on my chair. Generators start to clack madly in all directions. It's almost dark now. The girl throws some incense on the coals and the scent of frankincense swirls on the smoke. In the sky above Tim's head, the minaret of the town mosque glows from within. A young boy in ripped brown shorts walks by barefoot, two goats tethered behind him.

"You got a girl back home?" I ask.

"Yeah. You?"

"No. Not really. You miss her?"

"No. Not really."

I laugh. Tim lights a cigarette with the end of his last.

"We're going to see how things are when I get back." He exhales.

"One of those."

"Yeah."

"That's tough," I say.

"No. I mean, yeah. It's just . . . it wasn't that hard to leave, but it's . . . you know . . . hard to figure things out."

"Tell me about it." I've been letting Sarah's emails hang in the inbox. Too heavy.

"I mean, who knows. Do you ever know?" Tim asks.

"I don't think so, not really. I think your mind keeps on fucking with you. I remember an ex-girlfriend of mine. She was an occupational therapist, you know, helped people recover from strokes or accidents or whatever. Taught them to dress themselves again, make toast, stuff like that."

"That's cool."

"Totally. Anyway, she worked mostly with old people, of course, and whenever she met someone who had been married for years and years, she would ask them their secret. I don't remember all the answers, but one was from a woman who said, 'Well, you just can't fall out of love with each other at the same time.'"

Tim nods. "I kinda thought it would help being here."

"And?"

"Well, I don't seem to think about it too much. Mostly I just keep on thinking about how terrible the food is."

"And how hot it is," I add.

"And how there's no beer."

"And no girls."

"Which is probably good."

I throw my cigarette into the coals. "I think at some point, you just have to decide to go for it or not," I say.

"Yeah. I don't know. I'm just hoping for something that fits. But it's tough to find, I guess. Some people do."

"Maybe. You ever look around, like on the subway or something, at all the other people reading or listening to music or whatever, and think, how does everyone have it so sorted out? Am I the only one who's just trying to hold things together with, like, bits of . . . wood and white glue? You know? Why aren't we all freaking out, or making out, or something."

"But everyone on that subway's thinking that, about you."

"Yeah, exactly. Sucks."

The handset crackles. Tim takes his lighter from the table and reaches for the radio below his stool.

"Think we should get back?" I ask.

"Probably. Bev'll be worried."

We stand up. Tim hands the girl a crumpled dinar note.

"Thanks," I say.

"I never know what to pay," he says.

"Dude, when thirty years from now economists look at Abyei's inflation rate, you know, with a line graph? The first thing they are going to point at, right at the beginning, is a mark that says 'Tim' and below it will be your face."

"So true."

We start to walk back. The light from the stalls' naked bulbs shadow ruts from last year's rain. We creep along carefully.

"So, Tim. Paola, she has a boyfriend for sure?"

"Yeah. I think so."

"What about her friend, the one who works for the UN?"

"Think so."

"This is going to be a long six months."

We are nearing the end of the market and are close to the compound. To our right, a Misseriya man leans on his counter, his chin in both hands, a small selection of canned and dried goods behind him. We stop to buy some tins of pineapple.

"You know how much to pay for these?" I ask.

"Not really," Tim says, handing the storekeeper a 1,000-dinar note.

We turn onto the last market stretch and pass a group of armed soldiers sitting down, drinking. One of them stands up, lurches towards us.

"My friend," he says, extending his hand, "my friend!"

I have never seen him before. Neither has Tim. His hand is naked, dangling. The silence stretches. His smile starts to fade. I reach to shake his hand. He grabs mine tightly.

"My friend!" He takes a step closer, and I smell the booze on his breath and see his red eyes below the brim of his cap.

I pull my hand free.

"We've got to go, partner," I say, and clap him on the shoulder.

Tim and I turn and start walking.

He shouts, "My friends!" then adds something in a language I don't know. The rest of them start to laugh. We quicken our pace. He is shouting as Tim and I turn the corner, but as we draw close to the compound, his voice is lost in the generators.

28/02: all measles all the time.

that is not far from the truth. today i have seen and admitted six cases. the tally would have been seven, but the family of a young patient lived just a bit too far away, and he died before i got to the hospital.

the miserabled are exceeding our capacity to hold them, certainly to isolate them. yesterday, they occupied one veranda. today, they started spilling onto the lawn. they ignore the tent we have set up for them because it magnifies an already aggressive sun. despite our best attempts to keep the miserabled separate, several cases have popped up in other inpatients.

i am often asked why i ended up choosing msf from an armada of medical ngo's with whom i could work. for many reasons, but none more compelling than this one. at our morning meeting, i wondered aloud to the rest of the team about our space problem. a decision was made to do something about it. by 2 p.m., there were six men in the corner of the hospital compound, and by 5, they had built a shelter that would house 20 patients. we also decided to find a nurse, hire one if necessary, and devote him or her to measles care. within the day, the will was found, the money, and the hands. we did not need to add it to the agenda of another meeting, nor to a paper pile of requests on an administrative desk. within hours, it was hammers and nails.

my radio crackles beside me. i am on call to the hospital tonight, and am responsible for it all nights. and all days. i thought i left this call business behind me, and could just carry it around as a kernel of pride. "oh yeah. 30-hour shifts, i've done that. it's not so bad." it was bad, ok? i admit it. didn't like it. uncool.

but, speaking of uncool, and its opposite, the coolest . . . radios. they're the main reason i work for msf. every day, i get to say: "good copy. over and out." for real. so sweet.

Brian passes my tukul door on his way to the shower. He arrived a couple of days ago to help coordinate our response to the measles epidemic. A convoy of vehicles is working its way towards us from Khartoum carrying bullhorns, ice packs, vaccine coolers. We have hired translators, made site visits to places even closer to the middle of nowhere than Abyei.

There are several new measles patients every day. Some show up at the hospital on their own and we find them sitting in the registration line, feverish and spotted. We pull them out as soon as we can to sit on a bench beside Ismael's lab until we can find a place. Other times, Bev will pull up in the Land Cruiser, drop off a measled family she found in the countryside, and then speed away. We are running out of mattresses.

Mohamed and I no longer work together much. Most days, I round on the inpatients, he on the growing number of measled now housed in a series of traditional recubras, long huts covered with grass. We meet in the early afternoon to talk about the sickest, then leave for lunch at our respective compounds. His, compound 2, home to our national staff relocated from Khartoum or Juba, the southern capital, is becoming full as we draw more people into Abyei to help us cope. I visited compound 2 on my first day, with Bev. Haven't been back since. I don't go to the market any more. Nor anywhere else. I talk with patients through a translator, or Mohamed when he is around, and only some of the Sudanese nurses speak English. Most of the time I walk around in a bubble.

It has been good having Brian here. The team has been feeling adrift. We all have questions. About the children who won't get any better, about the dead bodies no one will claim. The end of the month has come and gone, and I don't know how to do the statistics. Sandrine has not sent me her handover. When Brian asked me how I was doing, I looked at his tired eyes and said I was doing all right. I probably am. A lot of dying people, though. I try not to think about that too much.

Paola is struggling too. She is trying to coordinate her large nursing team, to bring the nurses up to basic MSF standards. On top of this, she must manage the pharmacy, and plan an international order for supplies. Between the two jobs, and with the new measles drain on resources, her list of tasks is bottomless.

Brian has told us that more people are due to arrive to help with the vaccination effort, including another MD, from Spain. I will be glad to have Mohamed back.

The shower door slams shut. It is best to shower at least three times a day: morning, noon, and night. You never really get clean, at least not for long. As soon as you step from underneath the pipe and into your flip-flops, the dust between your toes changes to mud. In those few seconds, though, a lifetime.

I hear Brian turn the pump on. It pushes water from a tank on the ground to one three meters above it. Twice a day we receive water from the sloshing buckets of the donkey-boys, a term we all agree is pejorative, but one we use anyway. The donkey-boys are about twelve years old, dressed in rags, legs as thin as their arms. They turn the bent spigot of their donkey-drawn barrel, fill a plastic pail with water, then bend and strain to pour it into our tank. We pump it up, splash it down.

He's done. My turn. Brian is sharing Tim's tukul. I claimed that the constant interruptions in my night would be too distracting for him to find sleep. More true is that I wouldn't find mine with someone so close.

The spatter of water hitting cement. Shit. Paola must have beaten me.

I lie back down and grab a book from beside my bed.

What time is it? Nine. I should probably try to go to sleep soon. I'm on call tomorrow. How many cigarettes did I smoke today? One after lunch, one just now. Two. That's pretty good. Maybe, if I get to sleep, I'll try to run in the morning.

The water continues to splash.

I put the book on my chest and look through the crack of my door. Brian and Bev are laying out a map on the gazebo table. They did the same thing last night. I returned from the hospital late, and they were still up, talking vaccinations. Everyone else was hiding in their huts. I have heard that other NGOs are concerned about our approach, some wondering if our estimation of the populations in the countryside is accurate. They want us to delay. We won't.

Finally.

I walk outside. Paola passes me with a towel around her waist.

"G'night," I say.

"Uh-huh," she mumbles, not looking up.

The shower floor is wet. I kick my flip-flops into the dust outside and turn on the water. It's cooled a bit. This afternoon, the water in the pipe was so hot from the sun, it burned.

The water pours over my face, my back. I'm careful not to get any in my mouth. For a minute, the dust and the heat retreat. I let the stream thunder on my head. Feels like forever.

I reach for the handle and it squeaks as I twist it off. I grab my sarong hanging on the bathroom door and rub my hair, then tie it around my waist. The rest of me is already dry. I step into my flip-flops. The dust in them turns to mud.

The door to Paola's tukul is mostly closed. Beneath it, I can see a sliver of light. Don't know where Tim is. Bev and Brian look up as I turn the corner to my tukul.

"Going to bed?" Bev asks.

"Yeah. Think so. Hope so. Good night."

"Good night."

I duck under the awning of my tukul, and again under the door, turn on the light. A lizard skitters from under my bed to behind my metal clothes trunk. I hang my sarong on one of the roof's branches and sit down on my thin mattress.

My tukul's cement walls are bare. In the corner is a plastic desk, and on it, books I brought from home. The history of the twentieth century, *Ulysses*, *Zen in the Art of Archery*. Kapuscinski's *Shadow of the Sun* is beside my bed. I haven't read more than a few words of any of them. Too hot in here, the gazebo too full of work.

I turn off my handset and set it on the desk. The crackling keeps me awake. The guard will come get me if the hospital calls.

I open my clothes trunk. Since this morning, a thin film of dust has collected on it. It tumbles off the back and lifts in a fine cloud. I pick up my running clothes and put them under my bed, then set the alarm on my watch for 6:20. I turn off the light, pull up the mosquito net, slide underneath it, and tuck it in.

Behind me, through the thin grass of our compound wall, a song warbles. With each of its million plays in the past ten days, its tape is becoming thinner, tinnier.

A dog barks. Yipyipyipyipyip.

I'm sweating. I roll on my side. My hip digs into the string underneath my mattress. It was Sandrine's, someone else's before that. I slide closer to its edge to find more foam.

I wonder how that little girl is doing. The orphan. Aweil. So quiet. Can't read her. Fevers, not eating. Dehydrated, dry eyes. I can't stop thinking about her.

Dude, tomorrow.

I turn onto one side, then the other. The mattress is wet from sweat. An insect starts to crawl slowly over my leg and I swipe at it in the dark. Familiar thoughts circle, circle, circle.

What time is it? Ten. Okay.

Yipyipyipyipyipyip.

I curl the pillow around my head. The outside world grows quieter, the amplitude of my inner world louder. Circles. They slowly start to break, their lines becoming more oblique. I realize I am about to fall asleep. The thought wakes me.

Maybe I should just call the hospital and check on her. No. Tomorrow.

What time is it? Eleven.

I reach down to where my watch is, change its alarm to 7:15.

Won't have time to run. Whatever.

A mosquito whines in my ear. I swat at it. It whines again. I throw a corner of my net free and feel blindly for my headlamp. I turn it on and begin to sweep my bed for the interloper. I find him hanging upside down, in one corner, and smear him against the mesh.

I turn my lamp off, lie back down, wrap the pillow around my head.

Yipyipyipyipyipyip.

I've got to have a conversation with that dog.

Knockknockknock.

Huh?

Knockknockknockknock.

"Yes?"

"Dr. James? Hospital. Channel 6."

" 'Kay."

06/03: y-shaped sticks.

"may you live in interesting times" is one of the greatest curses. the measles vaccines have arrived. 43,000 doses. they sit in . . . oh shit, they should be in the fridge. i'll be right back.

while we were building recubras for our measles patients, we were setting up three tents for a vaccination campaign command post. one for equipment, one to house the extra team members flown in from geneva, and the other to plaster with maps and strategies. 4,000 kg of cargo for the measles emergency arrived from khartoum last night.

interesting times. we have made it part of our campaign to screen all the children we vaccinate for malnutrition. because the population of abyei has tripled in the past year, there is a food shortage. there is one harvest a year, and it happens at the end of the rainy season. that will be in september or october. abyei is about to enter its food gap, and starvation will worsen. if we vaccinate 35,000 children in the next few weeks, and we find 1% severe malnutrition (a local ngo estimates it at 3%), that will mean 350 children, perhaps 1/2 under 5. we will offer all transport to the hospital. if 1/2 are under five, and 1/2 refuse, we still might end up with 80 more children in the tfc. right now we have ten. interesting.

so, that's what we talk about over lunch, and that is why there is reason to be nervous. 80 children. it would double our current census, measles patients included. what about latrines? showers? kitchen? where would they sleep? who will take care of them?

right. the max capacity of latrines is 20 people per. we have five. we can build more. we'll send a car for more gas and stoves. build another shower. we shouldn't put children at the front of the hospital because they would be vulnerable to fighting or the chaos of a big accident. so they go in the back. away from the tb patients and the measled. ok. we'll set up a tent. no, they don't like tents. too hot. they like recubras. fine. big hut, back of the hospital, put starving kids in it. more latrines, a shower or two.

this could start tomorrow. wednesday. ok. maybe we'll get there and everyone will be so fat they can't even waddle to the front of the vaccination line. so let's wait and see. then move fast if we have to.

our logistician spoke up. "well, maybe one thing. those y-shaped sticks, you know the ones we use to make the recubra? they are hard to find. people have to travel to get them. we should go to the market right now and buy as many as we can so we are not scrambling tomorrow if we need them. i'll do it after lunch."

we'll sort it out as we need to. except for the y-shaped sticks. today it's all about the y-shaped sticks.

logisticians make things happen. if it wasn't for them, the rest of us would be standing knee deep in dust, waiting to get started but not sure exactly how to begin. we add things to their lists, and put request forms on their desks. yesterday i put one on jean's desk for "world's largest emerald." he didn't mention it today, so i guess it is on its way.

"WHERE'S HE GOING?" I ask Tim.

"Who?"

We're sitting at the table in the gazebo, eating our lunch.

"The emergency-team log, what's-his-name. He just went into our kitchen and took our kitchen knife."

The emergency team has been here for a few days. They are here to run the vaccination campaign and help take care of the infected measles patients. Right now, we have about forty in the recubra next to the cement fence. With their families, nearly one hundred people sleep there, hospital on one side of their buttressing wall, soldiers on the other. One noticeable effect is that, since we started flanking the soldiers with the infected, we have not seen them sneaking in to use our latrine.

The emergency team, thus far, has cut a wide swath through our normal activities. Three new people in our compound, five or six in compound 2. There are so many people there now, we have started to call it camp 2, because the number of people sharing a latrine exceeds the WHO standard for refugees. Our showers are flooded, our drinking water disappears from the fridge.

"I don't know where he's going," Tim answers.

I charge after him. I find him in one of the emergency tents, cutting open boxes.

"Bro. What? That's our kitchen knife. There's gotta be a better option."

"I need to open these. The ice packs."

"I can appreciate that. But that's our kitchen knife. It's our only one. It's already so goddamn dull. I'll help you find something else."

I take it out of his hand and feel instantly like an ass. Him chastened and me sorry, we walk to the logistics tukul to find a utility knife. I leave him there.

Tim is sitting, eating an orange. I set the knife down on the table.

"I'm a dick."

Tensions are high everywhere right now. We rarely eat together. Paola has retreated into her tukul, and if she's not there, or at the hospital, she is at the World Food Programme compound visiting her boyfriended friend. During the day, Jean is working hard to push forward a planned borehole. At night, he visits a friend of his who works for the UN. On top of her role as field coordinator, Bev has assumed that of vaccination campaign coordinator. I catch glimpses of her barreling past me in a Land Cruiser a couple times a day, cigarette in her hand, handset to her mouth.

I am at the hospital, mostly, and when I'm not, I'm trying to sort out the TB register, or make sense of the statistics. If the hospital is quiet, every couple of days I will sit in my tukul and write. The gazebo is full of bullhorns and maps.

The hospital is crazy. I think even more than usual. To this point it has been a controlled, smoldering chaos, full of unmet needs and slow revolts by patients and staff. As more people arrive at Abyei, as more people come through our doors, as the word spreads farther, the busier we become.

I was on my way home yesterday, hoping that there would be some food left. I had spent my lunch hour talking with the man who had brought the orphaned girl Aweil to us. He had intended to leave several days ago, to start school, but each day I try to persuade him to stay until she gets better. I found him that morning, his books bundled with a leather belt under her bed. She was still febrile, not eating. I convinced him to stay at least one more night. I was just turning right at the cannon.

"Dr. James for hospital."

Come on.

"Hospital, go ahead."

"Move channel 6."

"Moving. Channel 6."

"Dr. James, we need you at hospital."

"Why?"

" . . . "

"Hospital?"

"Dr. James, please come to hospital."

"Affirmative. Over and out."

Halfway home, I turned back. Outside the gates were two Ministry of Health vehicles.

The Abyei hospital is, officially, a Ministry of Health hospital. Though an MSF France section worked in Abyei during the war, it left as fighting slowed. This mission opened last year with the dual purpose of treating a growing number of returnees and watching for war. When we arrived, the hospital was so overwhelmed that there were dead people in the rooms. The few people who were working in the hospital couldn't keep track of who was alive. We signed a memorandum of understanding with the Ministry of Health. We would share their space and provide what resources we could to make the hospital function. We provided drugs, equipment, staff. We sourced a generator. We planned a borehole.

There were unavoidable problems. Some of the staff are MOH: a percentage of the nurses, all the cleaners. Their salaries, when they are paid, are lower than MSF's, so we decided to top them up. Though we pay them, we cannot discipline them. They are not our employees. If they miss work for a month, all we can do is withhold their incentive.

There is a skeleton administration, a director, a vaccination officer, and a hospital administrator. They each have their own offices in the hospital, but their salaries are as erratic as their colleagues', and their power to effect change small. They have neither a phone nor the right numbers.

Our flag hangs outside the gates. The hospital, however, is deeded to the MOH. In whose name were we working? In countries like Sudan, the government relies on NGOs, and at times leans on them. If there is any ethical imperative for a central administration to assume some responsibility for the health of its people, it is tempered by our presence. The people are getting free care. Why hurry? The presence of a Ministry of Health, from the North or the South, becomes a political game.

As I passed the MOH cars, I wondered how the hospital was being played. I already knew that the vaccination officer was unhappy with our campaign. We had called in the emergency team, trained vaccinators, and organized the vaccines, all on our own. By doing so, we removed the chance for others to make money from the endeavor and receive what they considered their fair share.

The guard was inside the gate, feet up on his small plastic desk, fiddling with the thick rubber antenna of his handset. As usual, not a lot of guarding going on. A guard's position is the lowest paid and least enviable. In a land of guns, we give them a walkie-talkie and then we rely on them to pass it to someone who can understand what we are saying. The other day I saw a group of guards underneath the tamarind tree looking at a blackboard easel with the alphabet written on it, practicing.

"So?" I asked him, shrugging.

He pointed lazily at a group of men walking towards the measles area. I ran to catch up to them.

"Wait a minute! Wait! Stop!"

They turned around.

"Have you guys all had measles?"

They had. I introduced myself. Together we walked through the measles area, row on row of infected children and adults, flat on plastic beds. Often, three or four children from the same household, at different stages of the illness, lay like puzzle pieces, their mothers fanning their fevers.

I explained to the MOH delegates how our team was out right now, north of Abyei, mobilizing the communities for the upcoming campaign. I told them that of all the patients so far, we have had only two deaths. Both under five, both showed up late, with a secondary infection.

"Are you sure of the diagnosis?" one of them asked.

I leaned over a small boy and pulled his shirt up.

"You can see the rash. Here, look from this angle. Little raised bumps, patches. After you see a few, you can spot it at twenty yards."

They murmured their agreement. One of them wrote something down in his notepad.

"Do you mind if we take some blood from some of them? Just to confirm?" he asked.

"I . . . um . . . I guess you had better ask them."

The patients, of course, would not refuse. I doubt they recognized their right to do so, the idea of autonomy in the face of authority as unfamiliar as everything else in the hospital.

I started to ask what had brought them to Abyei from Kadugli. A nurse grabbed me by the elbow.

"Dr. James. A woman in the emergency. Bleeding. Pregnant."

I left the ministry officials beside the little boy's bed and crossed the courtyard to the hospital. I stopped where the orange fence, used to separate the hospital from the measles area, had been loosened, stepped through, pulled it taut. A little girl, on the veranda, watched me.

"You didn't see that," I said.

In the emergency room were a woman and her husband. She had started bleeding that day.

"How long has she been pregnant? Is she cramping? Has she passed any tissue or clots?"

A nurse at my arm.

"Dr. James. Please come to the nursing room. A boy. Breathing problem."

I left the woman and her husband, their answers still in their mouths, and walked to the nursing room. Breathing before bleeding.

The child, about four years old, could barely draw a breath. Every few seconds, the muscles in his ribs would flicker and his stomach would pulse. He was unconscious.

"Vital signs?" I asked.

None had been done.

"Okay. Heart rate, temperature, oxygen saturation, and check his blood sugar. All of those. Grab that mask. No, that one. The small one. Give it to me. And the bag. Watch. Hold it like this. Like this. Just so his chest moves. No. Too big. Small. Good."

I hurried to the pharmacy and grabbed the oxygen concentrator. It was new, still in its box. I cut the top off and pulled it out, foam beads spilling onto the floor. I removed the plastic, kicked the pharmacy door open with my foot, and wheeled it past a queue of admiring inpatients who had gathered to watch.

"Out out out. Everyone." One of the nurses had taped an oxygen saturation monitor to the child's finger. It read 70%. Should be closer to 100%. He had a fever. His sugar was okay.

I unwrapped the plastic from the concentrator and threw it on the ground. I found a pediatric mask and affixed it to the boy's face. I turned the machine on.

The oxygen saturation crept from 70% to 90%. I looked down at his ribs. Flicker. Pause. Flicker. Pause. Pause. Pause.

His mother sat on the edge of the bed, looking from my face to the flashing numbers on the monitor.

The child couldn't breathe on his own any more. His ribs and diaphragm were too tired. He needed a machine to do it. We didn't have one. I removed the face mask.

"Michael, start bagging again. That mask. Yeah. Right. Like that. Perfect."

I grabbed a handset off the nursing desk.

"Brian for Dr. James. Brian for Dr. James."

"James, go ahead."

"Brian, I've got a kid here who needs to be intubated or he's going to die. Likely pneumonia. He's got a fever. I just don't know if I should do it. We have no ventilator. Over."

He would be right there. Sweet.

I returned to the pharmacy and fumbled through its shelves in the dark, flashlight in my mouth. I still haven't figured out where the light is.

What size of tube? Age over four, plus four . . . a 5. Suction . . . where is that? Here. Laryngoscope. What size blade? One miller, I guess.

By the time I got back, Brian was in the nursing room.

"Yeah, I agree with you. He's not really breathing. How long has he been this way?"

"Mother says he was fine this morning, but I doubt that. He's going to die any minute."

He looked at the laryngoscope and tube in my hand.

"I say go for it. We'll call a nurse from compound 2 and she can bag him."

"For how long?"

"I don't know. How long do you think he'll need it?" he asked.

"He's not going to turn around in an hour. Not if it's pneumonia. It would have to be at least overnight. Maybe even longer."

"Overnight, then."

Brian called on the handset to compound 2 and asked for our best nurse. I sat down with the mother.

"Your baby's not breathing very well. See? He's only breathing small. Not good. We need to help him breathe. Put this tube down his throat to push in air. I think if we do not do it, he will die. Even if we do, he might die. I don't know. It's the only thing I can do."

The nurse translated and the mother agreed.

I put the flat blade of the laryngoscope past his tiny white teeth and pushed his tongue to the side. I lifted the blade until I could see his vocal cords. They flickered with each breath. I pushed the tube past them, into his trachea, then attached the bag to it.

His oxygen saturation improved to 100%. His chest rose and fell with each small squeeze of the bag. I hoped the MOH delegates would walk by, but they never did.

Muriel arrived from compound 2. She's young, was trained in Khartoum, and worked with MSF for years in Darfur. She is interested and competent, the best we have.

"Okay. Like this. Just a gentle push. Watch his chest. In . . . and out . . . in . . . and out. This is the suction machine. You work it with your foot, like this. You'll need to suction him every hour or so."

I addressed the other nurses. "This is a hard job. You will have to help her. You too, Mom. She can't stop. If she does, the baby won't be able to breathe and he will die. Okay?"

We left them, Muriel pushing on the bag, twelve times per minute, 720 times per hour.

I wonder, in cases like this, if the battle is worth fighting. The war is a long one, and the odds are stacked so heavily that perhaps energy is best conserved. Maybe it's best to use likely defeats to increase our resolve to work towards a day when they will be easier to win. But then there is the other tack. Battle, every time, with everything you have. Do the best you can for the person in front of you. Persuade the family of every malnourished kid to get into the truck, to come to the hospital, to be fed until they're better. Track down each TB patient who left, frustrated, halfway through his long treatment and try to get him to come back even though the countryside is littered with tuberculosis patients we will never see and one case will not tip the balance sheet noticeably towards a TB-free future. To the world it doesn't matter that much. Until you remember that it means the world to the patient. One exact world, bright and full of sounds, per person. That's what is lost.

I attended to the woman I left in the emergency room. She was miscarrying, but not hemorrhaging too much. If she continued to bleed, we would do a D&C on her tomorrow.

I checked on Aweil. She was sleeping on the floor beside another child. One of the mothers was watching them both.

In the nursing room, the boy's saturation was still 100%. I went to the gate.

"Driver?" the guard asked.

"No, I'll walk," I said, and mimed legs with my fingers.

The night was thick, moonless. I made my way slowly back to the compound, trying not to trip into someone coming the other way. It was late by the time I arrived, and everyone was in their tukuls. There was some food left on the stove, and I ate a few spoonfuls standing over the sink. I crawled into my sweaty bed and called the hospital. The child was still alive, saturation 100%. I told the hospital to call me if anything changed, and left the handset crackling beside my head.

This morning, when I got to the hospital, Muriel was still pushing the bag. She had not taken a break all night. The mother was lying down on the bed, her hand resting on her child's chest, feeling its rise and fall.

I relieved Muriel, and she stumbled from the nursing room towards the waiting Land Cruiser. I explained to the mother that we needed to take the tube out, to see if her child would breathe on his own. I suctioned his small mouth, removed the tape from around it and from the tube. I stopped bagging.

He was breathing. A little. More than a flicker, more than last night. I pulled the tube.

On my way home for lunch today, I got a call from the hospital. His breathing was getting worse.

"Put him on oxygen," I said. We couldn't intubate him again. We didn't have the resources or the trained staff. Fifteen minutes later, they called again. He was dead. I sat down to lunch.

And now I am looking at this dull goddamn knife. Useless. Better for cutting boxes than tomatoes, that's for sure.

I am not going to intubate anyone else.

08/03: bounce.

so far, at this point in the day, twelve noon, i am having my first day off. well, i went to the hospital, but only to check on a baby i admitted yesterday who was so dehydrated that you could see his fontanelle from 20 meters. he was sleeping soundly, his mother beside him. she has two oblique scars on either cheek. like this:

```
      O    O
      // ^ \\
```

last night the "abyei jazz band" (and i use the already loose term "jazz" so loosely that one of the z's just fell off) played all night at volumes that greatly exceeded my 32 dB-rated earplugs. one of the rewards i had hoped to find this far from somewhere was a night full of quiet stars. no.

it is day two of the measles vaccination campaign. we are hoping for some bounce from the undetermined electorate, particularly the hard to reach 5-year-olds.

passed some of the queues on my way to the hospital yesterday, families standing outside in the hot sun, voting measle. we had some late-night drama the night before with our newly trained local vaccinating team. they demanded more money. our field coordinator had played this game before. "those who want to leave can. we'll pause the campaign, tell the community you don't want to do it, and train others. no problem." yesterday morning, they were all sweating with the patients, jabbing thin arms.

there are so many children, it is sure we are missing a few. yesterday i admitted only three for feeding. today might tell a different story. on the brighter side, we have the necessary y-shaped sticks.

i told the team, as far as i was concerned it was already a success. hundreds of kids will never, ever get measles. some of my enthusiasm is altruistic, but most of it is selfish. we need another 100 measles cases in the hospital like we need someone to crank up the heat. so whether it happens in an orderly way, people in rod-straight lines with smiles and sleeves rolled up, or if we have to run around in the middle of the market vaccinating everyone using some type of rapid-fire blow-dart scenario, it will be a success.

this morning, at 6:30, i woke up for a run. it is my only oblique entry in an otherwise linear day. my path is from the compound to the hospital. 460 paces to it in the morning, 480 on the return (so hot).

BRIAN HAS GONE BACK TO Khartoum. The measles team remains. Roberto, the Spanish coordinator of the measles effort, sits in the small recubra we built for him, typing out a growing catalog of measles patients. He eats only bread and jam, drinks mostly grape soda. A hummingbird.

I am just back from the hospital. For the moment, it is quiet. As my last order of business, I assessed a woman in labor. With my fingers I examined her cervix. She was 5 cm dilated. I struggled to feel the baby.

Oh. There it is. Tiny fingers. No, too short. Tiny toes. Yep. There's the heel. Footling breech. Wait . . . that's the head. Oh yeah, for sure. I can feel the sutures. Definitely not a bum.

So, one of two possibilities: some type of crazy somersaulting acrobatic compound presentation with the foot coming out just over the head, or there are two fetuses. I guess there is a third possibility. I can't tell my heads from my asses. The unfortunate part is that neither delivery would be straightforward, and it is late, and we cannot drive to a hospital that could do a caesarean section at this time of night.

Brian told me that he did his first when he was in South Sudan, sweating over a book, his heart in his throat. I went through our surgical tools before I left today, and we have the right ones. As I locked the door, I imagined myself standing there, Mohamed beside me, sweating over a book, the woman flat on her back, her abdomen draped with the cleanest cloths we have, twins waiting to get out into the world, Mohamed showing me the book, then again, finally taking the scalpel and drawing it smoothly through the skin of her abdomen, blood quickly blooming into the yellow crevice, "suction . . . suction . . ." My heart's in my throat.

For now I am sitting in the gazebo, watching the sun fall into deep red sunset. Whenever I see the sun come up in Africa, or go down, I think the same thing: it is easy to believe that life began here. There is just so much of it. The spectrum of light that runs from red to violet, from long to short, is proof. As the day's starting and finishing rays pass through the atmosphere tangentially, cutting across the dusty plains and the deep jungle instead of directly down, the smaller bluer rays are picked out by water vapor, or a piece of sand, or a tiny buzzing beetle. The reds and the oranges bend around, careening through. Each morning and each night, a collision of these, and a phoenix. When I run in the morning, thanks to the sand and the blinded buzzing beetles, I can look directly at the sun until it is well above the thick horizon. It is the most perfect circle.

There are so many living things on this continent. Not just humans, of course. Insects, lizards, birds, bats, baboons, spiders (one in Paola's tukul the size of a fist), big cats, loping giraffes, and with them a legion of viruses, parasites, bacteria.

I look at my arm. Bites march over it, and over these a series of small pimples from the bacteria that cover my bed, my sheets, my tukul, me. Perhaps, like the rest of us, the new twins will get their start here. But maybe they are too new. In some ways it is easier to be a spider in this place than a new human trying to make it out with your brother's foot in your face.

Bev rounds the corner.

"Hey, Bev." I start cleaning up my plate.

The last time I saw her was this afternoon. She sped up in the Land Cruiser, pulled me aside, and pointed at two young children in the back seat.

"Two more measles cases, from Akur," she said excitedly, and sped off.

They weren't. Just regular rashes. I sent them both home.

"Hi."

She sits down, reaches for the ashtray in the middle of the table, pulls out a package of cigarettes. She takes one, then slides the open package towards me.

"Thanks."

We smoke.

"How are you doing?" I ask, finally.

"All right." She looks worn.

"You're not sleeping much."

"The measles team. It's busy. First emergency mission for all of 'em. Fuckups all around."

"How's the coverage so far?"

"Can't really tell. We don't really know how many people there are around here. All we have is GOAL's data, and I don't know if it's any good."

The handset crackles on the table between us. We both look at it. It remains quiet.

"Hey, I wanted to ask you something," I say.

"Shoot."

"Um . . . have you ever heard of . . . This is going to sound kind of weird, but . . . uh . . . Ever heard of someone adopting a kid while on mission?"

" . . ."

"Like, is it possible? Or is it against the rules or something?"

"It's not a good idea, James."

"There's a girl in the hospital, in the TFC. The orphan. Aweil. Did I tell you about her?"

"Yeah. Her mom died from malaria or something a couple months ago, right? Here in the hospital. Dad's a soldier. It's a bad idea."

"Think so?"

"Definitely bad. It wouldn't be a popular move. You would make a lot of people angry."

" 'Kay."

"I get it, James. 'If I can't save them all, why not one?' Right? Everyone goes through it. Wait it out."

" 'Kay."

Pause.

"What about money? Are we allowed to give money to particular people? Like is it okay to give her some of my per diem? Or just some money so she can go to school, or whatever? Not even now. Later."

"People do it. But it's not a good idea."

I am half finished my cigarette. It tastes black. I put it out.

"Okay." I stand up, stack my plates together, and turn towards the kitchen.

"There's some beer in there. It's probably not very cold, but grab one if you want."

"Sweet."

I leave my dishes by the side of the sink, look into the fridge. Pushed to the sides are people's personal food reserves, each wrapped in a separate plastic bag, or labeled with tape. It seems odd not to share, but to one side, my bag. In it, a can of pineapple I bought for 60 cents.

To the side of that, 500 milliliters of beer. From Kenya. Warm as hell. Once the fridge is unplugged and opened, it quickly assumes the ambient temperature. Today it is about 104 Fahrenheit. I plug the fridge back in, and it sparks, then hums alive. I stick two glasses in the freezer.

A few days ago, I showed up and the man with the books was gone. I've since watched Aweil shuffle from one mother's lap to another's in the feeding center. She never smiles. Everything else about her seems normal for an infant. She will pick at things with her forefinger, track my movements. But she won't smile, as if in the ten months she has been around, she has only seen things worth mourning.

She remains sick. And listless. Yesterday, after everyone left the hospital, I went to her bed and sat down. She was lying alone, half turned over, blinking slowly. I touched her bare back. She had a fever. I turned her, pulled her up to my knee. She drooped.

"What's wrong with you, huh? Why all the fevers?"

I looked at her chart, as I had done that morning, and studied it. Her weight was falling again. I'd treated her for everything. Malaria, all the bacteria I could think of, intravenous, oral, all. I posited to Mohamed today that it might be HIV.

"How did her mother die?"

"Meningitis," he said.

"Did you see the spinal fluid?"

"No."

"Could be HIV. Crypto. Or TB. Dad's a soldier."

"Possible."

"So maybe Aweil's positive."

I left it at that. We don't routinely test for HIV unless we have a program. She's ten months old. To whom would I provide the counseling about what a diagnosis means? Or the possibility of lifelong treatment? We can't test CD4s, liver function, nothing.

But I put the thought in Mohamed's head, hoping that he would test her without my permission.

I open the freezer. The glasses are a little cooler. I take the beer from the fridge, pour a glass for myself, one for Bev.

Maybe she is right. Maybe I want to do it because I want one small island of control to cling to. But it isn't that simple. I don't want to only save Aweil, treat-her-malaria save her. I want to take her home with me, put her in school, let her decide who she will be. I think I might love her a little bit. I can't help it. It's bigger than me.

Could I do it? I would have to quit, particularly if she doesn't get better. Get to a hospital where she can be diagnosed. I would have to get a new place. Mine's too small. I would have to commit to Toronto, or move back to Alberta. Commit somewhere. No more MSF. Who would babysit for me during my night shifts. Steve? Greg? Jeff? No way. I would need a nanny. What if she is positive? Could I watch her die?

I leave the kitchen, beers in hand, and Bev is gone.

14/03: good news.

"whatever you do tomorrow, do not go to akur riang from where you will be. there are mines along the road. it doesn't matter what anyone says."

that's the conversation that is going on beside me right now. measles team talk. they are blanketing the countryside with vaccines. they leave at 7 in the morning, and are finished loading the vehicles by 11 at night. they are improving. at the beginning of the campaign, one week ago . . . wow, it seems longer . . . at the beginning, they were nerves on nerves, tracking back on the themselves, just unprepared enough for things to fray by the end of the day. now they are moving like a machine.

the other night, the foot-in-the-face twins, delivered by one of our midwives. one lived. one was too new.

i received the best news today. well, two good pieces. the first is that my mother is sending me a battery powered fan. if i am lucky, someone will be coming to khartoum, and have the space to bring it, luckier still if that someone drops it at the msf office in sudan, and even more when someone brings it as part of their 15 kg of luggage to abyei. in the meantime, i sweat. it is 10 p.m., and 100F in my tukul. it was 115 this afternoon. the only recourse one has is to minimize the surface area of his body in contact with the bed. for instance, the side-sleeping knee-elbow maneuver. or the scapula-butt pillow wedge.

the second piece of good news, if not enabling my sleep, will allow me to lie contentedly awake. a child i've grown fond of is not improving as well as i would like. last week, as i was sweating asleep, a dark thought crept in. "maybe hiv." could be. the fevers, and the weight loss. i hoped not. i held my breath.

while i was away from the hospital today, she was tested. negative.

i spent months traveling africa in 2005 writing about hiv, but i never understood how truly important it was to prevent and treat the disease until i felt that cool relief today. good news. may it happen more and more often to more and more people.

THE DAY IS ALMOST DONE. I have checked on Aweil. She was lying on the plastic mattress in the courtyard. No one was around, so I picked her up and held her. Her head lolled to the side, to the back. I leaned her forward, let her hot forehead rest in the crook of my neck, and listened to the breath whistle through her nose. I sat there for fifteen minutes. I set her down when one of the nutritional assistants came around the corner. I didn't want to show any proof of my investment, that on this one, I am betting everything.

I have one more thing to do today and I am waiting for everyone else to leave. Last night a nurse pulled me aside and told me that a friend of one of our cleaners was raped a month or so ago and is now pregnant. And sick with fevers and pelvic pain. Probably gonorrhea or chlamydia. She wants an abortion.

Nyanut is in her forties, and well known in Abyei's small community. She often comes to the hospital to bring the nurses tea. She does not want anyone to know about this. In the curious twist so common here, rape is the woman's crime. We spoke briefly this morning about her symptoms, through a translator, under the guise she is not pregnant, but only having abdominal pain. I asked her to meet me here this afternoon.

There she is, over by the emergency room, talking to one of the nurses. I want to catch her eye, to gesture her towards the operating theater. It's private there. I can lock the door.

Good. She sees me.

I walk into the dark hallway that leads to the small operating theater and pass two women lying on beds. One is about to give birth, the other did this morning. Her new infant is lying beside her, uncovered and ignored, mewling. I came across an article on the medical computer about the importance of "kangarooing" the newborn infant, and mean to start encouraging it, get the midwives on it. I haven't. It sits at the end of a long list.

I remove the padlock from the door and enter the theater. On the surgical bed, I put a plastic sheet.

The windows are open to the outside. Through the mesh I can hear the chatter of the mothers in the feeding center, and behind the hospital the splash of someone washing themselves. It is almost dusk, and the generator remains off. I don't ask the guard to turn it on. There's enough light for now.

Nyanut raps on the door. I gesture for her to come in, to sit on the bed. I pull up a chair.

"Baby?" I say, and point at my belly, tracing a pregnant abdomen. Nyanut knows some words of English. She doesn't want to use a translator for this.

"Baby," she says.

"How many days ago, last period, last bleeding?" I ask.

She counts back on her fingers.

"Twelve January."

I count on mine. Sixty days or so.

"Pain?" I ask.

"Pain," she says, pointing to her pelvis.

"Blood?"

"Tch." A shake of the head. No.

"Do you want to have baby?"

"No. No baby." She waves her finger. "Cannot. Bad man. Think friend but friend no. Sex, afraid, no." She holds up three fingers. "Me, many children. No husband. Husband die. Cut. Muslim. Pain." She points down towards her groin.

I nod. I take her pulse. Normal. I touch her forehead. It's warm. I put a thermometer under her arm and wait for it to cool. Her temperature's okay. I gesture for her to lie down, then place a sheet over her legs.

I push on her abdomen. I can feel the edge of her uterus jutting above the hard brim of her pelvis. It feels firm, not boggy. She winces a bit. I push a bit harder and let go quickly. I look at her face. No grimace, no peritonitis.

I sit her up.

"I'm going to look inside with this." I show her the bright metal speculum. "I look for infection. Okay?"

"Okay."

She lies back down and spreads her legs. I remove the sheet and pull up her gown.

Her labia are scarred together. The introitus is tiny. Perhaps big enough for one finger. The speculum would never fit. I reach to my side and unwrap a pediatric one. It is much too large. I pull her labia apart and do my best to look inside. I can see green pus. I pull her gown back over her knees and sit back. I'm silent.

What the fuck.

She must have been cut, her clitoris removed, and her labia sewn together. Again after her children. Torn open, sewn back together. Infibulation.

She sits up. "Small small," she says.

For the first time, a hard hot kernel of anger burns in me. We have patients who refuse to treat their contagious tuberculosis and leave the hospital coughing, families with malarious children who disappear when our backs are turned, and we make sense of it. They might not appreciate fully the choices, or their consequences, or maybe there's something we don't know. But this. It seems deliberate, irrevocable, unforgivable.

"You need to take medicines. For infection. Okay?"

"Okay. Baby?"

"Yes."

Her eyes widen.

"Oh, I mean yes, pregnant. But we can stop, okay?" Whatever it takes to help you, I want to do it.

She nods.

I've never done this before. I think you use prostaglandin to relax the cervix. I'll look it up. I'll ask Brian. He'll know.

"All right. If you wait outside, I'll get some medicines, okay? Wait outside, okay?" I point.

"Okay."

She leaves through the blue wooden door, and its hanging lock bangs as she shuts it.

She's getting to the end of the effective period for medical abortion,

I think. We can still try, but if it doesn't work . . . I guess a D&C . . . dilate the cervix, scrape out the uterus. Might have to do it anyway if the infection worsens, or she could die. I would have to ask Mohamed for help. He's done more than me. The secret would be out then. We would have to cut her open in order to get the tools in there. Use ketamine, cut open the scar tissue with a scalpel. There'll be a ton of blood. Then sew her together. Might heal wrong otherwise. Chronic pain.

I know we don't have the right meds in the pharmacy. Maybe in the market, but I doubt it. I'll look. If not, I'll find a way to get them from Khartoum. Maybe I can send some from Ethiopia. Addis. It hangs like a diamond in my calendar, a breath away from this place, the handset.

I'll need to give Bev and Nyanut clear instructions about how to use the pills, how to watch for infection. And when to tell Mohamed if things go wrong.

I shut the wooden windows tightly against their jambs, put the plastic sheet in the washbin and the speculums beside it. I close the door and lock the small padlock. The baby is still mewling beside his mother. I pick him up, put him on his mother's chest, and cover him with a blanket.

I leave the hallway and the hospital is quiet. No outpatients to be seen, all the visitors have gone. Nyanut lingers near the front gate. I hold up my finger. One minute.

I walk towards the pharmacy to gather her antibiotics, picking my way between children on the increasingly crowded floor of the feeding center.

15/03: dream.

i had a dream last night that i was finished my mission. i was sitting at a table, surrounded by friends. one said "wow, that went so fast!" i agreed.

i woke up to the sounds of the muezzin at 5 in the morning. i lay in my bed, smelling the dust.

i left canada more than a month ago. it seems longer. i have seen and learned so many things, lived one hundred stories.

i wrote in my first post that i had anticipated one of the lessons i would be taught. "be careful what you wish for, you just might get it." part of my motivation for coming here, to abyei, was to test my resolve. i didn't anticipate it would be tested so well.

in the pre-departure training, we are told of the well-worn personal trajectory we will likely follow in missions like this one. we arrive to the project full of nervous excitement. there are so many new things. new faces, new routines, roles, and rules. we are frenetic, and overwhelmed, but buzzing with energy.

this fades after a couple of weeks. the reality of the days starts to thicken like cement and initial momentum slows. new things become old ones and the weeks of work stretch ahead. we realize that this is not an exciting dash to a spectacular finish; it is a marathon. our mood ebbs. one day of work bleeds into another.

days become weeks. soon the midpoint of the mission approaches. after three months of working seven days, we are allowed to rest for a week. our mood improves. where are we going to go? we start planning tickets and departures. excited, we leave the country, lie on a beach, and sleep. we return somewhat rested, and take another blow to our enthusiasm. back here again. back in no(middle)where, treading water.

days find weeks again. soon we realize we have an opportunity to make a lurching step towards a better tb program, or a bigger feeding center, or having a borehole finally dug. what we don't have is much time. we become frantic again, and as the end draws nearer, we wish it were further away. but it isn't. and here comes someone else, full of nervous energy, and a new world rolls over him.

for the time being, for me, my respite is that half hour of silence before the generator starts. the sun is still down, and the roosters newly up. we leave our tukuls, walk quietly past one another, whisper "morning . . . morning." we go to the kitchen and boil some water, grab a piece of warm bread, and sit on the brick wall of our communal gazebo and look at the sky. for a few minutes, the world seems to stretch wide, much wider than the grass walls of compound 1. for a minute, we are who we are.

WE ARE SITTING TOGETHER, the Abyei team. All of us. Bev, Paola, Jean, Tim, and me. The measles team is meeting with itself, in one of their emergency tents. The Ministry of Health has asked us to finish our campaign. They want to begin one of their own.

It is rare for the five of us to be together like this. Since I arrived, we have been pulled in so many different directions, and because of it, pulled apart, not together. Difficult in a place like this where it is already easy to feel alone.

"Pass the ful," Paola says.

"I can't believe you eat that stuff," Jean says, giving Paola the pot of black and brown beans.

"I like it," she says.

"It makes me want to die."

"A piece of bread, too."

Paola is leaving soon. So am I. She is going on her R&R. She has planned it for months. I'm off to Ethiopia.

"So, Paola, when do you leave again?"

"Two days." The edges of her mouth start to curve up.

I know the answer, but ask because the thought of it makes her happy.

Questions about time are common talk. At least to me.

When are you taking your R&R?

When did you arrive again?

When are you finished?

When do I go home?

Will I get to a time when I don't want to?

When?

"Bev, when do you leave?" I ask.

"Not sure. Soon. Beginning of April. Couple weeks."

"What are you going to do when you get home?"

"Can't think about it. Still two weeks."

She's tired. Measles has taken a toll on her. I've asked her a few times if she is okay. She says she is. I've stopped asking. We don't talk about how we are doing, except to say we're tired.

I am reminded of visiting an HIV project in Zambia a few years before. I asked a first-mission nurse, disheartened midway through her nine-month mission, what she found most difficult about the job.

"No feedback."

This work is not what one does if he is interested in being told that he is doing the right thing. We are expected to know. The work is not easy, not for anyone, and it never ends. If you keep on looking over your shoulder, waiting for a pat on the back, you've missed the point. It's not about you. If you are expecting it to be, better you stay at home. Still, at the end of a long day, it is an easy thing to miss. My blog is good for that. I'm lucky.

"What about you, Jean?"

"Same as Bev. Couple of weeks. Paola will be the oldest one in the mission, hey, Paola?"

"I guess," she says, frowning.

"And after she's gone, it will be you and Tim. The pros."

"Yeah, right."

We finish our food, and stack the plates on top of one another. None of us are compelled to find the tasks we left behind before lunch. I grab the plates, walk them to the kitchen, and set them beside the sink. Our cook looks up grumpily. I ask her to make us coffee. It makes her no happier.

Everyone has moved to our makeshift couch. The wind blows hot through the gazebo.

"How are things in the hospital?" Bev asks.

"All right," I answer.

"How many patients now?"

"Seventy or so."

"Is Mohamed going to be able to handle them all while you're away?"

"Hope so."

I don't want to talk about it. Everyone is quiet. Tim takes a cigarette from Bev's pack.

"How's the girl doing, the orphan?" Bev asks.

"Still sick. One of the nurses found a mother in the TFC to take care of her. At least for now."

"What's wrong with her?"

"Don't know. Treated her for everything." She's heartbroken, that's the problem.

I don't want to talk about her either. I'm thinking about Ethiopia.

The coffee arrives. We each drink our glasses, linger for a minute, then, one at a time, go our separate ways.

(breath)

20/03: lucy.

i arrived in addis ababa late last friday night. my flight was delayed because of a sandstorm in khartoum so thick that it blocked the sun from the sky, and for several hours, our plane.

i shared a taxi to the hotel with a colleague from mozambique who was also attending the tb workshop. it is a strange but certain phenomenon that when you identify a stranger as someone who works for msf, you welcome them into your fold of friends. perhaps family might be more apt. you may not get along, nor agree, but there is a common ground and with it, some forgiveness. at least you know that the person wearing the msf shirt who stole the last cold pepsi has been through a metafilter, that they could be working somewhere else, somewhere easier, closer to their friends and family for a hell of a lot more money. so, you curse them under your breath, grab the warm fanta, and sit back down.

though i landed in africa more than a month ago, i didn't feel like i had arrived until i found myself crammed into an ethiopian minibus with 15 other people. it was so full i had to lean over a row of passengers and brace myself on the back of the driver's seat. the cross hanging from his rearview mirror swung left, then right, as he angled his way through a thick mix of cars, goats, and pedestrians to pick up more people, reggae music bumping from under his seat. it is no wonder that the largest single cause of premature morbidity for expatriates is road traffic accidents. i am sure the same is true for goats.

yesterday i visited the ethiopian anthropological museum. ethiopia's rift valley is one of the richest sites in the world for fossils. thirty years ago or so, they excavated a nearly complete skeleton of one of our oldest bipedal ancestors, lucy. she is 3.2 million years old. her bones lie in the basement of the museum here in addis. there is an older fossil somewhere, an even grayer relative of ours, but i don't think the skeleton was as complete as lucy's, and at the least it isn't just down the road from my hotel.

so there she was, a pile of old bones. 3,200,000 years ago, she walked in the mountains i can see from my window. there's no way to know how many children she had, nor what type of food she liked best, nor how she died. nor if she had a ringing laugh, or was afraid of the dark. we can tell that she walked, and that her brain wasn't much smaller than ours. she represented an important advance. once she was an adult, she walked on two legs for her entire life. some scientists suspect that it allowed her to search the savannah for prey or enemies. others believe it was a step towards being able to throw and catch a frisbee, the most perfect manifestation of human ability.

the environment applies somewhat different pressures to us now. rather than responding to it, we change it to suit us. we don't grow more fingers, we build tools. i wonder how we evolve now that instead of standing on our hind legs, we can see our enemies on google earth.

part of the process, effect or side effect, seems to be an increased recognition of a shared human condition. it began, perhaps, with the printing press, then the first morse signal, from there to radio and television, and has been most completely manifest with the world wide web. the perspective it offers more properly places us in the world. in that way, the internet is not an infinite series of portals, it is a mirror in which we can see ourselves reflected more perfectly than ever before, an iteration in the development of a collective consciousness.

lucy can be forgiven for not caring about what lay on the other side of the mountain. she could not have known. one hopes that if she had, she would have made the walk. i do not think that is a naive hope. i am sitting in a room with 32 people from 22 countries who have been pushed towards common ground like we were pushed onto our hind legs a few million years ago. there is room enough for more, for all of us.

"HELLO?"

"Hey. It's James. Can you hear me?"

"Hello?"

"Sarah, it's James. From Sudan."

"Oh! Hello! Wow. How are you?"

"I'm all right. What about you?"

"Wow. Good. It's good to hear your voice. You sound really close. Where are you?"

"Khartoum. Just got in from Addis yesterday. I'm on Skype."

"How was it?"

"Really good. Fun. I made a good friend, from Morocco. We dubbed ourselves the Addis Ababa exploratory team. We were out every night, checking out the city."

"And?"

"Cool. Our last night we went to this crazy club. I think it's one of Africa's largest. At 4 a.m., the dance floor was still heaving. It was good."

"That sounds like what you needed."

"Definitely."

"When are you going back to Abyei?"

"Day after tomorrow, I think. Got my visa in Addis. It was a gong show. It took, like, three days. The Sudanese sorely overestimated my desire to return to their country. I went to the embassy and stood in lineup after lineup. Every time I asked if I was in the right one, they pointed to another. At one point I was in a line where people were being weighed. I thought I was going to be eaten or something."

"That's funny."

"Yeah, it was weird. Anyway, it worked out. Turns out the guy behind the visa counter was from Abyei, so he sorted me. Finally. And I'm Abyei bound."

"How do you feel about that?"

"All right."

"Really? . . . James?"

"Yeah, no, not really. I'm not super-psyched about it."

"Yeah, you don't sound like you are."

"It hasn't been a very good time. I mean, I know it's not about good times, but it's harder than I thought it was going to be. It's like . . . I can't get away, you know? Not even in my sleep."

"You suck at sleeping."

"Yeah, I totally suck. But it's like . . . a kid dies or whatever, and you're like, 'Hmm, what should I do now? I guess I'll just wait around for the next one.'"

"Oh baby."

"Yeah. Whatever. It's cool."

"Doesn't sound like it."

"It's okay. Sorry. Didn't mean to harsh you out. It's worse to look forward to than it is to experience. Just a tough day today, I guess. I think it's why they don't let you go home on your R&R, 'cause there's always this feeling when you're going back to the field."

"You're not harshing me out. I don't hear from you much. Just through your blog, like everyone. So it's good. I miss you. If you need to talk, you can call me any time."

"Thanks. Sorry."

"Don't be an idiot. Maybe if you're miserable, you shouldn't go back."

"No. I'll figure it out. Anyway, Sarah, what's up with you?"

"The usual. Wintertime here. Spring is happening soon. February was brutal like always. Work is kinda slow right now, but that's okay. The boys are throwing a party soon."

"I thought everyone agreed not to have any fun until I got back."

"Oh yeah. I forgot. I'll tell them to cancel it."

"They don't have to cancel it. They can still throw it, but maybe no music or something. Everyone can just mope around, think about orphans or starvation."

"I'll suggest it."

"Okay. I should go. Office is closing. Thanks for listening."

"Any time, James. Really."

26/03: sand.

the speaker above me clicked on.

"ladies and gentlemen, we have started our descent towards khartoum. we ask you to ensure that your seats and table trays are returned to their upright position and that your luggage is stowed in the overhead bins or safely under the seat in front of you. the weather in khartoum is . . . um . . . blowing sand. the temperature is 90 degrees fahrenheit. local time is 1:50 a.m."

i was once again in the land of blowing sand.

right now i am sitting in the msf office, five minutes away from the guest house where i stay, just past the garbage mound, and down the road. there is a small desk near the entrance. it is surrounded by boxes of drugs and equipment destined for the field, but there is just room enough for me. i can hear the squeal of the hf radio as it picks up signals from abyei or darfur. i wonder what they are saying.

on our last night in addis, some of us went dancing. there were about ten of us who became fast friends. we shared a similar enthusiasm for what we were learning, but also about what there was to learn about addis. after the long days, we discovered yemeni restaurants, king melenik's old castle, got lost in africa's biggest market, found traditional music, little holes in the wall just down the road.

the last thing we found was the dance floor late on saturday night. i was surrounded by people i had come to know, respect, and like. every hour our number would dwindle as someone left for the hotel to pack for rural ethiopia, or mozambique, or geneva. i was talking with my friend maria, an argentinian doctor who had last seen me throwing my backpack on top of a crowded bus in zimbabwe the day i finished with msf last. she said she often wondered what happened to me.

"james, answer me something. this life, where you get to meet people and know them, and become friends, and then in a few days or a few weeks, either they leave or you do . . . we say 'well, that's msf,' but i don't know. is it worth it?"

i am not sure, i said. i think so. maybe having your heart broken like that is what keeps it open.

now maria is back in buenos aires. mohammed ali (the great) is in mozambique. anthony in uganda. all blown like sand.

i am looking at the departure and arrivals board. on it names, destinations, and dates are scrawled in felt pen. mine is there.

James KRT ⟶ AB 28/03/07

but there are others.

my field coordinator is leaving in two weeks, and there may be someone to relieve her. our logistician is leaving at the same time, but as of yet, there is no one to take his place. in khartoum, there are similar problems. we have been without a medical coordinator for several weeks. i saw our logistical coordinator in ethiopia and he told me he resigned. our head of mission wants to be gone by the middle of april. no news on his replacement. when i left from abyei, i shared the plane with one of the two sudanese medical technicians that work in the hospital and who, with mohamed and me, make up our four person medical team. i learned today she is not returning to the project.

i will send word from abyei. love the spring for me.

CHAPTER II

THE PLANE RUMBLES TO A STOP and a cloud of dust envelops it, then swirls away.

"Welcome to Agok," the pilot says as he opens the door. Two of us clamber down.

Planes no longer fly into Abyei. The runway is too full of donkeys and bricks. This is as close as they come now, forty-five minutes and three military checkstops away.

I step out onto the cracked ground. The sun presses down and a hot wind pushes past. I look around. Ah. There's our Land Cruiser. And the driver, Anthony. I wave. Here we go.

"Hello, Doctor," he shouts, an Arabic purr on the last *r*. "Welcome home."

The pilot deposits my bag into the dust. The other passenger, with whom I had not exchanged a single word, is already driving away in a UN vehicle. I walk to the Land Cruiser and shake Anthony's hand.

"Sir Anthony. Good to see you."

I open the rear door. A man is sleeping on one of the benches, his forearm over his eyes. At the creak of the door, he sits up, blinking sleepily.

"Mohamed? What are you doing here? I thought you were on your R&R already. Or did you stay because you missed me too much?"

"I missed you, man. Too-too much," he says. He shuffles forward and we shake hands, bent underneath the truck's metal chassis, grinning at each other. "The hospital is very busy so I delayed for a few days. Bev asked me to."

"She's on her way to Khartoum, right?"

"No. She delayed too."

"How is she?"

"Very tired."

"And everyone else?"

"Everyone is okay."

"Good. So, you're leaving today?"

"Yes. My plane is at three."

"Let's go find a Coke or something. I'll wait with you. And if the plane doesn't come, you can just take your R&R here, in Agok."

"If the plane does not come, I will walk to Khartoum."

I close the back door and jump into the passenger seat. "Anthony, take us to Agok's fanciest restaurant."

He looks at me, key paused in the ignition.

"Coca-Cola. Let's get some Coca-Cola."

The airstrip is deserted, and we rumble down its center. I don't mention the ruts we are deepening. We turn off at its end, and widely spaced tukuls begin to appear, some deep in the scrub between hills, others closer to the road. We pass a group of children walking side by side, laughing. A man with a hoe angled on his shoulder waves.

My time in Addis has helped me see Abyei more clearly. People I met talked about their projects in Uganda or Mozambique. Weddings, local girlfriends, weekend trips. In the five or six weeks I have been in Abyei, I couldn't tell you one particular thing about the place, one custom, one habit of its people. It has been closed to me, or me to it. This is partly because of my tendency to retreat when I need respite, but it's more than that. Every gathering is a military one, every second person you pass at night a soldier. People are building their tukuls, working all day, and in the hospital, I see the poorest, the ones with no mosquito nets, or no access to clean water. Not only does our language seem irreconcilable, so do our worlds.

"I don't know, Mohamed. This is pretty nice."

We pull into a row of stalls that is Agok's market, carbon copies of the shops we see in Abyei. Outside of them lean bicycles, their frames wrapped in bright tape, their handlebars draped with flowers.

Anthony parks in front of a stall and we get out. Seated inside a slanted recubra are three Dinka men, listening intently to a radio.

"Drink?" Anthony asks.

"I'll have a Coca-Cola. Mohamed?"

"Apple."

Anthony goes into the recubra and Mohamed and I sit down on the thick root of a tree. I turn to him.

"You said the hospital was busy? Measles?"

"Yes, still many patients."

"Any more cases of meningitis?"

"Maybe one. Lumbar puncture was negative."

Anthony returns with our sodas. I fumble in my pocket for some dinars. He waves them away.

"Thank you, Anthony."

He nods, returns to the recubra, and emerges with a three-legged chair. He sits on it, angles his long legs away, puts his chin on his chest, and within seconds, falls asleep. I marvel.

Five boys, all around ten or twelve years old, emerge from between the stands. As Mohamed and I chat, they slowly circle closer until one bravely sits beside Mohamed. Mohamed puts his hand on the boy's head and says something in Dinka. He can speak a few words. The boy smiles. The rest of them come closer, emboldened. They start to chatter brightly. Mohamed takes a final swig of his soda, then tosses the bottle across the dusty road. The children scramble for it, the fastest bolting away from the scrum, green plastic bottle in his hand.

"So, what else in the hospital? How is Mansood and his knee?" I ask.

"He is getting worse. He won't walk any more. He has stopped eating."

"Did you start him on TB treatment like we talked about?"

"Yes. Last week. Aweil too."

I look away. "Oh yeah. How is she doing?"

"She smiled the other day."

"Really?"

"Yes. She still is having fevers, but two days ago I was in the TFC, and I saw her laugh."

The boys have returned. They are now sitting on the lowest bough of the tree, swinging their legs. I drain the last few drops of my Coke onto the ground and hand my bottle to the youngest. He grins and hands it to the fastest. I take my camera from my satchel, gesture the fastest forward. He's shy.

Click.

A boy, about six years old, in sandals five times too large, comes barreling around the corner of one of the stalls. He is holding, in each hand, the thin ends of two sticks whose tips are brought together through the center of a tin can lid that rolls on the ground before him. He careens past us and around the corner of a recubra.

"What are you going to do in Khartoum?"

"Visit my uncles. Eat. Rest. Watch television."

"What about look for a wife? Aren't you supposed to be married by now?"

"I am still looking."

"I think the Dinka mother, the one on the veranda, I think she likes you. Maybe you should take your R&R here and go on some dates. I can chaperone. We can get you some cows. How many do you think you'll need? Ten?"

He laughs. "She is very tall. Maybe more than ten."

"I can lend you some of mine."

Mohamed glances at his watch. "I think we should go back to the airstrip."

"Why? What's the hurry? If we miss it, there's another in a few days."

Mohamed taps Anthony on the leg. He wakes with a start. He jangles the key from his pocket, stands up, and returns the chair to the recubra. We leave the boys swinging their legs from the thick branch.

We retrace our route. There are a few Land Cruisers at the airstrip now, their passengers waiting inside. We park between two of them. Anthony radios back to Abyei. We sit quietly and scan the sky. Within minutes, the faint buzz of a plane.

"Well, Mohamed. I hope you get a chance to get some good rest. And that you come back."

"I'll be back. See you soon." We shake hands.

The plane loops once, twice, and lands. The engines whine down, and the pilots step from the cockpit. Mohamed moves towards them and queues with the few other passengers. I watch him lean forward over the clipboard the pilot is holding and point at his name. He turns towards us and gives us a thumbs-up. Anthony starts the engine.

We roll smoothly through Agok. I have my hand out the window, pushing against the hot wind. Anthony offers me a cigarette. I shake my head.

We are on the red rippled road back to Abyei. We pass a truck coming the other way, its box full of grinning soldiers bent over the cab against the rushing wind. Women carrying buckets on their heads try to flag us down, motioning "slow-slow" by waving their hand towards the ground. We ignore them, and in the sideview mirror, I see their grimaces seconds before they cover their faces from the dirt.

This is a road I have never been on. In fact, I have seen nothing but Abyei. It seems like it is kilometers between tukuls. I cannot tell where these people are walking from, or to.

We round a corner, and in the middle of the road is a large log. Two soldiers sit underneath a tree, bored. They glance at me, at our MSF sticker, step lazily out to retrieve the log, and wave us on.

Scattered huts start to appear. I turn to Anthony.

"Abyei?"

"No. Tongsay."

I recognize the name. Bev talks about it. It is a town made of SPLA soldiers. The huts become denser. Between them I can see scatters of plastic bags, piles of garbage.

We pull up to a second military stop, huts on all sides. This time the soldiers do not remove the log from the road. A group of them sits by the side, and as we slow, they stand and come towards us.

There are ten or so in the group. Two are armed. Anthony reaches towards the HF radio and turns it off. It is better if they think we are not broadcasting.

They gather at his side of the car. An older man, large, wearing a gray tunic, appears to be their spokesperson. He is familiar. He places one hand on either side of Anthony's open window and leans in. He smiles at me. Now I recognize him. I met him on my second day, when I refused to transfer the man with the severed radial nerve.

He and Anthony converse in Dinka. I can't understand a word. Anthony appears nervous. He is repeating something.

"Anthony, what's going on?"

He doesn't turn my way, instead waves his hand at me. Be quiet.

"Anthony. What?"

He turns. "They want us to take a person to Abyei."

"We can't."

"I know. I say."

"Who is it?" I ask.

Anthony points to an old man sitting underneath a piece of thatch tacked up under a tree. The man looks at the ground.

"They say he is sick."

He doesn't look it.

"What's wrong with him?"

Anthony shrugs.

"He is dizzy," says the older man, leaning farther into the cabin. "He walked all day, from Abyei, to visit his daughter here and now he feels sick."

"I'm sorry, but we cannot take anyone in our car who does not work for us. It is against our rules. It is for security."

"But he is an old man. He is sick."

"I can make an exception for an emergency. But only emergencies. All others need to find their own way to the hospital."

"You're the doctor at the hospital, aren't you?"

"Yes."

"Yet you refuse to help a sick man? What is your job? Is it not to help the sick? How can you call yourself a doctor?" His voice starts to rise.

More people have come from the huts on either side of the road and are flanking our car.

"Listen. These are our rules. I can't break them. I would not ask you to go against yours. Do not ask me to go against mine."

"We let you pass here, time and again, and you will not do us this kindness?" Soldiers now stand both in front of and behind our car.

Anthony is staring directly at the steering wheel.

"I'll tell you what. I will contact my boss, Bev. You know her. I will ask her permission. If she gives it, I will take him. If she does not, I cannot. Anthony? Back up."

The car starts, and as we inch backwards, people step away. I turn on the radio.

"Bev for James. Bev for James."

"James, go ahead."

"Bev, Anthony and I are in Tongsay and we have been stopped at a roadblock. They want us to transport someone to Abyei. Do you copy?"

"I copy. Who stopped you? Over."

"I don't know. I never asked his name. They claim the person for transport is sick, but he appears well."

"We need to get you out of there. You need to go to the hospital right away. Grenade. One man dead, one boy wounded. Do you copy?"

"I copy."

"Okay. Sit tight. I'm on my way. Over and out."

I love that woman. I turn the radio off.

"Anthony, pull the car ahead again." We inch forward. "Let the patient come here," I say, and turn the latch on the door of the Land Cruiser. It swings open. I gesture to the man.

He comes towards me. His gait looks normal. He draws closer, his eyes wide. He's nervous. He is within a foot of me now. I reach for his wrist and feel his pulse. It is 80, regular. I open my mouth wide. He does the same. His tongue and gums are shiny and moist. For audience effect, I feel along the front of his neck, the angled sternocleidomastoid, reach behind its muscle belly to feel for swollen lymph nodes. There are none.

I walk to the back of the Land Cruiser where people are clustered, watching. I address the large man in the tunic, the one who was speaking English.

"He is okay. No emergency. I think he just needs to rest here for the night. Today was a hot day. He is sick from the heat. Give him clean water. And some bread."

"Do you have any medicines?"

"He doesn't need any. If he is still sick tomorrow, tell him to ask for me in the hospital. I talked with Bev. No transport. And I need to go. There is a sick boy in the hospital."

He steps away from the car, his face stern. Finally, he gestures towards the log and turns away. Two soldiers step forward and remove it. He walks back towards the piece of thatch and doesn't look back.

Anthony starts the car and drives away. He looks at me, smiles, shakes his head. I shake mine, and pick up the receiver.

"Bev for James. Bev for James."

"James, go ahead."

"Bev, everything is okay. Do you copy?"

"Affirmative. Where are you?"

"Past Tongsay. Moving towards Abyei."

"I'll see you in a few minutes. Over and out."

Anthony and I drive on in silence as the sun arches towards Sudan's flat rim. On all sides are brown scrappy acacia trees. I lean my head against the rattling door frame and watch the gravel blur beside our wheels.

We soon see the plume of Bev's approaching truck and slow to a stop. She leans out the window.

"Everything all right?"

"Yeah, it's cool. They tried to bully us into taking someone to Abyei. He wasn't sick. He just didn't want to walk."

"They know better than that. I'm going to go and talk to them."

"Give 'em hell. Hey, how did Nyanut make out? Did she use the meds I sent from Khartoum?"

"Worked fine. She's grateful." She drives away.

We rumble our way to Abyei. We turn down its one red road and pass compound 2. Its guard raises a slow hand. We stop at compound 1's metal gate.

I shake my head. "Mustashfa," I say, and point to the hospital.

Military compound, howitzer. We park out front and I leave my bags in the back of the Land Cruiser. I walk through the front gate and pass the nursing room.

Yusuf, one of our nurses, looks up from a fan of patient charts. "Dr. James! Welcome!" he says.

We shake hands, smile at each other. He leads me to the emergency room. I feel better here than in my hot hut.

A man is lying on one of the cracked plastic beds, his shirt red with blood. A small pool of it has clotted on the floor. A boy, about eight years old, sits beside him, a bandage around his lower left leg, a red target at its center. He's staring at me with wide eyes, tears at their corners, and as I come closer, they streak down his cheeks.

30/03: in the shade.

i've started sleeping outside. it's better.

most writing about africa touches on its heat. touches on it, then jumps back with its burnt finger in its mouth. i was determined to avoid the cliché, but today i cannot. today, it is smothering. but at least it's a dry smothering.

i woke up this morning, underneath my tree, grateful for my thin sheet. it was dawn. roosters shouted. murmurs of morning voices. i was covered in sand. i could feel its grit in my mouth and underneath my back. a breeze lifted a corner of my mosquito net that had come free.

the day brightened, this day, the one right now. the wind started to blow warm, and with it, sweat beaded on my neck. after a few minutes of lying and listening, i needed to move. i lifted the mosquito net, shook the dust from my sheets, and bunched them in a ball at the foot of my bed. i walked to the kitchen, to find coffee, to find some bread.

by 9 a.m., i couldn't sit in the sun. by 10 i had moved into my tukul. i decided to write before i walked to the hospital on this, my day off. and here i am. it is 10:39 and 104F in the shade. it will climb to almost 120. i am typing with pieces of tissue underneath my wrists because sweat pools on my computer. i have taken my headphones off because it affords me another fraction of uncovered body surface area.

i will soon leave my tukul and go to the hospital. i will step out into the sun, and touch the top of my head where i have just clipped it on the door frame. my hair will be hot even after these few seconds. i will look down at my scrubs and see dark sweat at my knees. i will walk 480 paces under a cloudless sky, walk it in zigzags, looking for any piece of gray shade, no matter how narrow. fence, lightpost, piece of barbed wire. anything. the last 100 meters is across a dry courtyard, and the wind will sweep across it, gusting heat into the hospital.

i will move through the different wards, each hanging with their different smell of sickness, the hot drafts stilled by the walls. mothers in the tfc will fan their babies, and the man in the back room—i can't decide what is wrong with him, why he is wasting away—he will lie on his back and stare at the ceiling. of the 51 patients, i will see the sickest ones. i will go back, sometime in the afternoon, through the courtyard and its hot wind, down the road, then left, and enter compound 1. i will go into the kitchen and drink a liter of warm water from the fridge that was just unplugged. i will leave because i can't stand the heat. i will walk to the shower and turn it on. the water will flow from the pipe, and, warmed by the white sun, it will be almost too hot to bear. i will stand in the doorway and towel my hair, and by that time, the rest of me will be dry. i will return to my tukul, take the thermometer that is hanging by my plastic desk, and take a photograph of it. i will then post it here.

you feel the heat like a real thing, something you must push against when you open a door. at times, you can't tell where your body stops and the air begins. in other places i've been, the heat seems like it comes mostly from the top. here it comes from all sides. you step outside, and it presses firmly on the back of your neck, scolding you. you pass the metal gate, and the reflection hits you like a punch. you bend to pick up a vaccine box left in the sun, and touch the metal handles and get burned. all sides.

that is my final word on the heat. my tissues are soaked through. sorry for the digression but i hope the telling will be an exorcism. perhaps with it i will be able to stop thinking of the white shock of diving into icy mountain streams, or sitting on a surfboard at sunset swinging up and down with the swells, or the clear silence before the snowboard lands ten feet below on a cushion of dry snow that stings your face in a million tiny points.

MANUT'S LEG IS SHATTERED. The story goes that he found the grenade, and his drunk uncle started fooling with it, pulled the pin.

Bang.

When I assessed the uncle, he had a hole through his stomach. His body lay in the baking-hot emergency tent for two days, much to the horror of the mothers in the nearby feeding center. We have no morgue, and Abyei has no discernible system for dealing with dead bodies. Bev sent our community liaison to talk to Abyei's paramount chief, and the body was soon removed.

Now the boy is lying in a bed in one of the dark rooms, his mother on a mat on the floor beside him. Her forehead is scarred with hundreds of arching dots. I am looking at his chart. No fever. The discharge from his wound seems clear. No infection so far.

I push down on Manut's lower eyelid. His conjunctiva is pale. I'm not sure how much blood he has lost since the injury. We took him to the operating room the other day and picked out as much shrapnel as we could. I couldn't tell if his leg was completely shattered. Some of his tibia was splintered, but there seemed to be a thick column that was intact. I needed to open it again.

"Can you tell Ismael we need to check his hemoglobin?"

I write it on the bottom of the chart, and then hand it to the nurse behind me. She nods and writes it down on a ledger pad, then bunches the chart with the thirty others I have given her so far.

"We're done, right?" I look at my watch. With Mohamed away, I have all the patients in the hospital, save those with measles. The emergency-team MD leaves in a few days, and when he does, the measles patients become mine too. Brian sent word that we might be able to borrow a Sudanese MD from Darfur. I am glad.

"No. One more. Mansood," says Alfred, my translator. He's new. Our previous translator quit last month.

"Oh, right."

We move to Mansood's room at the back of the hospital. His walking stick sits beside his bed in the same place it was a month ago. He has stopped eating normal food. We have tried to give him Plumpy'nut, a nutritional supplement we usually reserve for children. Two of the foil packets lie near his head unopened. He is flat on his back on a plastic mattress, his head inclined towards the small mesh window at the back of the room. On its ledge sit a half-dozen bottles of apple soda, their bottoms littered with flies. It is the only thing he will drink.

When Mohamed and I aspirated his knee joint, the fluid was clear. We have treated him for conventional bacteria, and tuberculosis, but he has not improved.

"Mansood," Alfred says, stepping into the room before putting his hand over his mouth and nose, and stepping back out.

"Mansood!" he shouts again, one foot on the threshold, the other outside.

A slow turn of the head, and he lifts a thin hand. I walk into the room. It smells of urine and feces. I gag. I put my hand over my face, grab the chart wedged underneath his mattress, and move back out.

He has been tested for malaria, hepatitis B and C, and HIV. The only other test we can do is a hemoglobin, but that will tell us nothing about his sickness, and blood is not the cure.

"What are his vital signs?"

The nurse leans over my shoulder and scans the chart. They haven't been done. Nor did he get his medicines yesterday. Forgotten by everyone except Alfred.

I feel his pulse. It is normal. He doesn't feel warm. I look at his eyes. No jaundice. His knee remains swollen.

"Mansood."

He raises his thin hand again, turns his head slowly towards my voice. His eyes are thick with cataracts, dull pearls.

He's probably uremic. Kidney failure. Can't confirm it, but seems that way. From what? Hypertension? Diabetes? His sugar was okay. Maybe he got a bunch of gentamicin or something before I arrived, wrecked his kidneys. I check his chart. No. Well, if he is uremic, then he needs dialysis. He's not going to get it. He'll be dead soon, and I won't know from what. No one dies from old age. It's always something.

"Why is he lying in his own urine?" I ask the nurse.

She shrugs.

"He's not dead yet. We can treat him better than this. This is not a way to die."

"Dr. James, we have no time for this. There are not enough of us. At night, we are busy trying to give medicines, and there are not enough nutritional assistants, and . . ."

I know. Some of the MOH staff are unreliable, our MSF nurses are haggard. We need one full-time in the measles area. Muriel has left the project, requesting to return to Darfur. Those who have worked there all prefer it to Abyei. Others have been talking of going back.

"We'll hire someone, then. But until we do, I want him cleaned. And I want someone to help him get up and sit in the wheelchair. I know it's broken, but we can just have him sit outside. Okay? This is bullshit."

I'm angry. I can't stop.

"Just because he is from far away, just because he's old, doesn't mean we can't care for him, does it? That's our job, no? Sick people. No matter what, or who, or where, or when. Right? It's not easy, but sometimes that's the way it is. If they can't bathe, we have to bathe them. If they can't eat, we feed them. Okay?"

She nods. I take the chart from her hand and look at it one more time. I can think of no more medicine to add, none to remove. I close it, hand it back to her, and turn away.

I am standing in the courtyard, in the hot sun. Patients line the halls, trying to find shade. Alfred lingers nearby, glancing nervously at me, seeing if he should step closer or effect some kind of retreat.

"Alfred, come with me," I say. "I want to talk to you."

We walk towards the front of the hospital and past the laboratory's open door.

"Hey, Ismael."

Ismael looks up from his microscope, grunts hello. Alfred and I sit down on a bench outside his door.

"Okay. I've been meaning to have this conversation with you for a little while. I'm sorry it's taken me so long."

He fidgets.

"I know you are new. How long have you been working here with MSF?"

"Two weeks."

"All right, very new. Now. For me, you have the most important job in the project. I can give people medicines, and do many things for the patients, but I can't talk to them. And they can't talk to me. Without that, it is almost impossible for me to find out what is wrong with someone. We say in medicine, the story is 90 percent of the diagnosis. And even if I get it right without one, I can't tell them. I am useless."

"Okay." He looks at me with a small bit of pride on his young face, in place of his nervousness.

"So I need you very much. Now, I also need you to understand something else. First, you must translate what I say exactly. All my questions. If you don't know what they are, I don't mind. Ask me. I can explain it again in a different way. It is very important."

"Okay."

"The second thing is this. I know I get frustrated sometimes. But I am not frustrated with you. I am frustrated with me. It is difficult to not be able to talk, or to understand. This is not my country. I can't meet someone in the market and make a friend, I can't make a joke with my patients. So when I seem frustrated, it is not with what you are doing. I promise. It is because I feel helpless. Okay?"

"Okay."

"I'm sorry I haven't said that before. I meant to."

"Thank you. I worry about my English."

"I know. I'll try to remember to speak more slowly, more simply. We'll help each other. The translator before you used to write down words, and we would go over them together. I have a medical dictionary and we can start with easy things."

"Oh yes, that would be very good. Very-very good."

"We'll decide on a time at the meeting tomorrow."

I am hungry. It is lunchtime soon. Alfred is long overdue for his. The Sudanese eat no breakfast, taking their first break at ten. Despite our best attempts to shift their schedules to ours, the hospital empties for an hour at this time. My translator sits and waits for me, stomach grumbling.

"All right, enough of that. Let's go for lunch."

We move together towards the gate of the hospital and out onto the hot red road.

"Where did you learn English?"

"In a refugee camp. In Ethiopia."

"When did you come back to Abyei?"

"Only this year."

We duck at the cannon. Across the flat flood plain, men in white robes walk between market stalls.

"Are you married?" I ask.

"Yes. I have two children. Two girls. Are you married?"

"No."

He laughs. "But you are very old! And rich! You should have many wives."

"Maybe I'll get one while I am here. A Dinka woman. So my children will be tall. How many cows do you think it would take me?"

"For a rich man like you, maybe twenty cows."

"Twenty! Would she be tall?"

"Oh yes, for twenty cows, you can get someone very good."

"Back home we have only one wife. We think that is enough."

"Oh yes. Even one is too many sometimes."

I laugh. "Why did you come back to Abyei?"

"Because it is my home."

I look around. To my right the barbed wire of the military compound, soldiers sitting idly in a covered house. To my left, the potholed path to the market. We turn down it together.

"Is Abyei better than before?"

"When I left many years ago you could not walk at night. Sometimes you would wake up and your neighbor would be disappeared. Soldiers would stop you and take you away, beat you for no reason. Maybe kill you. These days it is safe at night. For now."

We are drawing closer to one of two food stalls in town. This one is at the very start of the market, on one of the two paths that lead to my compound. I rarely take this one. Some of our nurses and drivers are sitting down and eating pieces of fried goat with their fingers, breaking off pieces of bread.

"Will you join me for lunch?" Alfred asks.

"Oh, no, thank you. Mine is waiting for me at compound 1. I have to talk with Tim about getting a helper for Mansood."

"Please, it would be nice for me."

"There are some things I have to do. Next time. Thank you, Alfred."

He frowns for a second, then shakes my hand. Some of the nurses look up. I wave. They smile.

"Well, I'll leave you to it. See you back at the hospital. Take your time."

I stop at a stand. I have been stealing Tim's cigarettes mercilessly and decide I should buy him a couple of packages. I pocket my change and look back at my translator. He is smiling and laughing with the others.

I turn around and walk towards my compound.

01/04: new normal.

this morning, during breakfast, a loudspeaker blared thick arabic. today was a cleanup day in abyei. everyone was to clean the space outside their tukuls, or face consequences. tonight the air is full of the sharp smell of plastic. fires line the road. you can see the black shadows of people tending them flicker and dance on the grass walls behind.

people fix flowers to the handlebars of their bicycles in bunches. roses, carnations, impossible pink flowers in rows. even soldiers. daisies pour off the front, a machine gun hangs from the back.

when an organism enters a new environment, with time the new stimuli elicit diminishing responses. as it inhabits, it habituates. in a conflict setting, for expatriates, it is called "immersion." at first, every soldier is registered, every weapon noticed. after weeks, in a new normal, one sees mostly daisies.

for years i was blind to flowers. it took a friend to show me how easy they are to love. in the hot morning, they hang for water. an hour after, they stand tall. when i leave the feeding center, i think about that.

THIS IS WHAT HAPPENS if you are a Dinka child, say thirteen months old, and you have around your waist a circle of beads looped twice, like Aweil's beads except some of yours are blue, and you are naked except for these beads and lying on the cracked plastic bed in the small emergency room of Abyei's only hospital at ten at night surrounded by your mother, father, a nurse, and a midwife who is trying ineffectively to blow air into your small lungs with a face mask that is four sizes too big and lets all the air slip out of the sides, and the Canadian doctor arrives just in time to watch you take your last ten breaths, and then they stop and then you die. This is what happens.

Your mother screams, turns, and leaves the room. The metal emergency door clangs behind her. Your family outside the emergency room, an impressive number of aunts, uncles, grandparents, and friends, start to wail.

Your father sits down on the other cracked plastic bed, puts his face in his hands, and looks through his spread fingers.

A nurse puts one hand over your eyes and uses the other to close your mouth. She holds them like that until a clean cotton cloth can be placed over your face and she puts her hand over that.

The midwife takes long strings of gauze and slowly wraps them around your head, again and again, until your mouth and eyes are closed fast.

The nurse removes the intravenous and cleans your skin of blood.

Your father takes a small piece of string and binds your large toes together, to keep your legs closed, then wraps your feet. Your hands are placed grasping each other, and your thumbs are bound. Your fingers sit neatly folded together like piano keys. Your hands and wrists are then covered in gauze. Last, he lifts you onto a piece of colored cloth and wraps you a final time.

Someone opens the door (your grandmother?) and takes you from the room.

I stand there useless, and once the emergency room empties, I am alone. I pick up the gloves off the ground, square the edge of the cracked plastic bed with its metal frame. I loop the padlock through the drug cupboard and click it shut.

I take my time. I secretly hope that you and your family are gone when I step out into the night air. I don't know what to say. I'm sorry? That after the tenth time, it is not getting any easier at all? I just want to walk home alone, eat my dinner leaning over the stove, and go to my tukul and not see anyone.

They're gone. So are you. To where? I don't know. Here, for me, your story ends. Mine goes on, rushes away from me in all directions, so many things in it I don't know where to begin.

I finish with the last of the outpatients and walk towards the gate of the hospital.

"Call driver?" the guard asks.

"No. I walk. Cigarette?"

He gives me one. The package has a picture of a soccer player on it. He lights the cigarette for me.

I start walking home. The night is moonless and black. The cigarette tastes terrible. I throw it on the ground. I strain forward against the dark and a soldier almost barrels into me.

08/04: easter.

the abyei night is black like thick ink. as you walk down the road pushing your face into it, trying to gain a centimeter or two of perspective,
it almost meets a soldier's leaning over his handlebars doing the
same. you both recoil like surprised fishes at the black bottom of the
ocean. he swerves, and the flowers on his handlebars brush your arm.

this morning, a sleep headache behind my eyes, i laced up my running
shoes and ran out of town. i wanted some open space; no people, no
cars, no zigzagging chickens, only the wide horizon. a few kilometers
north of abyei, the sun and the moon shared the sky with dawn birds.

here in abyei, outside the hospital and in it, i am witness to the most
beautiful things. today i was standing in the measles recubra holding
a child from the feeding center in my arms. measles had once again
swept through our hospital and infected his mother. she was too
feverish to move. paola was giving her a sponge bath, and i was hoping to find a mother to help feed her son until she was well. i watched
a woman take the most gentle care to offer her child water from a plastic cup, holding her hand under the rim so that not a drop was spilled.
the child refused, and the mother offered softly again. it was such a
beautiful, intimate act of love.

i asked the women in turn if they could feed the child i was carrying
along with theirs, even if just for a day, even if they did it in turns. they
roundly refused. i pressed, they resisted.

the fittest survive. here beauty and the hard truth of nature share the
same recubra. like when you watch a butterfly fold her wings once,
twice, then take off on her jittery way, and a swallow swoops in, eats
her, then wheels out of the frame.

i spent the morning on a mobile clinic about an hour from abyei. we arrived early, and there were no patients. we hadn't been there for weeks because of the measles epidemic. while i was waiting, i walked out into a field and a million birds flew by. the flock pulsed and changed like smoke. when i turned back, i could see bright flashes of clothing moving through the woods as people approached.

it is now midday. most of msf has the day off for easter. the temperature is 120F, by my thermometer. i don't see the falcon on my tukul any more, but up above, some drift on hot drafts of air. a few move so high that they become dust, disappear like untethered helium balloons. the other night, bev and i were talking about how we would like our ashes to be reanimated. "falcon," i said.

annie dillard once offered her opinion on whether birds fly for pleasure. she found her answer when she watched, from her window, a barnswallow fall like a stone from his nest in a barn's loft. just as he was about to hit the dirt, he spread his wings, skimmed the ground, and flew out of sight. of course they do.

it is easter. in lac la biche, alberta, my family will be sitting together and watching cold ducks test the ice of the lake. they will have an afternoon meal and talk about the things they are thankful for. being grateful is a lesson i was taught well. it is one that the world keeps repeating. each of us is lucky to be alive and to be surrounded by people we care about. there are a thousand million ways it could be otherwise. but somewhere an opaque reason met an impossible chance, and we are all here at the same time. it's such a lucky thing, it's hard to believe.

"ANTONIA? FUL?"

She looks into the red plastic bowl of beans Paola is holding and frowns. "No. Absolutely not."

Antonia arrived earlier this week. The last time I saw her, she was sitting beside me in Geneva, grumpy from having her visa refused. Brian must have convinced Geneva that a midwife was important. I am glad. The "maternity hallway" that lines the entrance to the operating theater is the event horizon of an obstetric black hole.

Of a half-dozen midwives, a number that seems to shift with the week, there is only one that has any specific training. The others are traditional birth attendants. They are all larger than me and make an intimidating bunch. Antonia, though a third their size, is a force of her own. She is Italian, in her late thirties, and has worked everywhere. Within twenty-four hours of arriving she had distributed to all of us our own laundry buckets. She called our habit of throwing the clothes we needed washed on the tops of our tukuls "filthy." Two nights after she arrived I heard the whir of a fan coming from her room. I was amazed. When I asked her how she persuaded Jean to let her have one, she looked at me like I was from another universe.

"*Let me?* It's 120 degrees."

I liked her immediately.

"Salad?" Tim passes her a bowl with onions and cucumbers in it. She looks at it and wrinkles her nose. He sets it down.

Antonia has brought her own tray of food to the table. On it, an orange, a tomato, and a tin of tuna. Beside these, a small bottle of white vinegar. She picks up a plate, inspects it, then looks at me and frowns.

"Terrible."

I agree. In general. Tim has lost 15 kilograms in his three months so far. I treated him for parasites shortly after I arrived, but he has continued to lose weight. I have been sick several times. Both of us, on our first missions, shrug and accept it like we did the fan.

"The cook hates you," Antonia says, giving voice to a suspicion we each silently share. She stirs the ful disdainfully. "Tonight I make a big pasta."

"I like ful," Tim says, lying, trying to stick up for our cook, or our failure to do something about it.

"We'll put some aside for you. What's in this bowl?" she asks, taking the lid off. Inside is a fried egg.

"Oh, wonderful! Perfect! I couldn't be happier!" Her thick Italian accent makes us laugh.

Our cook, Ruth, comes out from the kitchen carrying five plates of pudding. We fall silent. She glares at Antonia, correctly identifying her as an adversary. Antonia smiles shiningly back. Ruth sets the plates down with a rattle and turns on her heel.

"Hates us," Antonia says, opening her tin of tuna. She faces Bev, who has been silent through all of this. "I would like permission to take one or two days from the hospital to do a training with Ruth. And the cleaner. Basic cleanliness and hygiene. It's simple." She looks around. "Maybe better we take two days."

When I arrived here and dropped my backpack in the dusty center of the gazebo, my eyes were fresh. I saw some burned candles slumped against the corner of the cement wall, some paperbacks swollen from last year's rains, a torn roll of yellowing plastic. That evening, after I had met everyone, I stacked all these discarded pieces into a box, put them in the corner. Jean said how much better it was, that after so many months, he didn't even see those things any more. The box still sits there, yellow plastic roll flapping in the wind. I don't really see it any more.

Antonia's eyes are fresh. I'm excited for some change.

"Just principles of disinfection and food preparation. The mothers can wait for two days, no?"

We glance at each other. To this point, none of us has dared to take on Ruth or our cleaner. They both wear dark glares most of the time. We have tried the complimentary approach, lauding the cook for things we like, silently sending back full bowls of ful. It has had no effect.

Antonia is waiting for an answer.

"We'll see," Bev says, lighting another cigarette. She leaves in a few days, and has returned from Khartoum for the handover with her replacement. She is scrambling to get her final report together and has little interest in big changes. Jean is leaving at the same time. He is trying to sort out problems with the borehole contract. He hoped it would be finished before he left on the plane. It won't be started.

"We'll see," Antonia echoes, cuts up pieces of her tomato and mixes it with the tuna and some vinegar.

Tim and I talk about the compound often. How it would be better with this, or without that. We talk about the food that Ruth buys, how much money we pay for the little we get. Tim collects daily receipts from Ruth, but they are in Arabic and he has never been through them. I suggested to Tim once that we ask around for another cook. He laughed.

"You can't fire anyone here. Essentially, it's against the law. They will go to the SPLA humanitarian office, make big trouble. We're better to cook for ourselves."

"Pass the ful," Paola says.

"What are you doing?" Antonia asks.

"I like it."

"Well, you and Tim can have ful tonight. James and I will eat pasta, yes, James?"

I nod and reach for the pudding. I offer Antonia a bowl and a spoon. She looks at me warily.

"Try it."

She does. "Hmm. Not totally bad."

"Yeah, just 80 percent."

She laughs. "Yes, just 80 percent bad, 20 percent not bad."

10/04: twenty-four.

i am trying to paint a picture of abyei, but all i have are hurried strokes.

yesterday, after dinner i was sitting in the open space of my compound, compound 3. it is adjacent to compound 1. the measles emergency tents used to be here, and eventually a warehouse will be built. right now it's empty. except for my bed under the tree.

the night was ink. overhead a flock of white birds flew, fluttering like pieces of paper. they landed above me, and noisily settled in for the night. the shuffling wings mixed with the voices of my neighbors and the tinny music of their radios. the air smelled of dust and burning plastic.

i woke at dawn and the birds were gone. the sky was cloudless as i folded my mosquito net and shook the dust from my sheets. the smell of plastic was still in the air.

on my way to the hospital, 480 paces (tired), i passed children on donkeys and men on bicycles. i answered them, fine, how are you, i am fine. plastic bags blew by with gusts of wind and were carried into a nearby open field where they flapped, thousands strong.

i passed two sisters. the youngest, ten, was dressed in a white dress, frills on the shoulders. it was torn and its white was choked with dust. no princess ever looked more important.

i returned from the hospital for lunch and lay down. i was somehow sick again. in the middle of a feverish dream (organizing something, again, what, again), when i was called on the handset. a woman had been run over by a car. i opened the door to the emergency room and saw the piece of white bone pushed from her leg glistening brightly.

later, a large truck pulled into our road and backed up to our gates. they carried from the box a stretcher with a woman and her new baby on it. twins, we were told. one delivered, the other not. we took her to the delivery room and removed the blanket. between her legs, a tiny blue arm. i touched it, and the skin came loose. how many days ago was the delivery? six. six days ago, a baby was born, and her brother, almost. he made it to his shoulder, and finding nothing to hold on to, went no farther.

i saw a child in our feeding center whose mother carried with her two pieces of wood. what for? well, my translator explained, when she was born, there were three. now she is the only one. so her mother cut two pieces of wood and said, these, these are your brothers. how long will she keep them? forever, he said.

it is later that same day. near dusk. i am sitting in the compound, in the gazebo, typing on the medical computer. just to my left, paola is giving jean a haircut. he leaves soon. antonia has just handed me a mirror to inspect my own sorry state. i need both a haircut and a shave.

the radio just crackled beside me. i am on call. once i am done with whatever night business the hospital has in mind, i will walk to the kitchen, eat what i can, leave for my compound, shake my sheets, tuck in my mosquito net, and fall asleep. 24.

I T IS LATE, AND I AM leaving through the hospital gate when I hear the handset crackle with a call to Antonia.

"Antonia . . . there's a woman here who delivered a baby at home two days ago. . . . She has high fever and it feels like . . . like she has another baby inside. Can you come to the hospital?"

She will. I turn around, walk to the hallway that leads to our delivery room. In it, a young Dinka woman is lying flat on her back. Her eyes are closed, and she is breathing quickly. Her new baby is on another bed, crying. He appears healthy. She does not.

I put my hand on her abdomen and can feel the bulk of her uterus through her hot skin. It is so swollen it comes nearly to her chest. I reach for the pulse in her wrist. Can't find it. I move the sheet to feel for the femoral pulse in her groin and see an umbilical cord hanging loosely between her legs. The placenta is still inside, infected. She has been losing blood since the delivery and is now both septic and profoundly anemic. She moans, half-conscious.

Antonia arrives with our national midwife, Atol. Together we carry the woman to a delivery-room bed. She is limp. I ask Atol to put an IV in place, and call on the handset for Ismael. The woman will need blood.

Antonia finishes her examination. We agree there is little choice but to remove the placenta manually and risk the hemorrhage. I go to the pharmacy to gather the necessary anesthetic drugs, antibiotics for the infection, and ergotamine to help the uterus clamp to itself and staunch the bleeding. Before I clang the door shut, I throw two vials of adrenalin in my pocket. I can recognize last breaths when I see them.

By the time I return, she is worse. Why does it always happen this way? You move them, and . . .

She is now comatose. Her breathing is becoming noisy. I show Atol how to hook her fingers behind the angle of the woman's jaw, pull it forward, with it the tongue, the pharynx. She breathes better.

I cross the narrow hall to the operating theater and get a bag and mask, replace Atol, and start to assist the woman's breathing. Someone got an IV. I look at the bag of saline above it. It is dripping too slowly. I don't trust it. We need another IV. Better two.

I see Ismael, Mohamed behind him.

"Ismael, do we have any blood?"

"No."

"Are you O negative?"

"No."

"Mohamed, you?"

"B. You?"

"O positive. Okay, someone take over for me . . . no, like this . . . fingers under here, squeeze the bag like this. Here, give me a cannula, an 18, and a syringe so I can take some blood. Ismael, go and find some of the relatives, see if they'll donate."

The veins are tough to find. They are flat, slippery, move one way or the other as I try to cannulate them. Mohamed is working on the other arm. Can't get it. We need a central line. Don't have one.

I feel for a femoral pulse. None. Her neck? I don't know. Maybe. Barely. Her breathing is becoming intermittent, agonal. It stops.

"Keep bagging. Yup, like that. Faster. About ten times per minute. Don't stop." No pulse now.

I lace my fingers together, feel for the hard flatness of her sternum, and start compressions, try to squeeze her heart between her ribs and her spine, push whatever thin blood she has towards her brain. Come on.

"Someone take over for me. Like this. Push like this. One, two, three, four, five, six, seven, eight, nine, ten . . . Breath . . . One, two, three . . . Faster."

I take one of the glass vials of adrenalin from my pocket and snap its top off. I draw it into the syringe and push it into the slow intravenous. It might cause the small arteries and capillaries to spasm and cramp, push whatever blood they have towards the middle, maybe form a beat.

"Good. Okay. Now stop for a second."

I reach for her neck and feel for a pulse. None.

"Resume compressions."

I take the second vial of adrenalin, snap the top off, pop, and draw it up. I pull back her sleeve.

Above the cannula, her arm is a balloon. The fluid is trickling slowly underneath her skin, not into her vein.

No intravenous, no fluid, no blood, no adrenalin, no breaths, no pulse. I check her pupils. No response. No more.

"No more. Stop."

I look at my watch, out of habit, for the coroner.

Fifteen minutes. That's what it took, from the first crackle of the radio to no more.

No death is easy. If it starts to become that way, I'll change professions. But this one is more difficult than most.

The four of us stand for a moment, then Mohamed and I quietly bend to clean the ground of scattered intravenous lines and tossed pieces of gauze. Antonia takes the intravenous out, wipes the tiny bullets of blood that are scattered on the mother's arm from all of our attempts. Atol puts the bag and mask into a blue bin to sterilize later. We do not meet eyes.

I leave the room and walk down the hallway. The baby is lying on the bed, where we left him, crying. I push through the curtain and a man with wide, wet eyes looks at mine, and knows.

"Malesh," I said. I'm sorry.

Sorry I can't speak Arabic or Dinka. Sorry about the intravenous and the baby and your wife and the fifteen minutes and the no more.

He tells me, through one of our nurses, that he wants transport to the graveyard. I tell him we don't do that, we can't. We couldn't save his wife, and we can't move her body. He asks, What am I to do, hire a car, where, the market, where?

I don't know. Malesh. Sorry.

I return to the delivery room. Antonia and Mohamed are almost done. Together we carry his wife to the hallway and lay her on the bed.

I go to the back of the hospital, click the lock on the pharmacy shut, then move around sleeping families towards the front. I walk past the hallway, and at the entrance, the man stands, lost, baby crying beside him. I walk past.

"Malesh."

Ismael, Mohamed, and Atol are waiting in the idling Land Cruiser. Antonia is disinfecting the delivery room and will be a few minutes yet. I tell the driver to go to compound 2 and we will call if we need him.

I sit on the front step of the hospital and look across the flood plain to the broad hallway of light that is the market road. Shadows cross from one side to the other, disappear down it. Dogs bark. I rest my elbows on my knees and my chin in my hands. I feel flat.

Antonia sits down beside me.

"The driver is gone?"

"I sent him to compound 2. We can call him back if you want. I'm going to walk."

"Walk? It is safe?"

I shrug.

"So far. Do you have a cigarette?"

"Sure."

We sit on the step of the hospital, smoking. We finish our cigarettes, stand, dust ourselves off, and walk on the black road back to our compound. Antonia tells me that this is not what she signed up for. She came to help train midwives, not deliver babies. And the compound. The hospital. No hygiene. Not at all.

I listen. I agree. I'm not sure what I signed up for either. But I'm silently glad about one thing. I'm glad that we don't take bodies to the graveyard, glad that I am walking back along the black road instead of struggling to roll a corpse into the back of a pickup truck. It's not my problem any more. I can shut that door now.

We arrive back at compound 1. There is a meal prepared for Jean and Bev's departure, and they are waiting for me so they can begin. Many of our national staff are there, clustered in one corner of the gazebo. Mohamed is not among them. I eat quickly and move to my bed under the tree. I shake my sheets, tuck them under the corners of my foam mattress, then my mosquito net. I climb in.

I saw clouds for the first time yesterday. They hung around the horizon, lurking. Tonight they are still there. I can see flashes of lightning around the edges of the dark horizon. Flicker. Flicker. Finally, I fall asleep.

I wake up in the morning, too tired to run. When I return to the hospital in the morning, the body is gone. Later that day, the rains arrive in Abyei, one month early, and lash us, unprepared.

11/04: statistics.

to compare health between nations, one most often uses statistics. when i was working as an editor at a medical journal, i asked a potential author to explain what they really meant. numbers are meaningless. what lies beneath under-5 mortality rates? what shortens a country's life expectancy? what does maternal mortality really mean? why do the mothers die, what is the human cost? he wrote the article, and answered some of my questions. more have been answered in the past few months.

"Shit," jean says, stopping the Land Cruiser.

"What?"

"Tim, get out on your side. I'm too close to the fence. I think I hit the bulb hanging over the road."

Tim's door creaks open.

"Yup."

"So much for being discreet," Jean says.

Tim gets in and slams the door.

We are on a narrow donkey-cart path that carries off the main market road. I have never been here before, or at least can't recognize it this late at night.

"Think we should stop and find out whose light it is?" I ask.

"Probably," Jean says, shifting the truck into gear and driving slowly ahead.

We are on our way to buy beer. We had a dinner for Bev and Jean the other night, with our national staff, but on this, their last evening, we are throwing a party.

"Isn't it right here?" Jean says.

"Think so," answers Tim.

"Let's just stop and walk."

Jean stops the truck and turns it off. We don't want to be seen too close, in our MSF car. Without the lights, it is black all around us. I can't see a thing.

"I bet you guys this is where 'black market' came from," I say, stumbling into Tim.

"Here," he says, gives me a flashlight, then turns on his headlamp.

We work our way down a dirt corridor, lined on both sides with grass fences. The fences give way, and to our right is a courtyard. We bounce our beams off its two tukuls and long recubra. It is quiet.

"You sure, man?" I ask.

We enter the open space and stand, waiting for someone. No one. We step towards the tukuls.

In front of one, a young girl, kneeling on the ground, is tending to the coals of a small fire.

"Hello," Jean says softly, startling her. In Arabic, he asks her where her father is. She stands and hurries away, disappearing into the dark.

He shrugs. The town is mostly Dinka, but many speak basic Arabic, a few English.

A man appears from the blackness. "Hello, my friends!" he says, then roundly shakes our hands. "Sit, sit!"

He pulls up three chairs, their plastic backs removed to serve some other purpose.

None of us is wearing our MSF shirts, but there can be no question who we are. In all of Abyei, besides the UN, there are a dozen expats at most. He sits down beside us and smiles.

"So, welcome," he says, prepared to start a long conversation.

Jean is not.

"We want to buy some beer. Tusker. Forty."

The last party Abyei had, at an NGO near us, ran out of beer. MSF has a reputation to live up to. Back at the compound, we have taken the vaccine freezer from the hospital and plugged it into our generator. It has been running all day to freeze the ice packs.

Tim is fiddling with his headlamp, turning it off and on. I try to take in the shadowed surroundings. I can see a candle flicker inside one of the tukuls, little else.

The man stands up, disappointed the visit is purely business. "How many?"

"Forty Tusker," Jean says.

"No Tusker. Only pilsner and extra ale."

"That extra ale nearly killed me last time. It's terrible," Tim says. "I vote pilsner."

"Okay, as many pilsner as you have, and the rest extra ale."

The man's back fades into blackness.

Tim smiles at me.

"This is fun," I say. "Jean, getting beer is going to be so boring a week from now. You'll just have to go to the corner."

"I'll manage."

"What about extending your mission? Tim, can you get on that?"

"Oh, I've already started. You'll just need to sign some papers."

Jean laughs. To this point, there is no one to replace him and no one due. An MSF water and sanitation expert is being sent to Abyei to work on the borehole. We each secretly hope he will help us fill the gap Jean is leaving behind. While the hospital can work without me as long as Mohamed is there, if the radio fails in the desert, and there is no one there to fix it, no sound.

The man returns with a bottle of pilsner and hands it to Jean. It is covered in dust. He blows it off.

"Can you clean the rest of them? Too much dust."

Jean hands the bottle to me. I turn on my flashlight and look at the label. Its best-before date was last year. Whatever. I hand it back to our host and he leaves with it.

Jean looks at his watch and shakes his head. People will be arriving in a few hours, and the beer needs time to cool.

We can hear only the faint drone of the market generators. From behind one of the tukuls, I can see the shape of three children, looking at us.

"Hey, check it out."

"Hey, you guys, come here. Don't be shy," Jean says.

The first, the little girl we saw tending the fire, comes slowly, shyly, towards us.

"That's a pretty dress," Jean says. "What's your name?"

She smiles, continues to look at the ground. The other two inch forward. Younger. Sisters. They stand behind the eldest and peek around her.

"We're going to have a party tonight, with our friends. Dancing and music. You know, doooodooodaaaaaa . . ." he sings tunelessly, shaking his shoulders.

The girls all laugh. The youngest ones come closer.

"Dooooodooooodaaaaaa . . ."

The three of them are now standing between us and the fire, grinning.

"Doooodadoooodaaaaa . . ."

The oldest one starts to sing.

"Sheshashooooohh . . ."

Jean joins her.

"Sheshashoooohh . . . sheshashooooohh . . ."

Her sisters start to dance, moving their shoulders and hips. They can't be more than six or seven. Soon they are singing too.

"Sheeeshashho . . . sheshashooohhh . . ."

We can see their silhouettes, and when their faces turn towards the fire, their bright smiles. They are looking into each other's eyes, laughing.

"Sheeeshaaashoooooohhhhhh . . ."

We're all singing now, we're all smiling now. The girls dance.

After five minutes of the same refrain, the father returns with a crate full of beer. We stand up. He returns with a second.

Tim pulls out the sheaf of dinars we donated from our per diems, counts them, then hands them to the man, who does the same. Satisfied, he smiles.

We each pick up a handle and carry the two crates between us.

"Thank you. Goodbye, girls."

They smile, continue to sing. We move away from the fire, towards the black road and from there to our car.

We load the clinking crates of beer into the back and climb in. Jean starts the cruiser, turns it around, and we inch our way back.

"Sheeeshaaaashoooo . . ." he sings.

15/04: glass.

once, when i was fly fishing in the rockies, pushing through brush and over rocks, hoping my luck at the next spot would be better than at the last, a mallard started following me. it wasn't easy work for either of us, all thick trees, all upstream, but he stayed with me the entire afternoon. i would turn to look for him every so often, and he would be there, treading water, pretending to mind his own business, waiting until i moved. at the end of the day, as i started back downstream, he flew off.

i ran yesterday morning. as i left town, a soldier ran from between two tukuls, and kept pace two steps behind. i looked over, and he looked straight ahead, minding his own business. we ran together, me carrying my heavy handset and him with army boots and jangling pockets. when we reached the tree in the middle of the flat landscape outside abyei, i stopped and turned around. he slowed to a walk and continued on.

the team is changing. jean, the logistician, left today. he is returning to khartoum, and from there to london. our new field coordinator, marco, is arriving. he is italian. this means with the italian nurse and midwife, tim and i are surrounded. the food has improved.

tim and i were talking, just now, wondering what we were doing here. not simply as two men the same age, with friends left behind and a future on hold, but as humanitarians. as msf. there is no conflict, and though perhaps we are too immersed to notice small signs, things seem peaceful. there are no refugees. the returning population is not huddled together under plastic sheets, sharing latrines with 19 others. the hospital needs attention, so much attention, but isn't that true of nearly everywhere?

the memory of the precise chemistry behind supersaturated solutions sits fragmented like much of my premedicine studies. i think the founding principle is one of entropy, that as one adds energy to a system it increases its randomness. what it allows is for one to add much more of a certain salt to a heated quantity of water than it would bear otherwise. it requires a completely new and clean beaker full of pure distilled water. as one adds heat, and chaos, he also adds salt. it dissolves, and he adds more. and more heat. and then more salt. the salt dissolves into its constituents, and the heat makes sure that the molecules ricochet faster and faster, knocking other ones loose. soon, all the salt has been added, and it is all in parts that are flinging themselves against the glass borders of the beaker. if one removes the heat, and allows the beaker to cool, the disorder lessens. the ions slow down. they spend less energy bouncing off of one another, and in fact would form crystals again if they could, but they can't. there is no solid substrate. you are left with a beaker of clear water sitting on your lab bench, full of molecules waiting to precipitate, but none of them have anything to hang on to.

now, take a glass rod, and just touch the inside lip of the beaker. a small piece of glass dust flakes off, so small you can't see it, and falls into the water. in an instant, the water becomes a crystal. completely solid. the molecules are at rest.

i think, for me, that is the reason why we are here, to be that piece of glass. it doesn't matter if you are from the north, or the south, or a christian, or a muslim, or dinka, or misseriya, or soldier, or civilian. we deliberately don't care. our intention is to make a place that is safe and solid for everyone in abyei. and it is not just about medicine; that is only our tool. the hospital is not just a place to treat the dinka infant with meningitis or the little misseriya girl with malaria, but a place where their fathers can reach for the water barrel at the same time and say to the other, after you, no after you. and maybe, two weeks later, when they pass in the market, they will nod. and perhaps, two years from now, they might stop and talk.

I'M WALKING TOWARDS the pharmacy. I am going there, officially, to start looking through the supplies to treat a large number of casualties. I meant to do it a month ago, but haven't yet. Unofficially, it is the only cool, quiet place in either the hospital or the compound. Unofficially, I am going there to sit in the dark.

The pharmacy door clangs shut. I look at the wide hole above it. I had mentioned it to Jean shortly after my arrival, and twice before he left. It remains open, and through it, cool air pours out.

I look for something to put in the space. An old box. That'll do. I take some scissors from a shelf and cut the box into pieces, fit one of them into the hole.

It is nearly black in here now. Shadows of pill bottles and equipment surround me. It is Paola's drowning task to keep things organized, a task made even more difficult by my grabbing armfuls of medicine, scribbling down approximations on loose pieces of paper, and leaving the scraps behind.

I reach down towards a box near my feet. It holds about 100 energy-dense biscuits called BP-5. They do not have as many calories as BP-100s, not as fatty. They're quite sweet. I like them. My translator said he ate so many when he was living in a refugee camp that their smell makes him vomit. I open one. Paola's job gets worse.

I start thinking about the feeding center. I am having a tough time with it. Some of the children don't seem to be gaining weight well, particularly the youngest ones. Paola is trying to improve the procedures, to train the staff. To this point it has been neither easy nor successful.

I'm not sure how to help her. I'm not sure if she wants help. She hasn't asked me for any, nor have I asked her. We have developed a system where we work separately in the hospital on our own important pieces. We pass each other several times a day, hurrying from one to the other.

Her tasks are broader than mine, less specific. I suspect, sometimes, she doesn't know where to begin. When I arrived, she was trying to take care of the outpatient triage, sorting the round crowds that sat at our door from dawn into straight lines, sickest at the front. On my way to the inpatients, I would pass her scribbling vital signs on outpatient cards, shuffling them into order, then with frustration trying to rearrange patients.

I haven't seen her there in a while. The triage system is once again working on momentum. The loudest patients get seen first.

We see, six days a week, a maximum of forty outpatients. This is a number that was decided on before I arrived. From these forty, I or one of my team sees the most ill. The others are seen by Sylvester, an MOH medical assistant. He has been in Abyei for decades. He told me that during the height of the war, he would not leave the hospital for months at a time. Since we arrived, he works a few hours most days, prescribing pills for patients I never hear about.

He seems interested and careful. Beyond that, he seems a good man. I don't agree with his frequent use of antibiotics, or his choice of them sometimes, but am not his supervisor. I treat him like a colleague. In turn, he treats me like a consultant, asking me to comment on difficult cases.

It is our mandate to practice secondary care, to focus on acute illness. We see the forty outpatients mostly to appease the community's hunger for contact. In an ideal world, we would have a sign on the door that said "EMERGENCY" and would turn people away with minor or chronic problems, sending them to the one other health clinic in town, run by GOAL, another NGO. Already, in an effort to refine our forty patients to the sickest ones, we turn some away.

Word has filtered from the community, through our staff, that there is growing dissatisfaction with our project. The community wants more.

We cannot provide it. Between the triage system that is now forsaken, tabled for another time, to the feeding center and its flat children, to the patients with contagious tuberculosis that refuse to be hospitalized, to the missed doses of medicines, to the children shitting in the yard, Paola and I can't keep up with the things that need to change. We suffer from not having a medical coordinator to help us focus. Both of us are reluctant to bother Brian much. We know Darfur is higher on the list of priorities.

In truth, no matter how unpopular our approach happens to be, it appeals to me. It has the same merit as working in the emergency room. I get to deal with emergencies. Everything else, no matter how important, is not my business.

It is the contrast between relief and development. We put fingers in the dam until the water goes down or someone comes along to repair it. We are not here to improve the community's ability to thrive. We are here to save lives that would otherwise be lost. That's our expertise. When we are asked what we are going to do about unaddressed problems, we say: "We're going to do what we're doing. The question is, what are you going to do?"

I finish my BP-5. It's been two weeks since I discovered the supply and I can feel my stomach starting to turn.

I look at the boxes around me. Two of them are labeled "EPREP" emergency preparedness. I stand and open one. Inside are dozens of liters of Ringer's lactate, dressings, intravenouses. I try to lift it. Too heavy. Would make more sense to have five boxes, each for five patients. I start to unpack it.

Knockknockknock.

"Yes?"

"James, it's Mohamed. I brought the girl to the operating theater."

Oh yeah. The girl with the burn. We have to change her dressing. I open the metal door.

"Okay. Do we need anything from here?"

"I think the ketamine is expired."

"I'll grab some. See you in a second."

I put the bags of saline back in the box, get a flashlight, and move past the rows and rows of medicines. Towards the back, I see the bottles of ketamine. I take two and stop just before the door to write on a scrap piece of paper: "April 18 ketamine x 2 JM." I tuck it under the calculator, and click the lock behind me.

22/04: open.

the hospital is slowly filling again. today, i turned the corner to the tfc, and couldn't find a route between all the families lying on their mats.

last night, i could not leave the hospital. i tried. but each time i put my stethoscope in my bag and washed my hands, clapped the nurses on the shoulder and said "bukra . . . tomorrow," another worried family opened the gate. they carried an infant with pneumonia, a woman with a spike of metal in her foot, a teenager with a kidney infection. one family walked for six days to bring an old man who could not walk on his own. i saw a child i discharged one month ago, the one i promised not to when i arrived, and didn't recognize him. he was 55% of the proper weight for his height. he had lost all that he had gained in hospital and with it, his bright curiosity. he couldn't lift his head to look me in the face.

i found myself leaning against the door frame of the nursing room, waiting for the results of a malaria test. the light was fading. the patients had pulled their beds away from the walls and their radiant heat and were scattered like dominoes on the ground. the air was heavy and still. i think it might rain, i said, to no one.

i leaned there, on the door frame, and waited. around the corner, below the blue water barrels in the middle of the courtyard, came achol. she was running like toddlers do, a little off balance, listing to one side then the other, using her fat arms as ballast. she came into hospital a month ago, thin and feverish. we fed her and i treated her for tb. tonight, as always, she was running. her mother scooped her up, and she screamed with delight.

i turned to look for clouds. none. i caught the eye of a parent of a child in the feeding center. she smiled brightly at me. i don't think i have shared one personal word with her, though i see her child every day, examine him every day. but whenever our paths cross, it is always the same; nothing but the widest smiles.

an unfamiliar feeling started to seep in. what was it? foreboding? no, nostalgia. melancholy. no. unfamiliar. wait . . . is that . . . fondness? for this hospital? for . . . abyei? with all its hard, sharp edges, dust-dustdust, heatheatheat. no way. really?

the nurse picked her way through the beds littered on the ground and handed me the sheet with the malaria result. negative. i turned from the door and set it on the table. a gust of wind blew in, and scattered all the papers. outside, it whipped through the courtyard. i felt the sting of sand on my face, the grit in my eyes. an unattended mattress flipped end over end past the door of the nursing room. the soft dusk light disappeared. sandstorm.

i saw two more patients, and walked home in the dark, squinting through my fingers. still, even though the desert tried to cover it up, i am pretty sure fondness is what i felt.

"WHAT'S HIS HEMOGLOBIN?" I ASK.

"Six," Mohamed says.

"Six? Shit." I look down at Manut. His eyes are wide and worried. Today is the day we have to change the dressing on his leg. We've done it every couple of days since the grenade accident earlier this month. I was hoping that we could do this one under general anesthesia, using ketamine, so I could fully explore his wound, dissect some of the torn muscle away and see if his bone is intact.

A hemoglobin of 6 is too low for me. If he vomits and inhales it, or if he gets laryngospasm from the ketamine, a rare complication, the oxygen level in his blood will fall, and there's not a lot of hemoglobin in him to keep it up.

We had tested his mother as a possible blood donor shortly after he arrived. She has hepatitis C.

We tested Manut too. I looked at his result and could see a few clumps of antibodies near the margins of the test's blue circle. Weakly positive. He likely received the virus from her during delivery.

I asked his mother if she knew of anyone nearby who would be able to donate. She did not. The boy's father is far away, and she tried to send a message to him, but heard nothing. No one else in Abyei was willing.

People here fear giving blood, believing that once it is given, it is gone forever. I explain that it will grow back, that it is like their hair, but cannot convince them.

She wanted to go and find his father herself, but had no money. She tried for days to borrow some but could not. Finally, Mohamed gave her the dinars she needed. She said she would be back in two days. She has been gone for five.

Traditional beliefs here are strong, and we struggle for legitimacy. There are two health providers in town, both competing for patients with our hospital. One is a medical assistant who charges patients for his services, which, regardless of the problem, include an intramuscular injection of benzathine penicillin, one of quinine, and an infusion

of normal saline. Patients believe that intramuscular injections are su-
perseded only by intravenous ones in their potency and are often unhappy when they receive pills from us, and completely dissatisfied if
they receive nothing at all.

The other show in town is a traditional healer. I haven't taken the
time to meet him yet. I would like to. It would be better to have a relationship with him so he knows when to send people to the hospital.
As it is, frustrated mothers leave the feeding center because of the slow
growth of their children and visit his tukul. He either blesses them and
sends them on their way delighted, or keeps them until they fall more
and more sick. Near death, they come to the hospital and die, sullying
further our reputation.

"Well, I guess we'll have to do it with local. You want to grab him,
Mohamed? I'll open the theater."

Mohamed lifts Manut up from under his arms. The boy whimpers,
terrified.

I open the lock to the operating theater and lay a plastic sheet on
the operating table. Mohamed enters behind me and sits Manut on
top of it. He starts to cry.

"Nonononono . . ."

He wasn't this upset last time. Mohamed tries to comfort him in
Arabic, then shakes his head. Manut speaks only Dinka.

I leave the room to find Alfred. He is sitting at the front desk, arms
folded, eyes closed. I tap him on the foot and he starts awake. He follows me into the theater.

"Alfred, explain to him that we need to look at his leg, and we will
be as gentle as we can. Okay?"

Alfred speaks to the boy softly.

"Nononononononono . . ."

Mohamed and I prepare the necessary dressings and syringes full of
local anesthetic.

"Mohamed, do you know the maximum dose of lidocaine? It's 5
milligrams per kilogram. This boy is 20 kilograms, so 100 milligrams,
right? Ten cc's. Shit. Is that right?" It doesn't seem like very much.

We try to get Manut to lie down. He refuses, wailing.

"Alfred, tell him there is no choice. You know what, just hold him. Yeah, like that."

I remove the splint from his leg and Mohamed pours some sterile water over it, loosening the caked dressing. More crying.

"What is he saying?" I ask Alfred.

"Nonsense," he says.

I glance through the open mesh window into the feeding center. A feeding center mother is peering through, concerned.

"Shut that, will you, Alfred?"

Mohamed starts unwrapping the dressing. The boy sits up, trying to stop him. Alfred thrusts him down.

"Tell him he is being very brave. Brave like a man."

Mohamed has unwrapped nearly all of the dressing. The last bit remains adhered to Manut's flesh. Mohamed rips it away. Scream. I look at his wound. A hole the size of a golf ball in the anterolateral part of his shin, rimmed with brown, rotting tissue, and at its base, gleaming splinters of bone.

Mohamed starts injecting lidocaine through the periphery of the wound.

"Maybe if this doesn't work, we can try a Bier's block," I say.

The 10 cc's are quickly used. I try to lift Manut's leg by his toe. It bends at the wound like a tape measure stretched too long. He screams. Completely broken. No union.

"Well, he probably needs an amputation. We can transfer him if his mother ever comes back."

Mohamed and I set about trying to clean the dead tissue from the wound, but the lidocaine is not effective. Manut begs us to stop in a language Alfred is not bothering to translate. It is clear to all of us.

We're almost finished. Manut sits up with tears in his eyes, his hands in praying position.

"All right. That's enough. That's enough." Mohamed tries to wiggle free an ochre fragment of bone. Scream.

"Tell him it's over, Alfred." I walk around the end of the bed so I am close to his face. I look him in his eyes. "You are a very brave boy. When your father comes I am going to tell him how strong you were."

Manut's lips quiver as Alfred translates. He looks away.

"Alfred, if you can help Mohamed finish the dressing, I'm going to make a phone call."

I leave the operating room and hurry from the hospital towards the compound. The wind gusts dust in swirls. I clang through the gate, duck into the admin tukul. Tim is sitting at his desk.

"Hey, do you have the sat phone?" I ask.

"Yup. Here. Who are you calling? I need to write it down."

"Your girlfriend."

"Oh. Say hello for me."

"I'm calling our new medco. He's supposed to be in Khartoum this week. Finally. And he has tons of tropical health experience. I'm psyched."

I punch the numbers into the sat phone. It's my first time using it. We are allowed a free ten-minute call on our arrival in the field, but I haven't taken it yet.

"Hello. Hello? Hey, this is James, the doctor in Abyei. How are you? What is Khartoum like these days? Uh-huh . . . Uh-huh . . . Ha. So not much has changed. Hey, you have someone new in the office now, the medco from Geneva, right? Is he in? Can I talk to him? Great."

I move underneath the tamarind tree. Scattered empty pods crunch under my feet.

"Hello, Paul! Welcome to Sudan! It's James, the doctor from Abyei. Thank you. Trying my best. Listen, I have a question for you. Sorry to hit you with business right away. I just finished debriding the wound of a young boy who probably needs general anesthesia for me to do a proper job. In fact, he probably needs internal fixation or an amputation. Grenade wound. Yeah. Long story short, he's very anemic. We've looked for donors, but the usual, no one will give except his mom. But she has hep C. And so does he weakly positive. Uh-huh. So, my question. My assumption is that he got it from her. Yeah, no scars or anything. If I give him her blood, is it possible that she has a higher viral load or something, or if he contracted it elsewhere, might I be giving him a more virulent strain? Could I be making him worse? You know, 'First, do no harm.' "

The generator roars to a start. I glare at the guard and move farther away.

"Okay . . . right. That makes sense. They're both in their latent phase. Cool. Okay. I'll do it if necessary. Well, I must say, it's good to have you here. I've been figuring stuff out with textbooks, or by contacting Geneva. They've been trying, but they have so many different countries and . . . What's that? Oh. Really. No way. Shit. Well, I guess you have to do what you have to do. Uh-huh. Well, thanks for talking to me. Okay. Good luck to you too. Bye."

I duck into Tim's tukul and plug the phone back in.

"Was it good for her too?" he asks.

"The medco just told me he's leaving."

"What? Why?"

"I don't know. Something about the office being a mess, no records. Whatever."

"Man. That sucks."

"Tell me about it."

He holds up his hand and counts on his fingers. "No medco, no logco, no head of mission, no logistician . . . um . . ."

"No admin," I say.

"No doctor."

We shake our heads.

"What are we doing here again?" I ask.

"Sometimes I don't know."

"I mean, why not two hundred kilometers . . . that way." I point over my shoulder. "There's probably a hospital just like this one, maybe even worse."

Tim shrugs, turns back to his payroll sheets. I leave his tukul and pass under the tamarind tree. The generator shakes noisily behind me and from it, the thick smell of oil.

Each week we get an email from Geneva with vacant positions around the world. There are always several in Sudan, and lately, many in Abyei. I don't know why. Perhaps experienced people are fatigued from the long civil conflict, maybe most of them have already worked in the country and know how difficult it is. Or they know something else I don't.

I pass through the compound's open gate and walk back to the hospital. I don't want the work to be easy. I would feel I was in the wrong place if it was. I just want to know that of the many fights out there, this is a good one.

abyei is under water. well, much of it. the cracked fields that stretched from its sides are filled. in the middle of these lakes sit poorly placed tukuls from which women walk, balancing buckets on their heads, lifting their dresses to keep dry. trucks lie stranded, wheels spinning. it seems that either none of us were prepared, or we were waiting for the beginning to begin. our compound of dust is now one of mud, and we are watching for the first signs that cholera has found abyei's thousands of returnees in their new, wet land.

with the rain came a blanket of buzzing bugs in all forms. small ones that fit through your mosquito net and circle your headlamp casting tiny orbits on the pages of your book. larger ones who have bodies like an ant's, but longer, and who can stand on their back legs and survey the huge landscape of the dining table for sugar lodes; lucy's homologues. praying mantises made with sharp green seesaw angles fold and unfold themselves on our kitchen counter. and on the first heavy rain, insects that seemed a fragile, colorless cousin of the dragonfly lay waiting in their dry coffins for the water to wash them free. when it did, after thoughtless months, they took to the night air and carpeted abyei. in the morning, all that remained from their short, glorious season was their wings. they littered the ground like fall leaves and blew and whirled with the wind.

most of us in the project have contracts for six months. some are shorter, none are longer. though mine is only a couple months through, it feels like more. tim and i have decided on a slogan for this project: "for those who think life is too short . . . come to abyei! it feels like it lasts forever!"

i think in some way, we all distract ourselves to avoid the true experience of time because it is uncomfortable. i think that is why many of us dread going to the dentist. it is not because of anticipated pain, there is little of that. i think it is because we are never more vividly awake, never more focused on the present, never experience a longer minute, than when someone has their hands in our mouths.

i think some of the reason the time feels differently here is that there are few distractions. it was something i looked forward to when i read in the job profile: must have "interest to work in remote locations." there is no morning paper to read while we eat our breakfast. after dinner, there are no concerts to go to, nor walks to go on. we sit quietly, and the moments stretch.

the rest of the reason is the tumult of daily experience. emotions are cast through their full register. the delight of receiving a package and a letter from home is followed immediately by the anticipation of the thursday night meal, the one where we can stay up a bit later, the carpet being pulled from beneath you when you're called to the hospital to see a woman who has been raped. the world never lets go, and we are tossed about by its circumstances. like the first rain, with no protection, we feel more acutely its true weight.

"Mmm ... everyone ... welcome to our first ... meeting as a team," Marco says. "Mmm ... I'm sorry for my English ... it's out of practice ... Where's Antonia?"

We all look around.

"I'll go get her," Paola says, and leaves.

Marco smiles at all of us and shrugs. "Already, it's not so easy."

He arrived last week. In his luggage he had brought with him, all the way from Geneva, a package for me. It had inside of it a portable fan, several D-size batteries, and a box of cookies. It must have weighed at least 5 kilograms, a third of his allowed baggage weight. When I thanked him, embarrassed, he shrugged. "A package from home is important, no?"

For three days he was either bent over a map with Bev, reading glasses on the tip of his nose as she spoke in rapid-fire English about the military intricacies of Abyei, or roaring around in a Land Cruiser so he could see for himself.

He has worked in South Sudan before, but this is his first mission as a field coordinator. He told me that after he accepted the mission, he started reading my blog and changed his mind. Not because this project was any different from the one he had worked in before, but because it was so familiar. In the end, he agreed. We're lucky. Bev's lucky. She was hanging on at the end.

Paola emerges from Antonia's tukul. Antonia is behind her, brushing her hair.

"Sorry, everybody. Sorry. Terrible," she says, and lights a cigarette.

Marco looks at her closely, clears his throat. "So, welcome. This is our first meeting as a team. James, Tim, David, you are surrounded by Italians. I hope you are ready."

David pushes his chair away from the table and stands up. "No. I refuse. When I signed up for water sanitation they told me about the soldiers, but no one said anything about Italians. I leave immediately. Goodbye." He marches away.

Marco's eyes widen. A minute later David emerges from the kitchen, a large bottle of water in one hand, six glasses in the other.

"He's French," I say to Marco, as explanation. David has been here for a week now. He's a former logistician. No one knew he was coming. We got an email from Khartoum announcing that he would be arriving from the South in few days, then he was here. Officially, he is here to sort out the borehole. Unofficially, he is our new logistician, whether he likes it or not. Luckily he does. He spent today driving around, trying to find the best bricks for the new office Geneva just approved.

"Already it is not easy," Marco says again.

David pours water for himself, Tim, and me, then sets the bottle down, waiting for a reaction. He gets none and fills the other three glasses. Marco sighs.

I didn't get David at first. He talked too much. Then, one day, in the pouring rain, we climbed on the slippery walls of the gazebo, fixed yellow plastic sheeting to its sides, and shouted to each other over the storm "up a bit, down a bit." Now I think he's the best. Every doctor secretly wants to be a logistician.

"So." Marco looks around the table, surveying us all, drawing out a long pause. "Welcome."

I pick up Tim's package of cigarettes. He nods.

"This is the first of our weekly meetings. We will meet here Wednesday at four o'clock. To talk about our week. Or the problems. Is that time okay?"

We all shrug. Silence.

"Okay. Wednesday."

The generator clacks on.

"Before we begin, I would like to start this meeting off with a small game. It's okay?"

Paola sighs, Antonia continues to brush her hair. David is expressionless.

"Sure," Tim says finally.

"Okay. Everyone stand up. Everyone. You too, Paola. You don't like games? Okay. Move to the center of the floor. Good." He points at us in turn. "Remember your number. One, two, three, four, five."

"Why don't you get a number?" Paola asks.

"You'll see in a minute. Now, I want you to start moving around each other. Move. Walk. Faster. Don't stop. Faster. Try to use as much space as you can. Okay. Now, when I call out a number, that person, you make a loud sound, yes? A loud sound like you are dying and then fall backward. The others must make a catch to you. Okay? Faster . . . Two!"

Antonia lets loose a wide yell, "Oh! I'm dying!" and starts to slump to the ground. David grabs her under her arms.

"Good! Good! Okay, more moving. Move, move. Faster . . . Three!"

David gasps, "*Mon dieu!*" and falls to one knee. Paola and Antonia sandwich him, pull him to his feet.

"Good! Okay. Move . . . One!"

I clutch my chest, start to fall backwards. Tim, nearby, stops me.

"Okay. Well done. Very good. Let's sit down."

We sit back around the table, smiling.

"Antonia, very good dying," Marco says.

"Oh, yes. I am very wonderful at it."

"Good. Now, does anyone know what the game is meaning?"

We look at one another.

"Like, a trust thing? You have to trust your team to catch you?" Tim volunteers.

"Yes, a little."

"I know," Paola says. "It's about how you fall."

"More."

"If you make a big sound, like Antonia, people know how to catch you. If you make no sound, like James, no one knows you are going to fall."

"And then you hit the ground," Marco says, smiling at me.

30/04: .X.

the long-distance hf radio crackles beside me. a guard is resting his head on the desk in front of it. every minute or so, he lifts it and calls into the mic:

"mobile 1, mobile 1 for alpha bravo, over . . . mobile 1 for alpha bravo, over . . ."

he is trying to contact our land cruiser. we have sent a patient, urgently, to the nearest surgical hospital 3 hours away. when they arrived, they were told that there would be no operative cases accepted, and another hospital was suggested, hours away. it is well past dark, and outside of a hospital in northern sudan, in the back of a car, a woman in labor and in need of surgery is waiting to see if they change their mind, or if she will have to drive through the night on a dark dangerous road. we are sitting by the radio waiting for the same news. there has been no contact recently from the driver. we are not sure how to interpret this.

"mobile 1, mobile 1 for alpha bravo, over . . ."

marco was saying the other night that after you do one mission, and you go back home, you are ruined. there is a distance between you and others that is irreconcilable, things that you cannot share. when you try, the people you talk to either cannot place themselves there, or they realize they don't want to know after all. the rift becomes larger.

i am typing in the logistics tukul. i have just returned from the hospital. i got a call a few hours ago.

"dr. james? this is hospital. we have sick child. girl. 5 months. high fever. diarrhea. breathing problem."

"all right, hospital. can you test for malaria, give the child 80 mg of paracetamol, and some cool cloths. do you copy? good. is she drinking?"

"no."

"ok, start a cannula. weigh her and write the name down. i will be there in a few minutes."

"dr. james . . . i . . . um . . . i use bag for breathing now."

"i'm coming. over and out."

where is the driver? no driver. i grab my stethoscope, and jog 460 paces. i arrive through the gate, people are standing in front of me, waving outpatient cards. i brush past them to the nursing room. a young mother wearing a bright yellow veil is holding a limp 5-month-old. the baby's eyes are sunken, half open, and her small chest rises and falls with last breaths. two nurses are bent over one tiny, dangling arm that has a latex glove tied above its elbow, poking it with needles, looking for veins. the child doesn't flinch.

they can find none. no veins, no intravenous. (yusuf, can you use the bag again . . . no, like this, smaller breaths . . . no . . . do you hear that sound? it means there is no seal . . . you know what, i'll do it. tell the guard to start the generator for the oxygen machine.) no gas for the generator. (ok, prep the leg, the left one. with betadine. perfect. great. ok, take the bag. smaller breaths. push when she breathes. no, make a seal . . .)

i open the intraosseous cannula, landmark a little less than a cm below the tibial tuberosity, on the flat part of the shin just below the knee, twist and twist and twist until it pops through the thin shell of bone. marrow flows freely into the clean water of the syringe and i flush it smoothly back. the fans in the nursing room start to spin. i ask for fluid, and antibiotics. the child's head hangs loosely on my knee. she vomits, and breathes it in. (suction please.)

last breaths are like this:

. . . . hu. . . . . siiig-
ghhh. . . . . hu. . . . . sii-
iigghhhh. . . . . hu. . . . .
. . . . hu. . . . .
. . . .

so now i am blowing in tiny, tiny breaths through a tiny, tiny mask. i barely have to squeeze the bag, her lungs are so small. small, and full of crackles. three times my stethoscope dangles down and touches my knee, three times i feel a small pearl of hope, thinking it was her hand. i look down, and her arm hangs loosely by her side. i stay there for hours.

i think i would still be there if her breathing hadn't worsened, but it did. she was tired, her muscles burning and inefficient from the lack of oxygen, full of lactic acid. when i would stop, instead of taking a breath, all she could manage was a grimace, a shrug of her small shoulder.

i placed an oxygen mask over her cheeks and pulled it gently snug. i put my stethoscope on her chest, and heard her heart count quietly down.

5. . . . . (hu). . . . . . 4. . . . .
(hu). . . . . . 3. . . . . (hu). . . . . .
. . . . . 2. . . . .
. . . . 1. . . . .
. . . . . .

i don't think that i will end up ruined, but there are certain things that are going to be tough to share. things that would make poor dinner conversation (hey, have you ever heard an infant's heart stop? don't you think it is like the silence must be after a train wreck, deep in the forest? once the metal has stopped creaking? like all this activity, and then this final vacuum in place of all the sound?) i can imagine meeting people on the street, and being asked how my "trip" was. (. . . you know the feeling when you and your friends are cleaning up after some young mother dies and you can hear her baby cry and you're all praying to yourselves, please don't let anyone look me in the eye? you know that feeling?)

it was fine. it was all fine.

i cleaned up the emergency room, the nursing room, watched the family close the baby's mouth with gauze. i saw some outpatients. i took a seed out of a little girl's nose. i walked back to the compound alone. i went to the kitchen for a glass of water. paola came in to see me.

"is everything ok at the hospital? i heard the call on the radio. is the baby ok?"

"um . . . no . . . she's dead."

"are you ok?"

"yep, i'm good."

"you know, you don't have to keep everything right here," she said, and pointed to her sternum.

"i know," i said.

usually, as a doctor at home, it is rare to have one of these experiences, but when you do, you often bear it with others. another doctor, or nurses whom you know. you sit and talk about it. it doesn't make it go away, but it diffuses some of the weight. i don't do that here. i figure everyone has enough of their own weights. so, just now, from the kitchen, i walked over to the log tukul, and started typing this. instead of keeping it here, in my sternum, i am going to put it right here:

.X.

still no news from the car. we are all quite anxious.

i don't mean to burden anyone unnecessarily, but this is what happened tonight, just now, i am freshly back. the part of me that normally edits these stories out doesn't want to do it today.

KNOCKKNOCKKNOCK.

"Hmm?"

"Dr. James? Hospital. Channel 6."

" 'Kay."

The handset is below my bed. I sweep the cement floor for it. I have moved inside because of the rains.

"Hospital, go ahead," I mumble.

"Dr. James, we have patient here."

"I'm not on call. It's Mohamed tonight. Over."

"Dr. James. It is a gunshot. Over."

"Where is the patient shot?"

"To the chest."

"I'm on my way. Over and out."

I turn my light on, pull my clothes from the line in the corner, walk to the front gate. I check my watch: 2 a.m. The driver is pulling his seat belt on as I step into the Land Cruiser.

"Mustashfa," I say, as if there were anywhere else to go. He nods.

The guard opens the gate and we roll slowly past it, gravel crunching. The road is deserted. We turn right at the buried tire, pull past the military compound. It is quiet.

We stop at the hospital gates. The driver makes a signal with his hand, asking if he should wait. I nod. He reclines his seat.

There is no guard at the gate. Strange. I look around his desk. No sign.

I head towards the emergency room. No nurses in the nursing room either. A mother on the central veranda raises her head from behind a mosquito net.

The door to the emergency room is open. Inside is the security guard. And both the nurses. And four soldiers. Don't know which side, don't care. I glance at their hips. Unarmed.

Wait. Five soldiers. One is on the bed, his shirt off, dressings on the left side of his chest and his left arm. Both are red with blood. An intravenous has been started.

"Blood pressure?"

A nurse checks a list in his hand. "Um . . . 100 over 60."

I open the intravenous line fully.

"Heart rate, 90. Oxygen level, 98%. Respiratory rate, 16. Temperature, 97.5," he proudly reads from his list.

"Great. That really helps. Thank you."

I listen to both sides of the patient's chest. Air entry bilaterally. Less on the left? I put my finger in the notch of his sternum and feel the hard roundness of his trachea. It is midline. The veins of his neck are flat. So far so good.

I lift the dressing on his chest. In his mid-axillary line, to the left of the nipple, is a quarter-sized hole. I look elsewhere on his torso. No others. Odd numbers of bullet holes mean at least one is inside.

I unwrap the gauze on his arm. A small entry wound on the lateral side of his triceps, a wider exit wound through the medial side. Three holes.

"How many shots?"

My nurse translates. Maybe two. I think the one in his chest is the one that passed through his arm, judging by the size of the wounds. The damage done by bullets designed to kill humans is different than ones we use to hunt animals. When we fire a bullet towards an animal, we hope to kill and eat it, not destroy it. The ones made to shoot people are designed to tumble and fragment after they penetrate the tissue, transferring as much energy as possible to the body, creating as large a hole as possible.

There is a bullet in his chest, I'm sure of that. The entry wound in his ribs is small, which means the bullet must have yawed inside his chest, tearing up some lung. Could be anywhere though. Lodged in his heart. Neck veins flat. His spine. Is he moving his toes? Yes. I feel his abdomen. Soft. Diaphragm. Can't tell.

Trauma-room ultrasound and x-ray, chest tube, cross and type four units of blood, CT scan chest and abdomen. Call the surgeon for possible exploratory laparotomy to look for a diaphragmatic injury.

I decide to give him some antibiotics, a tetanus shot, and put in a chest tube. His lung has surely collapsed, at least a bit, and it will be bleeding. If it's not drained, the resulting inflammation from the clot will scar it.

I take my hands off his abdomen. "Can you tell him I need to put a tube in his chest? Tell him it won't hurt; I will give him medicines to make him sleep."

I leave the room as the nurse is translating and wind around the sleeping families cocooned in mosquito nets. I slide between the stacks of vaccine coolers left from the measles campaign and reach the metal pharmacy door. I open it, turn on the light. Lizards scatter.

I take a scalpel, some sutures, a vial of ketamine, and shuffle through the chest tubes. They are all too small. I pick the largest. I mark what I've taken on a piece of paper, sign it, and leave it on the shelf, under the calculator.

One of the soldiers has left, but the rest are still in the room. No one wants to miss any excitement. I ask them to go. One objects. He is the patient's brother. I let him stay.

I prep the man's chest with iodine until it is clean, and prepare all of my instruments. Lastly I draw up the anesthetic.

"Tell him this will make him sleep," I say, and inject the ketamine into his intravenous. By the time I am finished putting on sterile gloves, the soldier's eyes stop roving, and close. Beneath his lids, I can see his irises jitter back and forth. Ketamine works best in children, because they can manage better with the dream world it creates. Adults, as they emerge, can be disoriented and violent.

I make an incision in his chest, over the sixth rib, through skin and muscle. I take a curved forceps and curl it over the bone, and with a pop, push it through the pleura and into his chest. I spread the forceps apart, widening the hole, and then insert my finger, feeling for a piece of lung that might be adherent to the chest wall. There is none.

I slide the tube into the incision and guide it into his chest, directing it towards the back of his rib cage, cinch it with a thick suture, and tie it to his chest. I clean away the torn skin from the bullet hole, then wash it out and sew it shut. As I turn my attention to his triceps, he starts to moan. I give him more ketamine and with it, some Valium.

I finish. As the nurses are dressing his arm, I open the door to let the other soldiers back into the room. They are asleep on the veranda.

I ask the nurses to do another set of vital signs and begin to clean up the mess. I put the scalpel and the needles in a thick cardboard box, and bend to pick up the iodine-soaked dressings on the floor. Beside them is the bag I just attached to the chest tube. It is full of blood.

How much.

I pick it up. Easily 800 milliliters. Whoa.

"Can this guy give blood?" I point to the brother.

"He says no," the nurse answers.

"What? Why not?"

"He says he is too tired."

"Well, that disqualifies everyone on the planet. Tell him that his brother is going to die if he doesn't get blood."

"He says he had malaria."

"It doesn't matter."

"He refuses."

"Ask the other ones."

"They say no."

"What the hell."

It's four in the morning. I look at the bag of blood. Closer to 900 cc's now.

"Okay. Tell them they have to find someone who will give blood. They have an hour. Or he will die. And then start another intravenous and give him more saline. A whole bag."

The soldiers leave. The nurse turns to me.

"He was shot by other soldier."

"Oh."

I leave the room to find the guard and use his handset to call compound 2.

"Ismael, it's James. I need you at the hospital. Blood transfusion."

He's on his way. I call compound 1.

"Marco. It's James. Sorry to bother you. I need to do a transfer. Yeah, gunshot. No, don't know the details. Shot by another soldier. His own side, I assume. Wait, let me ask . . . No. I was wrong. Not his own side. You'd better come. Over."

I'm more awake now. I stop for a second and listen. I don't hear any gunfire. Wait. Is that—? It's tough to hear over the generator. I step out of the front gate and look at the military compound. No lights. Quiet.

Marco and Ismael arrive in the same car. There is no sign of the other soldiers yet. Ismael tests the wounded patient, still sleepy from the Valium. Marco and I start getting the car ready for transfer, hanging bags of saline and stocking it with medicines.

The soldier's brother arrives alone. He could find no one else and now agrees to donate.

"Ismael, how much blood can we draw, maximum? A unit? Maybe take a bit more."

Ismael draws half a liter of thick blood from one brother and we start to drip it into the other. The night begins to lift. It is five-thirty and we can be on the road soon. We call in a driver and an extra nurse. We carry the patient to the Land Cruiser on a stretcher and lay him on a mattress in the back. There is now a liter of blood in the bag.

I pull the nurse aside and write specific instructions on a piece of paper. How much of the medicines to give, how fast to run the fluid and the blood, how often to do vital signs.

"Is it clear?" She nods. "Call me if there are any problems."

Dawn breaks. The driver fires up the Land Cruiser, and the guard opens up the gate. The car pulls slowly forward, then stops.

At the gate is a small pickup truck filled with people. They are blocking the exit.

Our driver honks. The pickup pulls farther ahead. An impasse. Our driver gets out of the truck, begins shouting loudly in Arabic. The guard joins him. The driver of the pickup backs out of the way, and our Land Cruiser pulls through the gate and down the road.

The pickup enters the hospital grounds. Three men jump down from the back. I can see their uniforms now. Police. They reach into the box and pull out a heavy load that they carry between them. It is a body. They deposit it at my feet.

The face of the man is blue and swollen. I reach down to his neck. He is cold.

"He's dead."

"They want you to say how he died," the nurse beside me whispers. It is six in the morning now.

"I can't. I'm not a coroner. Tell them I'm only good with the living."

She translates. The policemen start speaking loudly.

"They say it is the law."

"No."

Marco comes from the nursing room. The body lies between me and the police, forgotten. We argue overtop of it.

"James?"

"These guys want me to determine the cause of death of this man. He appears to be beaten around the face, but I can't say for sure why he died. Broken neck, internal bleeding. I can guess, but we'll just get in the middle of something. It's a recipe for ending up in a Sudanese courtroom."

"I'll take care of it. You go back to the compound and get some sleep."

The hospital is waking up. People shuffle underneath their mosquito nets, toss them open. A baby starts to cry.

I grab my stethoscope and walk through the gate and almost bump into Mohamed. He has heard the entire story from Ismael.

"James, why didn't you call me for help?"

"I didn't think of it. I should have. Hey, can you do rounds today? I'm pretty tired. Wake me if there's anything, okay?"

He agrees, and I turn towards compound 1. Beyond it, the rising sun.

Bright.

03/05: cheap sunglasses.

one of the most difficult things for me to accept in sudan is that every-one has better sunglasses than i do. well, not everyone. mostly old men. in my other life, i live in kensington market in toronto. when i am not working or running from one place to the next, i am wandering the streets of my neighborhood trying to soothe that one hollow part in my spirit that the right pair of sunglasses would fill.

i don't think this is a sign of inner discord, representing a broader sense of dissatisfaction with the universe. nor do i think i should be looking for sunglasses inside my own soul rather than in second-hand store windows or on the faces of old sudanese men. i know this be-cause once i found the right pair. i bought them in new york on the street for ten bucks. they were like blue blockers, and on the bridge was a swordfish. with them on, the world was better. minty. i took them off only when necessary. last year, on my way to train with msf, sleep deprived and excited, i left them on the seat of a german taxi. as it took off, i felt a familiar ache.

it is a grand leveling that msf, as part arbiter of my sunglass woes, placed me in a country with such a high density of cool ones. i could even begin to forgive their role in the loss of my perfect pair if i could track some down. when i was in khartoum last, i spent an afternoon with a driver going from place to place, souk to souk, looking for some. he would pull up to a stand with racks of fake gucci glasses and look at me hopefully. no, i would say, i want old man glasses. confused, he drove on.

and now i am in abyei. the souk is full of carbon-paper stores. the one selling cigarettes, powdered milk, tomato paste, lighters, and biscuits abuts another selling cigarettes, powdered milk, tomato paste, lighters, and biscuits. there are two restaurants. at bashir cafeteria, one can take his chances with beans, goat, or if he is lucky, tomatoes. at the other, beans, goat, tomatoes. the worst part is, of course, the old man who takes your money has the best pair of sunglasses you have ever seen, but the market has none. i asked him one time where he got them. he smiled, and turned away. he could smell my desperation.

i need sunglasses. it sounds trivial, but that's the point. at night, it is getting tougher to sleep, and the next day, when i step from my tukul, the world is reflected in all of its sharp edges and the light is harsh and unflinching.

I'M UP. I DIDN'T SLEEP much after I left the hospital. It was too hot. I lay in bed, Antonia's fan blowing beside me. She has left the project early, frustrated by the compound, the drowning need in the hospital. Before she did, she gave me her fan. My portable one was no match for the heat. Antonia is now in Geneva, debriefing. I think with sympathy about the person who will receive her feedback.

This morning I approached sleep's black line, but could only dangle, so I got up, wrote about sunglasses on my computer, then left my tukul at noon to have a shower and wait for lunch. The team was gathered around the gazebo's plastic table.

The hospital has been evacuated. Minutes after I left, a military group arrived and laid claim to the dead body. The man into whom I put a chest tube, who arrived safely at our referral hospital, was a member of their opposing militia. While he, and possibly others, were beating the man in the pickup to death, a gunfight broke out and he was shot.

Marco called for Sylvester to examine the dead man's body. As the MOH designate, it is Sylvester's job to act as coroner. The arriving soldiers were not satisfied and demanded their own inspection of the body. They charged past, ignoring Marco's request to leave their weapons at the gate. Soon a swarm of armed soldiers was milling among our patient beds, asking questions. At least three of the families in the feeding center left.

We evacuated all MSF staff from the hospital. It was Marco's only card to play, to withdraw activities. If such impositions continue, we close the mission. They lose the free care for their soldiers and their families, and gain the ill will of a community.

In Germany, during our pre-departure training, we were reminded that the nature of conflict has changed. Wars no longer take their greatest toll on combatants, but on civilians. This means that our proximity to the fighting is necessarily greater. As war spreads its wide grasp, it erodes the space in which we work.

Once, being a humanitarian carried with it a certain privilege: if

you declared yourself one, you were not a target, not even on the bat-
tlefield. The red crosses and MSF logos no longer provide as much
protection. Some don't see them, and to others, they look like bull's-
eyes, a sign of wealth, of resources. Someone told me that in Darfur,
Land Cruisers get jacked at a rate of around one per day. A month or
two ago we got an email that cited a report claiming Sudanese Armed
Forces had painted some of their planes white, like the UN, and were
using them to transport supplies, possibly weapons, to Darfur. The dis-
tinctions were becoming blurred.

We were increasingly seen as part of the conflict, a potential pawn
in a larger political game. With one swift stroke, one could drive help
away from an enemy, or more likely, from civilian countrymen who
might be supporting them.

The problem is, once this humanitarian space falls away, it cannot
be rebuilt. The newer wars will have no memory of it. Those whose
only protection is this invisible margin of safety will be left defenseless.
It is why we keep our distance from anyone with guns, even the UN,
why we cringe when we see soldiers delivering food, or hear the phrase
"militarizing humanitarian corridors."

The space is not only for us. One of the reasons the worn red road
between the compound and hospital is safe at night is that if it were
not, we would leave. The hospital, once full of armed soldiers, was a
place where people could feel safe because if someone refused to
check their grenade at the door, we evacuated. We demand the space,
and with it comes air for everyone.

We left the hospital. When the soldiers did too, with the body, we returned. Well, two of our nurses did. A skeleton shift. At the suggestion of
the UN, Abyei is under curfew. No unnecessary movements until the
situation declares itself. Both nurses will sleep in the hospital. I will try
to handle things over the radio as much as possible, and go to the hospital for life-threatening cases only. Others will wait until morning.

From what we can glean, the fighting is between opposing militia.
Both armies, the South and the North, find it more politically convenient to use groups of armed civilians to do unofficial fighting to make a
point or to raise uncertainty without declaring war. They choose groups

with whom they have ethnic or historical allegiances, or to whom they can make promises of power, and arm them. What better way, for instance, to defer a census, or a referendum, than to claim a place too "unsafe" for it? Meanwhile, the oil wells keep humming.

It is unclear whether the recent spate of violence is a symptom of something larger. We knew tensions were high, heard that troops were mobilizing on both sides. Each week, Marco meets with the UN to discuss security, but at the most recent, no escalation was predicted.

If this is not a symptom, it could be a spark, a shard of glass. Like peace, sometimes war only needs a little piece to become real. If more fighting happens between these two groups, their mentors might show their allegiances. Or as in previous geneses of war here, a rebel group proves itself dangerous, and hornets fly from Khartoum.

These are our thoughts as we sit in the gazebo in the center of our compound, watching the season's first torrential downpour. The rains to this point have been heavy but short. This one is unrelenting. The compound is mud, puddles connected by small rivers.

We are all here. Marco, Paola, David, me. Tim is away on his R&R. I miss Antonia. Paola does too. She helped us laugh.

Paola stands up and runs to the kitchen. On our last trip to Muglad for gas, she got the driver to buy apples. This afternoon she volunteered to bake a pie. We are all grateful for something to anticipate besides war.

"So. If things get hectic, gunfire-wise, where do we go?" I ask. "The kitchen?"

"No," David answers. "The walls are too thin. Not safe. The bricks are very poor clay. Look." He leans over and breaks a small piece from the gazebo's wall.

We look at our security area, bags of dirt between Tim's tukul and mine. They had burst in the sun, and with the rain they are now mostly mud.

"I think Tim's tukul is best," David says. "We have the kitchen to one side, your tukul to the other, some protection from the bags of dirt. We would still be vulnerable on two sides, more or less." He looks at Marco, who says nothing, only shrugs.

Marco has been quiet for most of the day. I think the gravity of his position is becoming more real. As the situation threatens to worsen, we turn to him. He can turn to the acting head of mission in Khartoum, but the man has never visited Abyei before and will likely only support Marco's assessment.

We too are grounded in this place more firmly than before. This is, in essence, what we signed up for, to be in the middle. We are where we wanted to be.

The rain thunders on the roof overtop of us. Paola comes back.

"Not quite ready," she says, smiling.

I think about my thoughts. They meander, unhurried. Things are calm. The possibility of escalation still seems unlikely and, at the least, beyond our control. If something happens, we will rely on the UN for air evac, or leave by ground in our Land Cruisers, towards the North.

"Hey, what do we do about David? He can't go through the North. No visa," I ask.

Marco is silent. He has thought about it, but doesn't want to talk.

"We can put him on a donkey," I say.

"Yeah, we can give them rubber boots," Paola says. "Two for David, four for the donkey."

"And some BP-5."

"And an injection to make him strong."

David begins to intone one of his stories about Darfur, about how chaotic and dangerous it was, how much more so than here. We all find the story unhelpful. Paola leaves to go check on the pie. Marco asks me for the insect repellent. The plastic sheeting that David and I hung along the walls of the gazebo flutters, and the metal pole at its bottom swings away from the wall and into it again, clanging viciously.

Clang . . . clang . . . clang.

A guard runs through the rain, hugging a handset close to his body. He hands it to me.

"Hospital," he says. Marco and David are watching.

"Hospital, go ahead."

"Dr. James. We have another body. Gunshot. Over."

Uh-oh. "Um. Hospital, is it a soldier?"

"Negative. A civilian."

"What are the vital signs?"

"The patient is dead. Brought by police. Over."

There is no reason to go to the hospital. Marco takes the handset from me and tells the nurse to send the guard to find Sylvester. He can inspect the body.

Marco gives the handset to the guard. There is no way to tell what has happened. Not until the morning. No movements. Can't talk on the radio.

Paola returns with the pie. "Sorry, but there was no butter. Only flour. I tried to use some yeast, but I think it died from the heat." She looks disappointed.

After months of beans and fried goat, we are thrilled. She starts to cut it into pieces.

"Wait!" David and I run through the rain to get our cameras.

We sit together, under the tin roof, quietly eating apple pie, and strain our ears above the din of the rain to listen for gunshots. It's impossible. A mere 460 paces away, a dead body sits on the veranda, and our thoughts are there too, wondering if this is the beginning of what everyone in Abyei is waiting for.

05/05: the problem of the dead body.

i have been told that some years, in this season, a thin cloud appears on the horizon of an otherwise clear day. it approaches quickly with the wind and, minutes later, locusts cover crops, cars, tukuls, lie floundering in puddles. as i type this, one is doing a stop-motion crawl across my tukul floor. skitter-pause . . . skitter-pause . . . skitter.

last night i had a fever and lay in bed, sweating, plastered to my sheets. as i was drifting in and out i heard, above the usual noise, wailing. a chorus of cries from the hospital. another dead body. another throng of people at the gate and more, running from town.

we have been having problems with dead bodies recently. not because of their alarming number; this is something the abyei hospital is accustomed to. others.

where to put them? we replaced the dusty room at the back of the hospital, a makeshift morgue, with a pharmacy. now when someone arrives at the hospital ten minutes too late, we flounder for space. in the emergency room? occasionally. it does little to instill live patients with confidence in the hospital, or in my skills in emergency medicine. in the tent beside the tfc? once. the man with the grenade hole in his stomach. when the roof of the tfc crashed in from all the rain the women refused to move their children into the tent. haunted. on the ground, in the back? too wet. in the room at the front? nope, full . . . measles patient. in the pharmacy? over my . . .

dead body problems. when someone is sick in a village, they don't come to the hospital straight away. there is no road. transport is too expensive. often the family calls a traditional healer, and they spend their carefully collected money, likely saved for this exact contingency, for treatments that do not work. the patient worsens. there is no choice but to spend what money they have left to hire a donkey, or a car, and bring the patient to abyei. they don't have enough, so they sell their only goat, or a piece of their land, to their neighbors. they use the money to get the patient to the hospital, ten minutes too late.

they are grieving, and penniless. there is nowhere to put the body, nor for them to sleep. pleading, they ask for our help to take the body to the graveyard. they are heartbroken. we say no.

it is an impossible decision. we could easily take one of our cars, the pickup for instance, and offer the family some relief from a cruel day. but we don't. we cannot be a hospital and a hearse service. nor when someone knocks on our compound door, his eyes as big as moons, and says "my wife, she is delivering at home, but the baby is stuck, can you take her to the hospital," can we be an ambulance service. no, we say, you need to find a way, and quietly close the gate.

these are impossible decisions because their wisdom is easy to see, but they are contrary to one's spirit. once we start transferring bodies to the graveyard, the hospital becomes their destination. once we become an ambulance service, our resources become taxed, and we may go to destinations that are not secure. further, each time we are a band-aid, we simply cover the problem, and delay the slow work towards a tenable, permanent solution. but when a family comes kilometers over broken roads, carrying their dying daughter, and they arrive ten minutes too late, when you tell them that no, you cannot help them bury her though you have the means, the knowledge that you are being wise is poor comfort.

you want to drive each patient where they need to go until you run out of gas, use every last dose of rabies vaccine for the small chance the dog was infected and the child dies foaming, to give the starving family money even if it will only feed them for a day, drip all of the blood into this patient, the human (someone's father, brother, son, best friend) bleeding in front of you even though it means there might be none for the next ten, but today you have it, and today is his lucky day, and tomorrow you will worry about tomorrow.

but we don't. we are measured, and careful. it is what tomorrow's patients expect of us and the tomorrows stretch towards forever, and today is nearly done.

TIM IS SITTING BESIDE ME on a low chair. I look at him, and gesture towards the pots full of food on the table to our right. It is 11 a.m. and our Sudanese hosts are waiting for us to eat. This is early for us to take lunch, and late for their breakfast.

We rise to our feet and head towards the table. Paola does the same. Marco sits.

Lining the rest of the large, sturdy recubra are Abyei's nine Dinka chiefs. Some of them have a small entourage, and all are eyeing the groaning table hungrily. This is the paramount chief's recubra. He is the most powerful man in the Dinka tribal system in Abyei, the one who resolves disputes the local prefects cannot, and the food is made by his chef. One can assume that if there is to be a reversal in our opinion of Abyei's regional cuisine, this is where it will happen.

It is customary within this tribal system to solve disputes in a public forum. We are here to allow for the airing of grievances about our project. The word we have received, through our local staff and community contacts, is that there are many. This is an attempt to establish a dialogue, to improve our standing with the people we are here to serve.

The meeting has been organized by Ajak Deng, the man with whom I shared an airport taxi in Geneva, when I was halfway gone, and he was halfway home. He has been sent on behalf of Geneva to further illuminate Abyei's complex political and social situation and our place in it. Our understanding of the movements, tribal and political, that swirl around us is so rudimentary that we are lost.

The trouble from last week has blown over. The woman who was shot was a civilian as reported. She was killed in a retaliatory attack, the bullet meant for a member of the opposing militia. The night that we sat in the gazebo, eating Paola's apple pie, was a difficult night for the hospital. We were told the next morning that a militia had occupied the latrines, in anticipation of more wounded, so that they might spring a trap on their enemies. More patients left the hospital, and many refused to use the latrine for days.

Once more soldiers entered the hospital with weapons, and once more we left it. And then, as Abyei lilted towards a familiar chaos, everything became quiet. No more shooting, no more military intrusions. Perhaps part of it was Marco's convincing threat that we were an instance away from complete withdrawal. More likely Abyei's political importance trumped petty militia rivalries and the groups were reined in. The official troops, North and South, were legion, and well resourced. Neither was going to test the other's considerable mettle over what sounded more and more like drunken quarrels.

We kept the curfew for a few days, and because of it, we had to sleep in the hospital. The day it was my turn, the curfew was lifted and I slept in my tukul.

The hospital has been quiet. Part of it is the waning of the measles epidemic. Though small pockets still smolder in the shifting nomadic populations, the blaze is over. The rest of the decrease in hospital admissions is because of the recent military incursions. Even the market has been hushed. People are holding their breath.

I am not clear whether Ajak's visit is in response to the recent events, an example of MSF's quick capacity, or was set into motion with Bev's departure and debriefing. The mission is still new, and because our interim head of mission is more closely tied to Darfur and has never been to Abyei, clearer insights are welcome throughout this particular MSF thread.

As such, Ajak has been touring the countryside, meeting with the various Dinka chiefs. On his way to Abyei, he spent time in Juba, the capital of the South. His ties to this country are strong, his family name recognized as powerful. His access is complete.

His report to us about Juba did little to illuminate Abyei's future. The forecast is mixed. Some call for war, saying that the Khartoum government is not to be trusted, that it is not a dialogue in Dinka or Arabic that will bring freedom, but one in bullets. Others are wary but reluctant to let peace slip away after working towards it for so long. He told us something that we already knew: neither side is willing to back down.

"Black and brown," Tim says, wrinkling his nose and pointing to a pot full of beans.

"You have to take some. It's not polite," I say.

"Forget it."

Ajak is traveling back to Uganda tomorrow, this meeting his final task.

We already know what to expect. Dissatisfaction. When Ajak briefed us before the meeting, he told us this. The community wants us to do more. They are unhappy that we want to focus on the hospital and on secondary care. We either transfer people too much, indicating that our hospital resources are too thin, or we don't transfer enough, a sign that our transportation options are too few. Some want a helicopter, others an operating room. We heard that many are unhappy being told to go to GOAL for treatment of their non-acute problems.

We struggled with this. No matter how many days in a row we worked, it felt like we were getting further from being accepted. It had surely happened more often, but I can only clearly remember one patient's approval. I had taken a piece of glass from his foot, and when I apologized for the discomfort it was causing, explaining that local anesthetic in the sole is painful and often ineffective, he shook his head at me and fixed me with a broad smile.

"I am from Darfur. In Darfur, there is no one. No hospitals. No medicines. You are doing a good thing. I am a very lucky man."

We are not naive. We expect few accolades. The Dinka are a strong people. They have resisted incursions on their soil and on their culture for centuries. Through these last decades, because of the long conflict in Abyei and ascendancy of the NGO as the arbiter of the world's philanthropic wealth, they have become used to people driving up in Land Cruisers and asking what was needed. We should expect their chiefs to advocate for their people, to ask for as much as they could get even if they might receive a fraction. I would do the same. And after decades of former friends burning down their homes, they will be cautious about trusting new ones.

Tim and I sit down. As soon as we do, others stand up, queue, and begin to heap their plates. The food is similar to what we eat at compound 1, or find in the market. Oil-drenched okra, black beans, ground goat mixed with pasta or potatoes. There is a round piece of oily white gelatin in the center of the table that survived Tim's and my pass intact but is being whittled away by the Sudanese guests.

The paramount chief, for his part, has stayed seated and still. His chair is made of large pieces of strong wood that suit his mighty frame and booming voice. Next to him sits Ajak. Ringing the room on rickety chairs are the rest of the attendees. Between the district chiefs and their emissaries, our MOH staff sit across the room from us. When we arrived, Sylvester came over and shook our hands. The vaccine officer, the one with the office at the back of the hospital, didn't meet our eyes.

The paramount chief brings the meeting to order and everyone sits down. He welcomes us to his house, thanks us for our kind patience in waiting for this important meeting. He throws a meaty arm around Ajak, says he is sad his cousin is leaving so soon, but how good it is that he came.

He starts to make introductions.

"Majak Atem Atem, chief of Gumbial. Arop Atem Deng, chief of Abienton . . ." Each name leaves me as soon as I hear the next.

"We are each grateful that you have taken the time to come here. We know the hospital is very busy," he says. "It has been a long time since we have sat together, MSF and us. We hope this is the first of many such meetings."

Tim shifts uncomfortably beside me. Next to him, Marco smiles at the chief, nods.

"Many people in the community are unhappy with what MSF has done in the hospital. . . ."

And so it goes. From one person to the next, we are roundly reminded of the things we do not do. As one chief runs out of words, starts to pause, the man to his side starts.

Someone is describing the ire of a patient sent away without treatment, a patient who had some sort of hysterical paralysis that even the local nurses in the hospital called Abyei Syndrome. I interject.

"How many times do you hear from people who come to stay in the hospital? The very sick people?"

The chief dismisses this, shakes his head, and continues on. We slump lower in our chairs. The vaccination officer smirks.

It is an hour later. I glance at the rest of the team. Paola is looking at her feet, Tim leaning forward with his chin in his hands. Marco is trying to remain engaged. Across from him, one of the chiefs who has spoken his piece is leaning his head against the pole behind him, snoring softly.

The paramount chief looks at his watch. He has another meeting. He calls this one to a close. We stand, dejected, dizzy from the contrast between how hard we are working and our perceived performance.

We step out into the bright noon sun. Ajak decides to stay behind. He has more family to see. Tim, Paola, Marco, and I start back to compound 1. The road is rutted from the recent rains, but has dried in the morning heat.

"So?" Paola says to Marco. "What do we do about that?"

He looks puzzled. "What do you mean? Nothing. We do what we are doing. We work in the hospital like before. Until I hear something different from Geneva."

It is rare that we are this deep in the market at this time of day. Store owners glance up at us. We stop to buy some water. A group of children start to trail us, giggling. We walk on, and as a team, we lighten. That we are misunderstood, that our efforts seem unappreciated, makes the long hours seem even more virtuous.

"Hey, Tim," I say, pointing at a grass-lined compound and a hanging broken bulb. "Sheeshaashooo . . ." He laughs.

By the time we pass through the metal gate of compound 1, together, we feel tighter.

11/05: paradise now.

this is the part of the story when the character begins to get tired. when he walks his daily route, one that is so familiar he can do it with his eyes closed, he does it with his eyes closed.

yesterday, on the walk back from the hospital, a monkey loped past me. he cast a brief backward glance, then took a sharp left into the market. he was wearing the most amazing pair of sunglasses.

my morning run has been suspended recently so that i might concentrate more fully on smoking. unfortunately, i woke up over-early this morning, and could find no excuse to avoid it. my usual route, over a flat wide flood plain, has been made impassable by the rains. all that was left was to run along the red road that leaves town, and look over my shoulder for overfull trucks. i took it to its first junction, and turned south. it was very early and i could see a corona form over the fields, much clearer than on other mornings, no refracting dust. in an instant the sun blazed, burned my eyes. people walked from the trees towards abyei over the cracked ground that drained rainwater like a sieve, and their white robes were silhouetted by the sun, morning ghosts.

everyone in our mission smokes furiously. msf. part of the reason is the isolation, the idle minutes. as it has been said in many languages, when you have a cigarette, you always have a friend. the other part is that in the face of all the sickness and early death, one's health falls from constant focus. you look around at the other passengers, and from all accounts, if it looks like the plane is going down, smoke 'em if you got 'em.

I AM IN THE LAND CRUISER, on its plastic back seat. Marco is sitting in the front, Anthony is driving. We are grinding slowly past the tire at the corner, but instead of turning right towards the hospital, we drive straight.

In a few hundred meters, we are somewhere I have never been. We begin to pass half-finished tukuls ringed by a railing of thin sticks. A woman drops a bundle of grass from her head to the ground beside her tukul. It will be used to make a roof, or a fence.

This must be where the new returnees are settling.

We pass the last tukul and bump across an open field. Hundreds of plastic bags, bleached white by the sun, flutter on the rough ground.

"That's not getting any better!" I shout over the chatter of the car.

"What?" Marco shouts back.

"The plastic! All those bags!"

"I can't . . ." He shrugs, smiles.

"Later," I say, wave my hand. I turn back to the window.

This is my second time in the land that surrounds Abyei. The first time was when I did a mobile clinic a month earlier, to see what it was like. I had been a vocal opponent of mobiles. In my months in the hospital, I had watched the Land Cruiser return at the end of a long day with an exhausted team, and only once or twice had it carried an emergency. I worried that patients who were truly sick might delay attempts to find transport to the hospital if they knew we were coming in a few days. I struggled with the possibility that one day, because of the rain or the fighting or because we had closed the mission, the service would be stopped. Those people may have stayed where they were, farther from Abyei, because we helped them resist the tide of urbanization.

Further, I knew the type of medicine that was practiced. Pills were given based on the patient's complaint, often in the absence of a physical exam. At my mobile clinic in Cambodia, I found myself sifting through dozens of patients to get to a sick person. On the way, I would dole out pills that would be traded between patients. Two yellow for one red, my antibiotics for your paracetamol. After a few days, I gave out mostly vitamins.

Last month's mobile was the same. Queues of women and children, a few men, all mostly healthy. Of the forty or so patients I saw that day, I diagnosed a girl with a possible urinary tract infection, a young boy with a superficial eye infection. To everyone else I gave either paracetamol or vitamins.

Anthony turns onto a wide road, a proper one, and speeds up. The rippled clay rattles my teeth. It is too loud to speak.

We have three sites. We are on our way to the one deepest in the forest. We discovered the population shortly before I arrived, after we received a few cases of hepatitis in the hospital and found that they were from the same area, Bayom. Bev went with the first doctor, the one I had never met, and came across several hundred people, a mixture of soldiers and civilians, all desperately poor, living in the middle of a scrub forest, far from a main road. They had lived closer to Abyei once but, because of the war, had settled here. They had little access to food, less to medicine. It was difficult for them to get to us. We decided to get to them.

I am told that they have a local doctor, someone who has some official training, but we don't know what type. I am going to meet with him or her. I am going to get the fuck out of Abyei.

Anthony points out the window.

"Bricks!" he shouts.

On the side of the road, stacks of gray clay bricks, formed by hand. They will be fired in a wood kiln and turn red with the heat. The only people who can afford them are NGOs and the government. Local huts are plastered with clay.

The scenery changes back to brown scrub, the land flat and austere. No bricks, no birds, no animals, fast glimpses of an occasional hut. Trees flick by. The sameness is hypnotic. We drive for miles. Flick. Flick. Flick.

The Land Cruiser slows down. To our left, a small dirt track appears, so faint that I would have missed it. We turn. After a short distance, we see that it will not be passable in the rain. The soil is loamy, and the path dips below the water table in several places. Once the daily rains start, these people will be on an island.

We wind on the path for an hour, scraping between trees, scattering occasional troops of monkeys. After an hour or so, I see a hut. A few more. Roofs of grass held up by walls of grass, and inside them, beds of grass. No clay. Families stand to watch us pass.

"Bayom," Anthony says.

It is my first real glimpse of the larger world that surrounds Abyei, one where many of my patients live. The other mobile I did was just off the main road.

All this space.

When I said I was interested in being somewhere remote, this is what I imagined. Not Abyei, its generators, its military rallies, its roving UN vehicles.

We climb a ridge and see huts scattered on gently sloping hills. At the top of one is a large tree. Underneath it sit several men.

As we get out of the Land Cruiser, they rise and step towards us. They shake our hands eagerly. One of the men, my age, is introduced to me as a doctor. We smile at each other, then sit down. There aren't enough chairs for everyone. Two of the men remain standing.

The chief begins to speak in Dinka and the doctor translates.

"First, to our guests, thank you for coming such a long distance to meet with us."

Marco nods.

"You have brought medicines to these people who have suffered so much because of the war, and without them we would have none at all. We are glad you are here, to sit with us, because we are worried about the rains."

Their worries for the rainy season are the same as ours. Not only will it choke their access to the larger world, it means disease. Malaria, cholera. When the rain starts and before things grow, the chief explains, his people have no food. They eat grass and it gives them diarrhea, and some of them die.

Please, could we bring them food? A box of medicines? Could we build a proper school? Dig a water pump?

Marco listens carefully, nodding throughout. When the doctor is done translating, he answers with the only thing we can do: we will drive on an increasingly muddy road until the truck will go no farther, and once that happens, we will turn around.

The chief nods solemnly. Our limitations must seem like refusals. Marco speaks again.

"Someone told us of another road, one that goes to Bayom but from the other way, from Twich. Do you know that road?"

The doctor translates and the men begin to talk excitedly.

"Oh yes. Another road. A very good road. Someone was on it with a car like yours the other day. It is this way, down the hill. Past those tukuls. I will show you. It is very very good," the doctor says.

The meeting is nearly over. I ask them if there are any particular illnesses they are seeing right now. Diarrhea, hepatitis, measles. The doctor answers that there are only a few cases of malaria, nothing else. We stand to shake hands again, and Marco talks to the chief. This time Anthony translates. The doctor and I step towards each other.

"Michael, I'm glad to meet you," I say. "It must be difficult to work here. I find it difficult to work in Abyei, and I have a hospital."

"Yes. It's difficult," he says. "I have no medicines. Sometimes I can go to Abyei and get them, but mostly I have to tell people what they need and let them find it."

"Where did you go to school? Are you a medical doctor?"

"I am a nurse."

He did two years of training in Ethiopia, and once his certificate was done, he came to help during the war. That was four years ago, and he's been here since. He's not from the area. He is from near Juba, the capital of South Sudan. He wanted to help his people.

"I have a small clinic. It's on the way to the road, just down there." He points down the hill. "You will pass it, just before you get to the road." He glances over my shoulder. The chief needs him to translate something to Marco. He excuses himself.

I move back under the tree. Most of the men have left, carrying their chairs back to their homes. A few are still sitting and smoking. We look at one another and with no way to say it, have nothing to say. They start talking to each other.

The edge of the hill is rimmed with patches of scrappy acacia trees. Underneath a large one, I notice three families standing, looking in our direction. I watch another woman walk towards them, a baby balanced on her hip. They must have heard the car and think we are here to do a mobile.

Marco and the chief are finished. Michael and I go back to the Land Cruiser. We discuss Bayom's people, about how poor they are. I don't ask how much he charges them for his consultation. We shake hands a final time, and I climb in.

Michael speaks with Anthony, and then the engine roars on. We circle around the tree, away from the way we came, and past the waiting women. Anthony shouts something to them in Dinka, and when I turn around, they are walking back through the brush.

We pass Michael's clinic. It is made of grass. I ask Anthony to stop, and jump out. Its entrance is made of thin sticks, designed to form a series of hallways, like a cattle gate. Inside it is cool and dark. The ground is covered in grass. There are two chairs, nothing else.

I get back into the Land Cruiser, and Anthony finds a road that stretches north. On it, we can see a pair of tire tracks. Huts flank it at first, but as they disappear, so does the road. It changes from a road to a bicycle path. Several times we are blocked by trees and must reverse, retrace our route to the previous fork. We push through the brush for an hour. The sky starts to darken.

"Do you think we should turn around?" I ask Marco.

He looks at Anthony, who shakes his head.

"Are there any landmines around here?" I ask.

Marco looks straight ahead. I shut up. Anthony picks up the radio to call compound 1 to give them the hourly update on our location, then sets the handset down. We don't know where we are. The prospect of getting lost becomes more real. I start to get excited.

We enter a wide clearing, and in the center of it is a large grass tukul. A man, having heard our approach, stands outside. A pair of children's eyes peek through the gaps in the wall.

"Twich?" Marco asks.

The man points north. We drive on until we find another hut, another man.

Twich? That way. Twich? That way.

The path finally widens. Underneath a tree, four men are talking. One of them has a bicycle.

"Twich?" Marco asks.

The man with the bicycle answers in English.

"You're not far. Just that way." He points north.

"The road. This road. In the rainy season. What is it like?" Marco asks.

"Water. All water."

"Oh."

"You should build a proper one."

Anthony puts the car into gear and we drive on. One can interpret these requests in two ways. The first, that these people expect others to do everything. The second, that they believe that we can do anything. If we can drop food from the sky, why not knock down a bunch of trees, push some dirt into a road.

We enter more clearings, pass more tukuls. The walls are no longer grass; they are clay. We must be getting close to the main road. Like the dry riverbeds I saw from the plane, green trees on their banks, roads spill energy from their sides. The man on the bicycle is right. Of all the ways we could help Bayom, a road would be the best.

We drive from yard to yard, and finally bump onto a red road. I look at the odometer. Twelve kilometers. Two hours. And with the rains, no chance.

We drive back to Abyei deep in the afternoon, and watch the clouds stack. As we turn into town, raindrops start to spatter the windshield.

13/05: mother's day.

one of the members of our team is approaching the end of her mission. she has been here for five months. i have watched her go through some of the same stages i have, some i have yet to approach. right now, she is stifling the excitement she has for going home, trying to save it for when she steps onto the plane, for when she will be able to believe it. marco was talking about what it is like when one's mission ends. you leave from khartoum and step off the plane in geneva, and the world you left . . . collapses.

i am not surprised. we completely inhabit it, focus our entire energies on it, but as soon as you queue up in the airport to get a starbucks latte, it will seem as far away as the moon. but that is why i am writing this. to convince us all that it is not.

of course, i can't bring you here, as much as i would like to. as such, much of the perspective gained is mine, and i might only realize it for a split second as abyei disappears into the horizon of my memory.

part of the secret to being here is to think not of the future, nor the past, but to imagine the day only as it folds into the next. every thought that starts about my vacation, or how much i miss careening around toronto streets on my bicycle, i let out what little air my happiness holds, like a balloon.

but, if i could be anywhere else today, i would be in alberta. i would be driving down the country road to my home, the one i left more than a decade ago, the only one i have ever really had. i would pull into our driveway, and drive slowly up it, stones popping from beneath the tires. i would stop, shut the car off, and hear only smooth silence. i would open the door, then the trunk, grab my bags, unlatch the gate, and go inside.

almost tough to type that, i can imagine it so clearly. and as clearly, the delight on my mother's face. mine would be just as strong, but i have learned to hide it. it burns brightly, but under the surface. hers burns like a star. she is the most famous person in the world. trust me. if you met her, you would see it too.

"WHY DO YOU PUNISH YOURSELF?" Marco asks me, a piece of bread in his hand.

"What?"

"The book. Why do you punish yourself?" He points at the thick copy of *Ulysses* that sits beside my morning coffee. Each morning when I don't run, I pull it from the wall of my tukul and sit down to read five pages. After three months, I am a few hundred pages into the annotated edition. I left the SparkNotes in my tukul. I use it to read about what I just read.

"No, it's good. Well, okay, I can't say I like it, but it's worth it. It changes the way I think about thinking."

Marco shakes his head and disappears into his tukul, returns with a book. He sets it down on the plastic table.

"This is better for you. If you are a writer."

I look at it. Paul Auster, *The Invention of Solitude*. Seems to fit.

"I'll take it, but I can't start it. If I do, I won't read this. I'm looking for an excuse to stop."

Marco shrugs and walks away towards the shower. It is Friday and our day off. Our cook's too. Our day to starve. I tried to ration the almonds Sarah sent me from home by only taking a small handful in the morning. A small handful in the midmorning. One after lunch. Another just before dinner, and then one just after. They lasted three days.

I push my chair back from the table, and it scratches in the sand. My coffee cup wobbles on the brown plastic table etched with scattered grooves. I grab it and look in its bottom. Coffee grounds. Cardamom.

Why do they do that here? Cardamom. That's an Indian spice. It comes in pods. I saw some in Zanzibar. I have that picture, the one with my guide with a red bindi dot on his head from the ink of a flower. I wonder if the spices began in Africa and were brought on the spice route, or vice versa. Probably vice versa. Why does food suck here so much? I don't get it. Instead of just boiling a chicken, why doesn't someone just chop it up and fry it with some onions and some cardamom? Must be a poverty thing. Either you don't get the chance to sit around and come up with creative ways to cook, maybe risking a meal because the next one might be tough to come by, or it doesn't matter that much, you just want food and it all tastes good. Could be a taste bud thing too. But Zanzibar had a wealth of spices. Wonder why they didn't make it this far.

I wonder what happened to that girl I met there, the one working for the UN. She was in Sudan, I think. Or Chad. She was cool. Oh shit. I sent her a poem. That's right. Jesus. Why would I do that? So embarrassing. I didn't even know her.

I put the coffee cup down and turn my book over.

The gazebo is completely different after we sawed those legs off that table. Now it looks like a coffee table. It's funny how something so small can change the whole vibe. More comfortable. Those metal chairs are shit. I don't understand why we don't just throw them all away.

I fish for my sandal with my right foot.

What am I going to write about today? I should write something. What did I write about last? Mother's Day. Sunday. Do they have Mother's Day in Europe? I should have reminded Tim. I don't remember him mentioning his mom. I think he has a family. I hate when you do that.

I fish with my left.

What the hell am I going to eat today? I hope someone else makes something. I haven't cooked once since I have been here. I wonder why. I don't even care about it. Oh, I made some eggs. A while ago? Bev was here. We made them together. I cracked one, and its yolk fell out pink. The next one too. Then the third. I cooked the shit out of it anyway. How are you supposed to tell if an egg is bad? The yolk falls apart, I think. These ones smelled like metal.

I'll work out after breakfast.

I'll work out, then I'll write and then . . . I'll clean my tukul. Maybe I'll go to GOAL and check my email.

I walk to the kitchen.

I can't believe those bags of dirt are still there. They should just be a garden, then I can tell Grandpa I planted a garden. I should write about him. Like when I told him I was going to work in Cambodia, he didn't say, "Don't go, it's too dangerous," he said, "Don't go. It's too far." That's funny. Or how when he was a kid he would put on those skates, those double skates, and just after the lake froze and the ice was thin, skate around with an axe handle and try to stun muskrats through the ice as they swam underneath, bubbles in their whiskers, streamlined smoothing under the clear black ice, and then whack, a star of cracks. He would sell them for pocket money, for candy.

Grandma's brother is deaf from measles. I think she had a sister die of it. Maybe I can come to it that way.

Wow. Our water tank is filthy. Everything is square. The clothes washing sink and that stupid metal table. Was that worth the fight? The cleaner hates me because I took it into my tukul without asking. It was MSF's table. Whatever. Should just smash it.

I wonder when the foundation of the new office is going to be finished. It looks like a mosquito farm. Can't they clear the dirt away? It just makes mud. Last week with the hole in the kitchen. Dust was everywhere. Oh, look, someone stacked dirt to make a little ramp. The satellite antenna is crooked. Tim and I . . .

I step into the kitchen. The guard has delivered our morning package of bread in newspaper, the pieces on the outside black from the ink.

A piece of bread. I wonder if that ink is bad for you. Not as bad as cigarettes, so who cares. I wonder if there is some Nutella left. I wonder whose it is. Everyone eats it. Sarah sent me some. That's a mess. Don't think about that.

What am I thinking about? A billion things at the same time. A billion blind pathways.

Quiet.

I open the lid of the freezer.

An orange. One left. So what. I'll get another later. Nutella. Sarah. No. Bread. Cigarette? No. Yes. After lunch. See if it tastes good. Maybe I'll stop.

I take the Nutella from the rack at the top of the freezer, grab the orange with my other hand, let the freezer door slam shut.

Ants in the sugar. Shake them out. Wonder if their brains live on glucose like ours. Probably.

I unscrew the Nutella jar, and take a spoon from our cutlery can. Beside it is a sink full of dishes, dashes of blue wash powder by its edges.

They use that powder for clothes. I wonder if it's safe to eat. So slippery. I should do the dishes. Corrugated metal roof. Hot in here. No breeze. Plastic over the windows. Tear a corner open.

I pick up the jar of Nutella, the spoon, the orange, and sandwich a bottle of water under my arm.

Why do I always need to make one trip? I wonder what that means about me. Something. Beer bottles with candle wax on them. We're supposed to take those back. Should we? We said we would. I wonder what they do with them.

I step out of the kitchen and onto the flat ground. The compound is quiet.

Where is everyone? Plants. Wish the generator was off. What am I supposed to do? Cigarette. No. Write something. Shoulda washed my hands.

I walk back to my plastic table, set my food and water down. The orange rolls off the crooked table and lands lightly in the sand.

I pick it back up, blow it off, and start to peel it. I turn Ulysses back over and notice that its binding glue has melted from the heat and pages are coming loose from the spine. I tug at one and a section fifty pages deep slides free.

With satisfaction, I stand up and walk the thick book over to the garbage can and drop it in. I return to the table, peel a section of orange, tilt back my chair, and look up at the sky.

14/05: half.

at this point in the story, the character's eyes are closed nearly all the time. despite the fatigue, sleep eludes him. he is replaced with a half-ness, a part of him awake, part of him not. at night he sleeps in fits. he approaches dreams, but never arrives.

this morning, while walking to work, at the corner, the one with the half-buried tire, the character saw a mini cyclone pick itself up off the road. it whirled dervishly in widening ellipses, then blew itself into a closed green door, opening it. his eyes met those of the man seated behind it who calmly stood from his chair and closed it again, as if cyclones came knocking all of the time. the character thought to himself, who needs dreams when days are so extraordinary?

i am more than halfway through my mission, and am overdue for a break. though my time in ethiopia was more about tuberculosis than rest, it did allow me to step away from abyei. so i delayed a vacation partly because i wanted a true experience, to spend my full time in the field, to arrive at all the important points in the mission so that i could better understand them. i have discovered that fatigue, however, is like the personal experience of illness. though being sick is valuable, particularly as a physician, because it increases one's empathy, only a fool would court it. so too exhaustion.

but, here it is. a halfness. i remember talking with friends about how i could manage to work, during my residency, 30 sleepless hours in the hospital, leave it to sleep, then return. i explained that the last thing to go was my capacity to perform medical duties. i could sort out a high potassium at five in the morning. what i lost was my ability to offer the patient something beyond the task. i would walk in, inject the proper drugs in the correct amounts into their iv, mumble something neither of us understood, then stumble out to do something else.

the tiredness i feel now is different. it has been a slow erosion. bits of sand have ground me down. i can still recognize the best things in the day, but am just not able to participate in them fully. half.

some members of my team have suggested that i not take call, that we have enough staff to make it possible. i have thought about it, but i think i would miss it. often, it makes up the best part of my day. i get to meet someone, someone new, listen to their story and feel their anxiety. i get to touch their child's forehead, then quietly listen to his heart. and sometimes, i get to put my hand on the father's shoulder, tell him that everything is going to be all right, and i get to feel the coolness of his relief.

one of my friends told me that once, when she was having a personally difficult time (someone in her family was sick and her relationship was crumbling), she poured herself into her general practice. the more she worked, the more patients would stop on the street and say "hello, doctor soandso," the more they would send flowers. not only was she caring, she was being cared for. of course, in the end, this was not an equitable relationship, not the true contact someone needs to feed their bruised spirit, and after several months, she burned out.

i will not, though i can feel the heat. i can understand it better. i am due for a break in 16 days. i started counting yesterday.

MOHAMED AND I ARE sitting beside Aweil, watching her play. The woman who has unofficially adopted her, a relative of a child who was in the feeding center, sits close by wearing a new necklace. We have been paying Rebecca to stay in the hospital with Aweil and she seems to be spending the money wisely. I have never seen her drunk and Aweil is wearing a new red polka-dot dress. It is likely she has some children at home, and is using some of the money for them. I don't care. Marco has agreed to continue the arrangement for now, and each time I suggest to Rebecca that Aweil could probably continue TB treatment at home, she says her home is too far away. I never press.

We have sent word about Aweil to the military area where we last knew her father to be. So far, we have not seen him. Our discussions about her care have been exclusively with this woman, and we are reluctant to complicate things any further. Mohamed and I are in no hurry to take her from our daily routine.

To our other side is a mother with her starving child lolling in her lap, his eyes half open, hands taped over so he cannot pull at the feeding tube in his nose. He probably couldn't manage the strength anyway. Today he hasn't been able to muster anything but a thin cry.

His story is typical. Already malnourished, his mouth last in line for whatever small amount of food the family could afford, he got diarrhea. What little energy he had left, to tug at his mother's skirt, to cry from hunger, to hold his head up to be fed, was washed away.

Her child mewling and taped, tubes in his nose and his arm, the mother sits embarrassed. I'm not sure if it is because it marks the tenuousness with which her family is hanging on, ten hands scrabbling to find purchase, or if it makes evident her necessary neglect of this child in favor of the others. I wish I could talk to her, I wish Alfred's English was better. When I walk past and she looks at the ground, I could say, "I know what you were trying to do. I do. You were trying to save as many as you could."

We can't know how many children die in the mud tukuls because the family cannot afford to bring them to the hospital. The only thing we know is how difficult it is to get them better once they do. Diarrhea is a killer. It runs children dry. The work it takes to keep their machinery turning with the desert outside and the one inside becomes too much. They creak to a stop.

I don't have the necessary investigations to determine what the terminal cascade of events is. Could be a problem with potassium. They lose it in their diarrhea, become hypokalemic. Or their kidneys fail from having to work so hard with such little fluid. Could be acidosis, the pH of their blood so low that the proteins in it unfold, their cargo bobbing uselessly a million cells away from where it is needed. Could be all three. Or none.

Aweil shakes a rattle of beads at me. I try to take it, but she won't let go. She grins.

On rounds earlier today, I pulled down the boy's lower lid. It was white from anemia. I remembered talking with someone in Ethiopia (a month ago, two?) about how many malnourished children they saved with transfusions. Today we are trying it.

The mother agreed to donate. Ismael drew some blood from her this morning, and we are trying to drip it into a small vein in the back of her son's hand. We are running it slowly. If we give the blood too quickly, it can overwhelm his homeostatic system, the extra volume filtering into his lungs.

I hand Aweil to Mohamed, stand up, and dust off my scrubs. I take the small bell on my stethoscope and put it on the boy's chest. His mother stares. I feel the taptaptap of his heart before I hear it. It's the size of a cherry. I listen to his lungs. Clear.

I unwrap the cool towel that we have wrapped around the blood bag and look at the drip set hanging below it. A thick clot hangs from the filter.

This is the second time today we have tried this, the second time it has clotted. I went over the process with Ismael after the first failure, made sure he added the correct amount of anticoagulant. He did. I went back at lunch to try and find an answer in a book. Ismael did the same. We found none. Brian is gone. We're unlikely to get a response from Geneva in time.

Shit. Maybe the intravenous is too small. Or it's too hot outside. Perhaps it affects the heparin. If we store it somewhere too warm . . .

The boy's breathing is getting faster. I've seen it this way a dozen times by now. If you do something as simple as put in an IV, worse an intraosseous, sometimes if you even turn the kid over to wipe at the diarrhea, they spiral. They cry, and that withdrawal of energy, from the pain and the distress, puts them into debt and they die.

I stop the IV. The mother looks up at me.

"Mohamed, can you tell her that the blood is too thick, that it won't flow?"

While he is translating to her, I go to the front to find a nurse. I find one hunched over the desk trying to read our orders, then drawing up medicines into unlabeled syringes that litter the desk.

"How do you know which syringe is which?" I ask.

He looks at me and smiles. "I remember."

"Right. You know the baby with the blood transfusion?"

"I know."

"It's clotted. Not working. Can you take it down and put in a saline lock?"

"Yes. Right now."

He leaves the room and I sit down on the blue metal chair behind the desk. My foot bumps against something. It is the cardboard box we use to hold all of the charts from all of the patients that leave the hospital each month. It is nearly full.

I lift it onto the desk and take the top chart. It is for a patient who died last night. One of two. She was a young woman who came in with a sudden fever and a headache. We treated her for both malaria and meningitis. Her fever never left, and in the past forty-eight hours, she drifted in and out of consciousness. Mohamed was on call last night and he told me that the nurses called him at four in the morning to say her blood pressure was 220 over 140, and as he prepared to come into the hospital, they called back to tell him she died.

Probably a brain abscess. No way to know for sure. I have scrawled at the top, as a diagnosis, "FEVER." When I tally the births and deaths at the end of the month, hers will be classified under "Other."

The next chart is in sequence. It is that of a man who also died last night. He started feeling weak a few days ago and saw a local doctor, who gave him some antibiotics. He continued to worsen. His weakness became so profound he could not walk, and by the time he rolled through our doors, he was having trouble breathing.

Mohamed saw him last night, on call. The man started to vomit, and inhaled some of it. He stopped breathing shortly after. Guillaine-Barré, probably. Could be botulism, I guess. Myasthenia gravis. On the top of his chart I write "WEAKNESS." Other.

I start to comb through the charts, remembering the people through their scribbled stories at the tops of their pages.

Oh yeah. This one. Little boy, came in with a sore throat. Seemed to be all right, but got worse. Didn't respond to antibiotics, stopped eating. Breathing became noisy. We finally transferred him to Heglig, where they airlifted him to Khartoum. I heard he died on the tarmac. "SORE THROAT."

Mansood. His chart is thick. He was here for months and never got any better. The caregiver we hired worked for a while, but after she found out I was treating him for TB, I never saw her again. I checked on him a few days ago. His eyes were still and unblinking, the skin on his face taut, his last expression a toothless grin. On the windowsill of his room was a stack of foil Plumpy'nut packages and three or four half-finished sodas swimming with ants. "WEAKNESS."

"MALARIA." "MALARIA." "PNEUMONIA." "SNAKE BITE." "MEASLES." "FEVER."

"GRENADE WOUND." The boy's mother finally came back, and we transferred him for an amputation. Don't know if it happened, or where in the world he is.

I put the old charts back in their box and start going through the active ones, the ones on the desk, to make sure I haven't missed a stool or urine sample.

The nurse comes back, the blood bag in his hand, coils of tubing looped over his arm. He shakes his head gravely.

"The baby has passed."

I nod, shuffle back through the charts to find his. Aywan Chan. Sixteen months. Male. From Anet. I write as his discharge diagnosis "MALNUTRITION" and beside it, circle "Death."

I finish going through the pile. There is one stool sample from this afternoon that needs treatment. I calculate the dose of metronidazole. In the chart I draw half a pill, twice a day, and show it to the nurse. He nods.

Mohamed shows up at the door. He is tired. It is the end of a long, difficult day for him.

"James, are you finished?"

"Yup. I should get out of here before any business shows up. You?"

"Halas." Finished.

I stand up from the table, put the cardboard box under it.

"Let's go."

"I need to lock the theater. I'll be right back."

Mohamed goes to the back of the hospital and I walk towards the front. It is late in the day and the sun is angling towards the horizon, its light soft and orange. Across from the hospital road a football match is being played on the wide flood plain. I can hear a soft thud as the goalie kicks the ball away from his net, deep into his opponents' territory. Players race for it, kicking up clouds of dust.

In the space beside the hospital road, a group of younger boys is playing their own match. The ball they are using is nearly flat, likely discarded by their older brothers. One of them kicks it, and it makes a loud *pock* and careens erratically.

Smoke is coming from some early-evening fires. High above Abyei, on the hot drafts of a rainless day, hawks circle.

I turn around. Mohamed is standing behind me, watching. We sit down on the hospital step and watch both games.

"James, do you believe in God?" he asks after a few minutes.

I think for a second.

"Not really."

Mohamed often excuses himself, if we are at the hospital through lunch, to go pray.

"What about paradise?"

"No. Not really."

"Most religions have theirs."

"I think this is it, Mohamed. Paradise, I mean."

He shakes his head. No.

"The way I figure it is that I didn't know what life was before I got here, and if there is something after this, I won't know it either," I continue. "And this world, the one here, the one with that ball being kicked up in the air, and above it those birds, I can touch it with my hands. I can taste it. And I can change it. It is the only miracle I know. You and I, sitting here, every bit of us from some distant part of the universe, filtered through a star, and put together just like this." I hold up my two hands.

"No, I don't think so. Too many babies die here, too many of us are fighting. This is not what God, praise be to Him, wants of heaven for us."

"You could be right. I don't know anything. It seems too hard. But maybe that's the thing. Maybe we're supposed to make it."

The game closest to us is winding down. One by one, the younger boys are leaving for home. Now there are only two boys, kicking the wounded ball back and forth.

Pock . . . pock . . . pock . . .

Mohamed shrugs, stands, and brushes his pants off. "I am going to walk home."

"Me too."

We move step in step towards our compounds, both of us lost in our thoughts. As we draw close, Mohamed stops.

"I'm going to pass through the market."

"Okay. See you tomorrow."

"Yes. Good sleep."

I watch him walk, head down, hands in his pockets, until I lose sight of him in the fading light.

18/05: arrival.

this morning, i opened the honey jar, and inside floated an ant. i held the jar up to the sun, and his wire frame swayed gently. for an ant, the sweetest of deaths.

i have been in sudan for over three months, but i have yet to fully arrive. i wonder at times if i ever will, if it is even possible. it seems part of me remains in canada, watching my friends and family through a thick glass wall, unable to hear them or touch them. another part of me is waiting on the plane, looking at his watch, ready to leave as soon as the rest of me shows up. it is an uncomfortable feeling, one i am not accustomed to, having parts missing.

i also work on avoiding the future because i will never catch up to the part of me that is already waiting on the plane. when i make it there, he will be through customs, and on the cab ride home, he will be having a glass of wine on the roof, watching the sun set, surrounded by friends. if i spend my time running to catch up, i'm only running.

so, i work on here. 11:09 a.m., friday, may 18, in my tukul, compound 1, abyei, sudan. the sky is mercifully cloudy. a bird is tapping for termites on one of my posts. a small lizard poked his head around the corner, and just now ran underneath my clothes trunk. a larger one, a foot long or more with a yellow head and tail, is clambering up the brick wall of another tukul, and is doing push-ups, peering around the corner, looking for locusts.

every now and again, it rushes in. not just for me, but for all of us. we arrive, completely, even if just for a short time. we sit in the middle of our compound, reading, and the donkey-boys show up with our water. the glass falls away, and you remember, right, i am in rural africa. donkeys deliver our water. a boy walks to the hand pump, waits his turn, grabs the hot, sweaty handle, and pulls up cool water hidden beneath the sand. he collects it in dirty plastic buckets, heaves it onto the back of his donkey, and together they walk to the msf compound, through the gate, to our water tank. there they stand now. such hot work.

someone calls your name, and you are gone.

Tɪᴍ ᴛᴀᴘs ᴏɴ ʜɪs ᴋᴇʏʙᴏᴀʀᴅ, frustrated. "You get any signal?"

"No," I say. "Nothin'."

"Shit. I'm supposed to Skype."

"You want to stick around?"

He looks at his watch. "No. Let's get back. We should help Paola."

We pack our laptops into our bags.

"You wanna walk?" I ask.

"Yeah. You?"

"Definitely."

We pick our way past the moat that has become GOAL's driveway and wave at the guard. None of GOAL's expats are around. Their current manager is on vacation, their health manager has quit. The compound is mostly empty.

"So, what do you think of Angie?" I ask.

"She seems okay. Different than Paola. But cool."

"Kinda revved up."

"Yeah."

A bicycle, two boys on it, pedals slowly past us, front tire wobbling.

"It's good for me, though. She was a pediatric nurse. That'll be useful. Lots of kids in the hospital, man."

"Yeah," Tim replies.

The ground along Abyei's road is now verdant green. What was once a dry field between bunches of tukuls is now filled with rainwater and grass. In the middle of this little lake, two girls are taking turns hammering the handle of a water pump. They jump in the air and land on it with straight arms. Once, twice, three. The other's turn. Once, twice, three. As Tim and I pass, a girl waiting in line points to us. The pumping stops, and they all turn and stare.

"I think they like you," I say.

"Think so?"

"For sure. You're tall and thin. You're like an albino Dinka. You just need a djellaba and a walking stick."

Tim laughs. He has lost so much weight that on his way back from his R&R, Geneva made him check into a hospital in Nairobi. He was given a clean bill of health.

"Who were you Skyping?" I ask.

"Oh. Just someone back home."

"Just someone, eh?"

"You know. What about your relationship? The one you didn't know you were in?" he asks.

"What are you talking about?"

He laughs. A little boy comes running out from a hole in a grass fence, his little legs turning so fast he stumbles. He picks himself up off the ground and runs to us, crumbs of food on his fat face.

"Kywyja! Kywyja!" White person! White person!

The word irks me. Paola used to answer, in Dinka, "Hello, little black boy."

"Hello," Tim says, holding his hand out for the boy to shake. The boy stands there wide-eyed until we pass.

"So what are you going to do?" I ask.

"Figure it out when I get home. Too hard from here."

We stand to the side as a truck rumbles roughly past.

"Well, man, I was thinking about it the other day. I'm thirty-three, not in a relationship—shut up—and I was thinking that, you know, part of it is to do with me. I mean, we're all looking for love. You, me, everyone is. It's kinda what it's all about. But there's this part, this grass-is-greener part, that only ever wonders if something else is better than what we have, you know."

"And then you just want and haven't got."

"Exactly. So maybe the next . . . I don't know . . . iteration of my spirit is to realize that to find peace, with someone or just in my day, I gotta ask fewer questions, to tap into the happiness of the current moment, 'cause that's all there is, you know?"

"Yeah, man, totally."

"So that's true, right? But there's just one other thing."

"What?" he asks.

"Maybe it's not that fucking complicated. You meet someone, she says something, then you say something, and you start to fall in love.

And I think I would be always . . . kinda . . . sad that I was so afraid to be alone that I thought love was something I could figure out. That it was about me. You know?"

"No."

"Yeah, dude. Me neither. Sucks."

"I'm going to stop and buy some cigarettes."

Tim stops at a wooden stand, its awning made of grass. Behind its counter, a Misseriya man in a white cap smiles at him, his back framed by batteries. He pulls two packages of cigarettes from a hanging basket. Tim makes a flick-flick motion with his thumb, and gives the man a Sudanese note. The man with the white cap hands him a lighter and a handful of change.

"Want one?"

"Sure. I'll give it up when I get home. You?"

He pulls one from the pack, hands it to me, takes one for himself. "When am I going to stop smoking? Here," he says, and points at the filter.

We are halfway back to compound 1. To our right is the muddy path to the market, its ruts filled with water, garbage, and half-buried bags.

"Here, dude, hold my cigarette. I want to take a picture of this.

"And, ladies and gentlemen," I say, as I put my camera back in my bag and retrieve my cigarette, "that's where diarrhea comes from. The end."

Tim claps his hands. We continue on.

We can see some of our national staff sitting in chairs alongside the road, their backs to the sun.

"Wanna stop at compound 2?"

"Sure," I say.

Most of the national staff are recruited from Khartoum, a handful from South Sudan. Everyone in compound 2 has relocated from somewhere else, many of them leaving families behind. One of the medical technicians on my team has been in the compound for almost a year. His newest baby was delivered in Khartoum a few months ago. He was here.

We walk to the side of the road.

"Gentlemen," Tim says.

They all stand up, shake our hands warmly.

"You guys watching for girls?" I ask. They laugh.

"No, Dr. James. Just trying to keep cool. Compound 2 can be very crowded."

"You mean camp 2," Tim says. More laughter.

"Oh, Dr. James, I am verrrry tired," one of the nurses says, his *r*'s trilling. "You know, Mabel, the nurse, she sleeps the whole night. She doesn't do anything. I can't work with her any more. I told Paola. No more for me!" he says, slapping his hands together.

"I'll talk to Paola about it. But you know the new nurse is here."

"Oh yes, I met her. Angela. Like angel. With one more *a*. Very nice. Very good," he says, proud of his English.

"Maybe we'll give her a day or two to get settled in. Does that sound okay?"

"Very okay. I have no more night shifts this week. Very okay."

"We're going to go inside. You guys yell if you see any pretty girls."

Tim and I turn towards the metal gate. The guard stands up and opens it.

Inside the grass wall of compound 2 are eight tukuls, all shared.

Over their doorways, bright printed pieces of cotton ripple in the warm breeze. Earlier in the year, when I first came here, I saw that their beds were pulled into the middle of the courtyard. All of them slept outside. I soon did the same. We have all moved in because of the rain.

Their kitchen is a white emergency tent. To the side of it is the flat cement base of a planned concrete kitchen. To the other side, a brick shower, similar to ours, surrounded by a large puddle of water, the ground underneath it too saturated to drain. In the small pond, bright blue birds twitter and splash, then dash to the low-hanging branch of a large tamarind tree.

Mohamed is sitting down, playing dominoes with three others. He rises to his feet as he sees us, excited.

"Hey! Man! Welcome to compound 2." He grips Tim's and my hand in turn, pulls each of us closer to the table. He pushes his stool towards me, and turns to the kitchen tent to grab two others. "Sit down. Sit down. I'm just about to make some tea."

"M-m-mohamed m-m-m-makes the b-b-best tea," says the man to his right, John, a nurse. In the hospital, I rarely hear his stutter. He must be nervous.

"No, no, thank you. Tim and I are just stopping by to say hello. We have to go and help out at compound 1. Paola's party tonight, right? She leaves tomorrow. Insh'allah."

The men around the table are disappointed. Despite promising, we don't make the visit to compound 2 very often. It is about five hundred meters from our compound, and this is my third time. They rarely come to ours. Too full of work.

"Tim? We have time for a cup of tea?"

"Nothing but time."

"Two teas, please."

Mohamed disappears into the kitchen tent. Tim and I sit down, inch closer to the table.

"Dominoes, hey?" Tim says. "Who wants to teach me?"

Each of the three men starts to offer advice, pulling pieces from the pile and laying them out in sequence. I am having trouble following their enthusiastic instructions. I turn my attention back to the birds.

Mohamed returns with a Thermos and carefully pours three glasses of tea, sugar swirling at their bottom. He picks one up by the rim and hands it to me, the other to Tim.

"Shukran . . . shukran," we say. He nods.

Mohamed and I sit sipping tea, a few feet back from the table, watching Tim and John angle dominoes into a growing maze. Every now and again, the metal gate creeps open and one of our staff walks in, blinking in surprise at seeing Tim and me this close outside of the hospital.

A chorus of generators begins to ascend, and I drain the last grains of my sweet tea.

"I think we have to go. Paola's last day, and we promised we would help her. You guys coming?"

The men around the table shrug. Tim pushes his stool back.

"Thanks for the tea. We have to come here more often. It's like paradise. Tea, games, birds singing," I say.

"You're w-w-welcome an-n-y time."

We shake everyone's hand, and they return to their game. We open the gate. The sun is setting, and now that it is no longer in their eyes, the men have moved their chairs to the other side of the road. We wave to them.

"See you tonight?" Tim yells.

"Oh, maybe. I'm verrry tired."

"Come if you can. We are making lots of food."

We wave goodbye and walk towards our compound.

22/05: cows rule.

if one is lucky, he might witness the extraordinary, maybe even the magical. if he sees it just once, he will spend the rest of his life looking for it.

today, the sun was high and hot, and it burned through bands of thin white clouds. i sat watching them, trying to determine whether the wind would hold the darker ones on the horizon away or shuffle them in. i couldn't determine which direction they were moving. north . . . no, south. wait. north. the narrow strands of cloud were being blown back, and forth, and back, and forth, stuttering, a glitch, a loop in time. they stayed there, tossed around from side to side, for a minute or more. dizzying.

the life around abyei is not linear, it is curved. it moves in ellipses and arcs. the huts are round. the cattle paths meander back and forth. there are no straight sidewalks when one nears a home, but a gently angled padded approach. in canada we can trace our lives with a ruler. our doors, our stairs, our house, our property, the shortest path to work, to the movie theater. whenever i arrive home after months away like this, my first thought is always "wow. everything is so square."

as i have mentioned before, many of the paths in the part of sudan where i work are made by the dinka. they are one of the largest tribes in the south, and make up a majority of the patients that i see in the hospital. consequently, i know them the best. easily recognizable, tall and thin with high cheekbones and almond eyes, they are nilotic cousins of the more famous masai from kenya. among the most famous of the dinkas is manute bol, who, at seven foot seven, was the tallest player in nba history. anthropologists wonder at how they preserve their unique height. someone once told me that the dinkas in southern sudan changed weight/height charts for the entire world.

historically, many of the dinka were pastoralists. they spent their time herding cattle from one grazing area to the other, looking at the clouds and following the seasons. if the unit of human understanding is the story, the story at least in this part of the world includes the cow. they are of the highest worth. they are used to pay a woman's family for permission to marry. their number is a measure of social status, of power and wealth. they are tended and loved. often, a man will favor a particular cow, befriend it, write poems about it. on the full moon, some tribes tie colorful bands to the bulls' horns, and sing and dance until morning.

in abyei, there is one large bull that is free to roam about town. his horns are incredibly large, difficult to believe. they are as disproportionate to his frame as mantis antennae, and very heavy. unable to find equilibrium, his head bobs from side to side.

cows are rarely killed for food. usually, only their milk is taken. traditionally, at adolescence, a dinka boy is relieved of his childhood duties, of which milking the cows is an important one. with an initiation rite, he is welcomed into the world of men, and with this arrival, the permission to accumulate cattle of his own, and to take a wife.

many of the men who i work with bear the marks of this initiation. on their foreheads are deep scars, tracing the brows and meeting in the middle. they are intended to resemble horns. at thirteen or so, after an adrenalin-filled night of dancing and singing and homage to ancestors, an elder takes a sharp knife and cuts deep into the forehead of the initiate, who neither cries nor flinches; a jitter in a smooth scar would be a permanent sign of his cowardice. the blood is then wiped away, and his forehead bound. the cuts are deep. i have read that sometimes when a skull is discovered one can tell the tribe it belonged to because of the marks left in the bone.

i have not found out why some of the people i see have different patterns of scars. delicate series of lines, dots, circles stretching from their faces, down their arms, over their chests. they are remarkable, elegant, and final. occasionally, i will see women with such intricate scars, but haven't been able to glean their significance. i will do more research.

there are other unique, distinguishing features particular to some of my patients, as well as some of my colleagues. some, for instance, have their four front teeth removed. i have seen it done both on the top and the bottom. others have their teeth pulled to right angles from their jaw. completely perpendicular to their face, they jut beneath their lip. it is thought that it makes women, in particular, look beautifully fierce.

i remember asking my translator in cambodia why he kept the nail on his fifth finger so long. he shrugged. "i think it looks good," he said.

it is an unfortunate thing that i will not be in abyei long enough, and am unable to mix with its population well enough, to get more than glimpses into the complex patterns of human history and beliefs that surround me. already, one can see ties to the past loosening. in abyei, 50 cent shirts are more common than traditional garb. one of the people i worked with asked how much it would cost to have his teeth reinserted. such traditions are relics, part of an old sudan that has no place in a global future.

as i often do, i wonder what we lose as we drop another piece of human pageantry, another extraordinary piece of our history. perhaps nothing. and it makes good sense to me as a canadian, good rational sense, to not give a fourteen-year-old boy scars on his face he might be ashamed of fifteen years later. however, i suspect the part of us that encourages uniformity, that engenders such shame, that puts as arbiter a sensibility that sees differences as deviances, is more to blame than his parents. north americans do not need to look far to see how easy forced integration, borders, and culture is for a native, nomadic population.

however for now, and for the foreseeable future, no matter how many eminem and wwe shirts parade around abyei, cows still rule. the dinka are slowly recovering from the turmoil of africa's largest war, and they are moving with their growing herds to find green grass and to celebrate marriages. change may be inevitable, but here at least, it will be slow.

"ALL RIGHT, SO PAOLA showed you most of the things, right?"

"More or less," Angela answers in a heavy Australian accent. "I've got to say, though, I'm completely lost."

"It won't take long to figure it out."

We walk past the veranda on the far side of the hospital. Under the thin gauze of a mosquito net is a woman who has second- and third-degree burns to her torso and arm. She is sitting there quietly, as always, her head hanging. Her back is a mass of early scarring and open wounds. One of the nurses has covered it in gentian violet, the blue dye staining the white bandages on her arm. Flies buzz around her.

"Jesus," Angela says.

"Yeah. She's been here for a month. We keep on bandaging her arm. Full-thickness burn. She'll need a graft, but I don't know anywhere that will do it. Once she heals, I guess we'll tell her to go to Khartoum. When I first got here, I would debride these types of wounds, but they all got infected. One little kid died. Too dirty here. Okay, this . . . this is Abul. She got hit by a car a few weeks ago and fractured her leg."

Mohamed sits down beside a woman with white hair, a long cast on her leg. Scattered beneath her are white chips of plaster.

"She got hit by a car in the market because she was lying on the ground there. That's where she lived. She must have schizophrenia, or Alzheimer's or something. Anyway, she broke her leg, and now she keeps on picking off her cast. She has no family or friends. Except us. Right, Abul?" I take her hand away from the hole she is digging in her cast. She smiles.

"What are you going to do with her?" Angela asks.

"I don't know. The mothers around here are getting frustrated because she is so bizarre. She grabbed one of their children yesterday and hugged him too hard. We have to figure something out."

Abul starts picking at her cast again. I pull her hand away.

"Marco and I have been talking with her chief. Usually they take some responsibility for people in their chiefdom. But that could take a while, so we're thinking we will take her to compound 2. For the time being."

Mohamed looks up.

"Mohamed is looking for a wife anyway." He shakes his head.

Angela and I move on. Mohamed stays behind to chat with Abul. They find each other delightful.

"This is the TB office. I do a clinic here on Wednesday and Thursday, for the outpatients. We have about eight or so inpatients at the back of the hospital. We've had some people stay persistently TB-positive, and I couldn't figure out why. Then I thought maybe it's the rifampicin pills. They're heat labile and have been sitting out here in, like, 104 Fahrenheit for I don't know how long. So I moved them to the pharmacy. Like, yesterday. They're just kinda sitting there in the middle of the floor. Sorry."

"Right. No worries."

"This room here, the broom closet, is cursed. Or so people think, anyway. We had someone stay there for three months, and he just got worse and worse. The next patient was this old woman with diarrhea. She died last week. Right now it's empty. Nobody wants to be there. We are talking about making it our morgue. Long story."

"Okay."

We pass the women's ward, patients sprawled out in the hallway. A girl with a freshly amputated limb looks up at us.

"This is the maternity ward," I say, standing at the doorway. "Basically, I have no idea what is going on in there. We had a midwife, but she split."

Angela's eyes are wide. Around us, children cry, mothers mill about, forty outpatients are queued at the front, some holding babies, others with their heads in their hands. One of our cleaners starts our gas water pump, and it roars to life. He puts one end in a blue barrel, filling it. As he pulls it into the next, it sprays loudly, splashing us in the transition. Chaos.

"Don't worry," I say. "It gets smaller."

"I wasn't expecting this," she says. "Where do you start?"

"I'll help you out with that. Paola, before she left, was working mostly in the feeding center. It's a good place to work. You'll see. Maybe just give yourself some time to get used to things before you start making changes. Once you feel you're on top of it, you can decide where to begin. I think basic nursing tasks might be a good place. Vital signs, medical assessment, medicine administration. That kind of thing."

"Right. No problem."

"And, just personally, it will be good to have someone else in the hospital."

"Well, I know kids. But in Australia. I have a lot to learn here."

"Don't worry. I was the same. I'll help you out."

"That would be great."

I look at her and see myself, new, lost in this huge place.

"It's a lot, hey?"

"Yeah. A lot."

"Just do what you can."

"Right."

"And take care of yourself."

"Right."

"Because if you think you are going to change it all in six months, you're going to leave sick with regret."

We pick our way through the feeding center, towards the kitchen. The floor is full of families and listless children with loose skin, paper bags of bones. One of them is crying hoarsely, pulling at the feeding tube in her nose with gauze-wrapped hands. Her mother watches us pass.

In the kitchen, one of the cooks is stirring a large pot of beans. Several of our staff sit at a table, drinking tea, cleaning up the dregs of the morning meal with pieces of bread.

"Dr. Jam-es!" the cook says, grinning, and slaps my hand. She likes me for some reason.

"So, people in the hospital get two meals a day. Mostly beans. The ones who are here for more than a few days hate it. Paola and I were talking about switching it up more. Especially for the TB patients. There's calorie guidelines and stuff. We'll talk about it another time."

"Right."

We turn back towards the nursing room. We pass Aweil. She

squeals at me, puts her fist in her mouth. She started walking a few days ago.

"And this is Aweil. She's basically the best." I continue on, too shy to stop.

In the nursing room, an infant is screaming as a nurse places an intravenous catheter. His mom cradles his body and he struggles weakly against her. Mohamed is writing orders on an admission sheet.

"Pneumonia," he says, pointing at the child with his pen.

"Basically," I say, "everyone gets antibiotics no matter what, and most kids get IVs whether they need them or not. At first I was trying to convince everyone to use oral antibiotics, but nurses like IVs, patients' families like IVs, and we can dose once a day. MSF, pushing antibiotic resistance forward, one viral infection at a time!"

I pick up a finished chart from the desk and turn to the orders.

"Okay, and then we record the . . ."

Angela's face is pressed forward, her eyebrows arched. I put the chart down.

"You know what," I say. "That's enough for now. Let's go back to the compound. It's almost lunchtime."

She nods. "That would be good. I'm hungry."

"Don't get your hopes up. Mohamed, we'll see you after lunch. Don't forget to take Abul back to compound 2."

We leave Mohamed to finish the orders and walk out the front gate.

"I've never seen anything like that."

"Like what?"

"That kid, the one with the NG tube in her nose."

"Oh yeah, she came in last night. She's going to die. Probably today."

The sky is cloudy. The wind picks up, gusts across the road.

"How do you get used to that?"

"I don't know. I'm not sure if you get used to it. You end up just kind of . . . not accepting it. . . . More . . . you just . . . put up with it, I guess."

"I don't know if I'll be able to."

"You will."

25/05: six days race.

tired.

at the entrance to compound I, there is a whiteboard on which all of our movements are recorded. it has room for 2 weeks of mondays through sundays. when a week runs through, it is wiped off the board and replaced with seven more days. it flips through time like those old clock radios did numbers. i watch people arrive from two weeks away, and from days back, watch them leave. underneath may 30, in scrawled felt pen, sits my name. "Agok-Krt: Dr. James R&R." like a marathon is a 20-mile jog to a 6-mile race, so too this latest push. one foot in front of another, one day at a time, and on may 30, i will meet myself leaning against the plane window pane, and fly away.

six days. now it's a race.

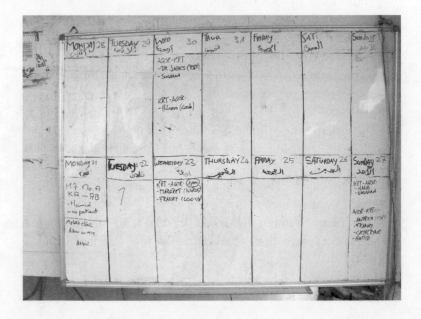

I AM IN AGOK AGAIN, looking at the sky for the metal glint of a plane. It was easier an hour ago, before the clouds started to build. They were white at first, and flat. Now they stack black and thunderous. We have been told that flights will soon stop leaving from here because the landing strip is too rutted.

I am sitting on a white plastic chair underneath the flat grass roof of Agok's arrivals/departures lounge. Other accoutrements include an overfilled latrine and . . . an airstrip. My driver sits in the Land Cruiser listening to a radio.

Ours is the only vehicle here. I wonder if we have the latest flight schedule. Usually there is more than one person from the area trying to leave it.

I am trying. This morning I packed my backpack with two changes of clothes and a book. I will pick up some swim trunks in Khartoum and, tomorrow, leave for Nairobi. I will be glad to be moving in something other than circles.

A fat drop hits the dust beside my chair. I look up. Thunderous. If it rains, or if the wind picks up too much, the plane won't land. One must not get too attached to the future. I stand to get a better look at the sky. We joke that WFP stands for "Where the F*** is the Plane?"

I can't see it. I scan the runway back and forth. To my left, two hundred meters away, a boy is crawling on the ground. He is maybe thirteen or fourteen, difficult to say from this distance. He is crawling on the ground, his belly flat to it, pulling himself forward with his forearms. A man in army fatigues is hitting him with a thin switch, shouting something I can't hear above the wind and wouldn't understand if I did. It doesn't matter. I know what it is. He is yelling "Lower! Faster!"

A second boy is standing farther back, a rifle-sized piece of wood balanced on his right shoulder. It is now his turn. He hands the wood to the first boy, extending his arms fully, as he has been taught, and drops to his belly.

Lower! Faster!

He finishes his crawl, and marches back. I consider taking a clandestine photo, but refrain. I sit back down.

A second Land Cruiser pulls up, "UN" stencilled carefully on the side. Marissa, one of the directors from the World Food Programme, climbs out, pulls her bag from the back seat. She is talking excitedly on a satellite phone. She waves hello to me.

"So, did you hear?" she asks.

"Hear what?"

"The fighting in Abyei?"

"What?"

"In the market, at eleven-thirty. What time did you leave?"

"Like, eleven-thirty exactly," I answer.

"And you heard nothing?"

"No. What?"

"I guess someone started shooting up the market, shot some police. Killed them. I can't believe you don't know. My whole staff is in our compound, waiting for word whether we should evacuate."

"Is it still happening?"

Her phone rings. She answers and moves away.

The market is a flashpoint. Its merchants are largely Misseriya traders, its denizens mostly Dinka. Surrounding it are the military compounds, and next to it, between them all, is MSF's.

I walk over to the Land Cruiser.

"Anthony. Have you heard from compound 1?"

He shakes his head.

"Call them. See if you can get Marco."

He calls into the handset, "Alpha Bravo, Alpha Bravo for Mobile 2. Alpha Bravo, Alpha Bravo . . ."

Marissa's off the phone. I hurry over.

"So, any news?"

"Well, no one's heard any more shooting."

"You guys going to evacuate?"

"I don't know yet."

"I've got to figure out if I should go back," I say.

If this is the start of something larger, I'm not sure they'll let me through the checkstop. If the call is made to evacuate, they might just want me to get on the plane anyway. One more seat on the UN helicopter for someone else.

But what if there are a bunch of wounded, and it's just Mohamed and Angela? I want to be there. I'm going.

I don't want to be there at all.

I walk back to the car. Anthony is on the radio, speaking in Arabic.

"Marco? Can I talk to Marco?"

He shakes his head. "Marco hospital."

"David?"

He calls into the handset. I hear David's voice, "Go ahead."

"David, it's James. What is the situation? Over."

"Shooting in the market, several wounded, two dead." He cannot elaborate on the radio. Our transmissions are public.

"Any further casualties?"

"Negative."

"David, do you need me to return?"

"At this point, negative."

"Are you planning to evacuate?"

"Negative."

"Can you talk to Angela and Mohamed in the hospital, to see if they need my help?"

"Stand by."

Marissa is talking on the phone again. Still no sign of the plane. It is an hour or more past its scheduled arrival. The spaces between the clouds are thin. A few more fat drops.

"James for David. James for David."

"David, go ahead."

"I spoke with Marco. He says the situation is stable. Do not return. Repeat. Do not return."

I am relieved, as much that the decision has been taken from my hands as with its result. Marco wants me to leave. He said so this morning, as he shook my hand.

"Good copy. I'll stand by in Agok. Over and out."

"James, we need to make two transfers for surgery and we need Mobile 2. Over."

"All right. Stand by."

I walk back to Marissa. She is sitting in the seat of her Land Cruiser, her phone on her lap.

"Marissa, if the plane doesn't show, do you think I could get a ride back with you?"

She hesitates for a second. We are well known for keeping our distance from other organizations. We can't speak to their motivations, nor their methods. Ours, from the training of our logisticians to the malnutrition guidelines, are developed from years of experience. We remain responsible to them, to our headquarters. By doing our own thing, we remain focused and flexible, rarely on unfamiliar ground. Our distance from the UN is even greater. They are not an NGO; they are the opposite, a GO. When we can get it, we need our space.

"Sure. Why not."

Anthony has already started the truck. He is returning, no matter what. I take my pack from the back and slam it shut. With a wave, he bumps across the rutted runway and disappears.

I have no Land Cruiser. No radio. No sat phone. No stethoscope. I'm free.

(break)

04/06: contrails.

after six flights, i am on kenya's coast. i feel like a poor traveler. after years of throwing my backpack on the top of local buses and bumping from country to country, i have forsaken discovery in favor of renewing pleasures that abyei does not afford. yesterday, immediately after my sleepless arrival, i ate fresh ocean fish in a sour coconut sauce, drank a glass of white wine, and fell asleep on a wide, white bed with a mound of pillows and an air conditioner whirring above me. 24 hours later, i have left my room only to swim.

operation boredom: accomplished.

it didn't take very long. one day. in an attempt to liven things up, i have unsuccessfully tried to find trouble in paradise. there is no conflict, no disease, no problems to solve, no situations to talk yourself out of. i have looked for seediness, for shady characters, and found none. i have even begged the hotel staff to hunt me for sport but have been politely refused. i figure if i continue to insist, they will do it for pleasure.

traveling is best done on the ground, bus to bus, and planned only when necessary. it allows for the greatest number of oblique entries.

traveling is also best done on the ground because it avoids it in the air. flying is for the birds. for me, putting a hundred humans in a metal cylinder and propelling it into the atmosphere using combustion is not a miracle of modern aviation, it is stupid.

my discomfort with lifting off the ground with a thousand kilograms of gasoline and navigating incredible distances at incredible speeds while avoiding incredible numbers of other missiles with similar trajectories does not improve with the number of times i fly. i fly all of the time. the only thing that has improved is how quickly i accept my inevitable end with every unanticipated click of the aircraft.

(click)

"well, i guess that's it. i've led a good life. seen amazing, beautiful things. i knew it was just a matter of time. should have taken the bus."

the flights in northern sudan have done little to quell my belief that i am flying on borrowed time.

the sky had shifted from blue to gray when the plane dropped from it. we would have a two-hour flight to kadugli, the nearest tarmac landing strip, where we would refuel. after boarding we climbed through the gathering wind, our tail waggling from side to side, and flew north. wind whistled through the door behind me. we ascended to several thousand feet, and as we reached the base of the clouds, we bumped against it. bump. bump. as we were being thrown up and down, one of the passengers turned to me and said, "i'm going to get some shut-eye," and i was like, "what? in this tin coffin? fine. you sleep, i'll use my mental energy to keep the plane aloft." so we flew to kadugli, our heads brushing the clouds, one of us fast asleep, one of us fast awake. below us, the scorched earth raced by.

after circling kadugli for what seemed like an inordinately long time ("is this normal? they would tell me if there was a problem. i'm sure they would"), we bumped shakily down. "crosswind," the pilot explained as he opened our door. we stepped out onto the tarmac. "um . . . ," he said, "refueling takes about 15 minutes, but we've gotta watch that, see what it's gonna do." he pointed his thumb over his shoulder. lightning sparked in a black horizon. "which way is el obeid?" i asked. he gestured over his shoulder again.

the tiny airport was full of un soldiers and staff waiting for a plane that, when it arrived, made our plane look like a toy. theirs was big and muscular. ours was made of balsa wood. i joined our pilot outside. we sat, smoking, as the wind gathered, and watched the storm. "what happens if we fly into that?" i asked, over the shh of blowing sand. the pilot made a breaking motion with his two hands.

it came towards us, but never hit the airport. we could see it dash the hills only a kilometer away, feel the weight of it on our skin, but it never crossed the runway. after several minutes, the un plane loaded its passengers, and smoothly lifted off from the runway with a certainty that must have been contagious.

"i think it is blowing itself out," the pilot said. "let's give it a shot."

a shot. perfect. a college try. and if it hasn't blown itself out, we'll just . . .

shhhh . . .

we lifted off in the wind. this time we were all bolt awake. we flew, certain, straight towards el obeid. the storm had shifted, but had not gone. as we rose past the hills, it stood in front of us, an angry purple bruise. mounds of clouds. flicker. flicker.

a day or two before, i had sat in the compound and watched storm clouds roll in on top of each other. i imagined being up there, not in a plane, but just hanging in the mist, feeling the crackle of electricity, looking for sparks amidst the twisting gray fog. perhaps nature had interpreted it as a wish.

instead of flying into its blackness, we circled back towards kadugli. i could see the jagged silhouette of the nuba mountains as we turned west, away from el obeid, away from the storm, and i wondered where i would sleep the night.

we did not land. we flew past the airport with one eye on the storm, and started to circle its margins.

we followed the sun, over the mountains, just outrunning the storm, moving west . . . west . . . north a bit . . . north . . . west . . . north . . . north . . . northeast . . . northeast . . . around it, into a bright blue pocket. we unclenched our hands from our armrests and smiled at one another.

i wonder not why i feel this way about airplanes, only why everyone else doesn't.

it is raining now, and i'm inside. i guess i should find something to do. wait. is that the gardener peeking through a shrub? oh, there is the concierge, trying to sneak up the steps. it appears my entreaties have worked. it appears the game is on. finally.

IT IS MY LAST DAY IN KENYA. I am sitting in the dying sunlight at an outdoor restaurant in the town nearest to where I am staying. Thus far, I have seen little of the country. I arrived sleepless in Nairobi, and flew eastward to the coast. At the airport, I waited for a shuttle that never came and, in the end, struck a bargain with a taxi driver to take me directly to my hotel.

This is my first time outside of it. I have spent the last four days sleeping, turning up the air conditioning, and drinking white wine. My first day I walked along the beach as far as I could in each direction, and was turned back by late-morning rain. The ocean is murky and swollen, thick with seaweed. I am one of five guests in a hotel that holds four hundred. It is ideal.

The events on the day of my departure are now clear, thanks to emails from Tim. A soldier, drunk already at that early hour of the morning, started firing randomly in the market. He was scheduled to go to court later that day and was determined to avoid it. People say he was mentally unwell. Probably schizophrenia.

Two policemen were killed in the market, and another died en route to surgery. The soldier turned the gun on himself, but succeeded only in blowing off his jaw. Tim also reported that when the shooting happened, armed men, dressed like civilians but obviously trained, marched across the open fields in Abyei and assumed strategic positions in town.

We evacuated the hospital again, because the soldiers stormed in with guns. This time, there was gunfire in the hospital.

It was a good time for chaos. Geneva had finally sent someone from their office to assess Abyei. She had arrived the day before I left. She will be gone by the time I get back.

For now I'm still here, in the last of the sun's rays, sitting at a corner table, drinking a beer. Two tables over is a group of people my age half watching a football match on the screen above them. One of them just said something funny and the man closest to me laughed loudly and slapped the table so hard the glasses clattered.

I haven't had a conversation with anyone in days. The last time was in Khartoum, the night I arrived. I went out for dinner with the new logistics coordinator and his girlfriend. Slowly the Khartoum office is filling.

A Land Cruiser pulls up with "Tour Company" written on the side, and a broad-shouldered blond man steps from behind the wheel, then hurries into a store.

There is a whole world right here, people criss-crossing paths, having chance encounters. On the way to this restaurant, I stopped at a store and bought shaving cream like a regular person. I just paid for it, and walked out of the store.

"Another beer please. Tusker."

How many weeks to home? Six. Maybe a bit less. Closer to five. When I get back to Abyei, Tim will be leaving. I will be the oldest one in the mission. I never thought it would come to pass. Makes sense, though. I feel oldest.

I glance down the road. A group of children are walking towards me. There are five of them. One, two, three, four, five. I can see the expressions on their faces so clearly. Everything is clearer. I can do this. I can go back.

My food is done. So is my beer. All that is left is this wooden cutting block, stained with grease. My friends at the table are moving on. I wonder what they are doing. I wonder if they are going dancing.

I pay my bill and walk back along the road towards the bus station. Along the way I see men and women sitting together on plastic stools at other outside restaurants, talking and laughing. Set back from the road are poorly lit signs that promise discos. A gringo, a woman about fifty wearing a sarong and Tevas, passes me going the other way. I try to catch her eye and smile, but she doesn't meet my gaze. It's the opposite problem of Abyei. I'm invisible.

A local bus drops me off at the dirt road that leads, after several kilometers, to my hotel. At the intersection, a man is washing his car. I ask if I can hire him to take me back.

"Yes. Of course. It is not good to walk around here. Especially for you. Very dangerous."

I wait for him to finish washing his car, then climb in.

10/06: space.

i am back in khartoum. how? i just finished waiting for the plane in agok, then the storm, then the middle of the night flight, then kenya, then back, and it seems like a minute, and soon i will be back tucking the mosquito net under my flat foam mattress, handset crackling beside me. time. it can't be trusted.

i was thinking about my thoughts as i walked into the kitchen in abyei one time, about how many we have as we carry out the most straightforward tasks. pouring a glass of water, for instance. for an observer, it takes us ten seconds, but inside, it is an infinity. but of course it must be. our concept of the universe, its largeness, its distant stars and the black, cold vacuum between, our outer space, is exactly proportionate to the largeness of our inner one.

i was glad to find some space. for the first time in months, my every thought was not of abyei. distance afforded me perspective. the difference between circling a storm and being at its center. i was able to glimpse a larger world.

i am glad for whoever replaces me that he or she will have a clearer idea of what we are there to do, and how to accomplish it. they will better see the goals, and how to achieve them, just as i did because of the work of the person i followed. things have already been made noticeably better by the dozens of people piling effort on top of effort consistently on one side of the scale, tipping the balance of the project, and even abyei, towards an easier future.

it is one of the ways that i make sense of the world, to believe that it hangs in a grand balance. but no matter the distance, no matter how much i travel, no matter how much i read, no matter how carefully i look, i cannot determine which way it tips. good, or bad. success, or failure. hope, or despair. i can't say, and it doesn't matter. all i can do is pile as many efforts as possible, no matter how small, on the side i want the most.

while i was away, lying on my bed shivering, the air conditioner whirring above me, i read a book by ryszard kapuscinski, one of poland's greatest writers and one of the world's best african correspondents. in part of it, he describes arriving to a town in ethiopia that is suffering from a severe drought. people lie on the side of the road, their eyes half open, starving. with that simple sentence, he picked me up and rushed me back to abyei. it was the half-open eyes of the starving. half open. half closed. mostly closed. closed.

i sat there, holding the book, and realized that no matter how much i try, i will never go back to being the person i was before i left. i can try not to think about it most of the time, and most of the time, i will succeed. the memories will fade from video to short sepia snapshots, but from nowhere, a simple sentence will throw all the hardness forward and with it, that helpless, sleepless, lonely drowning ache.

i will send word from abyei. i think the airstrip in agok is washed out, and i will have to be picked up in kadugli, a day away from abyei. i am looking forward to the drive, to the movement, to the space between.

CHAPTER III

"PLEASE THIS WAY," Anthony says, and turns between two wooden stalls, stepping expertly on a flat plank placed across a long puddle.

We are in the market of a mud town, halfway to Abyei. We left at dawn this morning in an MSF Land Cruiser sent to pick us up. All of our air movements now would require at least two days.

"The owner is friend to me," he explains.

We have stopped for lunch. There are five of us in the truck. Anthony, myself, two nurses returning from R&R in Khartoum, and Helen, the Ethiopian cook from the Khartoum guest house. She has been sent, at our request, to improve the food. She has brought with her an array of spices, some butter, cheese, a few different types of pasta. She's young, twenty-two or -three, diminutive. I don't like her chances with Ruth.

We pick our way through the market on planks of wood, right-angled like dominoes, mud to either side. We pass a butcher, a goat split in half on the wooden table in front of him. Flies cover the meat, and he swipes lazily at them with his newspaper, then goes back to reading it. It is raining lightly.

We stop at a covered stall, big enough to hold two low tables.

"Sit, sit," Anthony says, smiling proudly. The owner emerges from a back room, rubbing his eyes. Anthony grabs his hand and shakes it vigorously.

"Dr. James, Coca-Cola or Fanta?"

"Um . . . Coca-Cola."

Anthony takes orders from the others and walks into the back room. He emerges with five bottles, and hands them to each of us, waves away our money.

The owner pushes a gray pile of coals together and fans them with a piece of cardboard. They glow red. He takes a jar of murky oil and dumps it into a large steel pan, then places it over the embers. It starts to smoke.

A boy of seven or eight stands paused in the puddle next to our stall, staring at me. He is wearing a long dirty shirt, ripped at the shoulder. Around him, raindrops spatter into the water. Anthony sees him.

"Pffft. Pffffft."

The boy leaves. He steps onto a plank barefoot.

Everyone is talking to one another in Arabic. I can't understand a word. Behind us, the owner throws a bowlful of chopped goat into the pan. It hisses as it hits.

I lean towards Helen. "So, are you excited to go to Abyei?"

Her eyes tell me she is not. She is nervous. Until this morning, she had never been on a plane. She came from Addis to Khartoum by land and has seen cities mostly. This is the only town we have passed in half a day, its existence made possible by the large gravel pits nearby. It will be one of the last before we get to Abyei.

"Is Abyei like this?" she asks.

"Smaller."

"Smaller?"

I nod.

"What can you get there?" she asks.

"Malaria." She doesn't laugh. "For food? Well, not much. You'll see, I guess. It's probably better to talk to the cook when you get there."

"Is she a nice person?"

"Oh yes. Very nice."

A tray full of gristly goat pieces is dropped between us. With it, five pieces of bread. A flurry of hungry hands reach for them. Mine stay in my lap.

"Dr. James? You eat?" Anthony asks.

"Not hungry. Thanks. Coca-Cola is okay."

"You don't like? Not good?"

"Oh no, it's good. I like very much."

Anthony is not convinced. The rest of the table is waiting. I break off a piece of bread and scoop up a piece of goat. They start talking again.

I tear off another piece of bread. I have been sick enough times in the past four months. A picture of this market is hanging on the walls of *E. coli* travel agents around the planet. I went to the bathroom before we entered the market, and the latrine was flooded.

The food is soon finished. We need to get on our way. The drive is from dawn until dusk, and there is little time to pause. We thank our host, and pay. Anthony refuses to take my money.

We balance our way back to the Land Cruiser on the planks. One tips, I spill off, and sink into the thick mud.

The nurses jump into the back of the truck before I have a chance to protest. The ride in the rear is even more teeth rattling. Helen and I share the front seat. My right thigh digs into the handrest, my shoulder pushes uncomfortably against the metal chassis.

Helen is squeezed between the middle armrest and me. She is tiny. She is wearing short sleeves and her bare arm is against mine.

I have not touched a human being for a long time. Felt a few hundred, but it's not the same. I forgot. It's good. Soft. Simple.

I answer more of Helen's questions about Abyei, but it is difficult to hear over the din. The road is rippled, and no speed, fast or slow, lessens the tumult. We stop talking, and she soon falls asleep, her head resting on my shoulder.

I put my earphones in, and watch the trees whiz by. My left arm is fast asleep, but I don't move it.

13/06: open stretches.

after 10 hours on a chattering road, i arrived into abyei as planned, two days ago. the first thing i did after setting my bags down was to fall headfirst into a fever. i spent my first morning back shivering in bed.

today, i am better. at first i was worried i had disco fever, which in abyei, because of a lack of discos, is incurable. i considered lotto fever, spring fever, saturday night fever, johnny fever . . . pretty much all the fevers, but couldn't confirm any of them. we simply don't have the necessary tests, ones that would be readily available in canada. there, let's say someone has, i don't know, johnny fever. we just get the johnny fever guy on call, he rolls in with that episode of wkrp where mr. carlson decides to rain down turkeys on the thanksgiving parade, and the patient is cured. in abyei, it is much more difficult. the best we could do, if we even made the diagnosis of johnny fever, is to try to explain the episode from memory. it is poor treatment, and very rarely works.

on a hunch, i started taking antibiotics. today i feel better. i guess i'll never truly know which of the fevers it was. i'm just grateful it wasn't disco because there would have been little chance of staying alive.

the long ride from kadugli was exhausting, though the chance to see a landscape i had only flown over made it worthwhile. in ten hours of rocky red roads, we passed only a handful of towns. it is in one of them, the one where i ate lunch in a mud market, that i likely picked up one of the fevers. another one we passed was home to a hundred people or so. they shared their village with birds, large ones, three feet tall at the shoulder. they landed, evolutionarily, between a crane and a pelican, and walked stooped, their heads hanging between their bony shoulders. most of them lingered in the groundwater near the side of the road, trying to siphon frogs. a few of them, however, padded back and forth between houses like hunched old men, as if they were returning to the market to pick up something they missed the first time.

the rest of the journey, except for these few small blinks of people, was through acres of uninterrupted wilderness. the landscape reminded me of northern alberta, in the jackpine and the tamaracks, wide spaces between narrow trees standing on sand or marsh. some of my favorite. occasionally we would pass someone walking with a hoe dangling over his back. from where? to where? we had passed no homes. he was walking for miles, endlessly.

i thought, was this what the fighting was about? these spaces where no one wants to live, and those that do have to struggle and struggle just to get a stalk of corn to poke out of the ground? the blaze of the bombs at night, a second before the sound. the bullets splintering the tamarack trees, whining away, frustrated at not finding a human. people running ahead, just ahead of the fighting, to where, anywhere, just not here. these marshes? that's what it was about? here?

sure. and because of resources. history. politics. because humans are war-like. all of these, and for other reasons i will never know. but also over those empty stretches. because, at the end of each long day, as dusk fades to dark, somewhere in this flat land, a woman sits down and sighs, glad to be home. and when the bullets come and drive her from it, her thoughts are full of return, of the peace she once felt with her back to the wide sky on a quiet road that stretched towards forever.

"Y OU NEED A TRIPOD."

"What if you climb up here . . . like this. No . . . the tukul."

"Over here."

"Oh, I've got it . . . Come here. Right here. Up like this."

We are in compound 1, taking pictures of Saturn. Right now David is balanced between our kitchen table and the rough edge of the gazebo window, holding his camera steady on the rafters. Julie, the new administrator, Tim's replacement, is tryng to join him. Tim and I have taken a different tack, setting our cameras up on Marco's angled roof. Saturn, for its part, looks like it just spilled out of the cup of a waning moon.

On our makeshift couch, Marco sits talking with Laurence, our new logistician, about the Congo. Both of them did a mission there, at separate times. Laurence is telling a story of how he was invited to spend a weekend in the jungle with a group of pygmies. As they were walking, he looked away, only for a second, and was lost, their path indistinguishable between the trees.

"What did you set your shutter speed to?"

"One-tenth of a second."

Click.

Both Julie and Laurence arrived while I was on my R&R. They became fast friends on the long ride, on the open stretches. Tim and I finish taking our crooked pictures and sit down near Marco and David.

"So," Tim says, leaning forward from the couch, reaching for the ashtray.

"So," I answer.

He ashes out his cigarette. "Glad to be back?" he asks.

"Gladder than when I left, I think."

"Yeah. You look a bit better."

"I got some sleep. And it was good to see that there is more to the world than compound 1."

"There is? What's it like?"

"Ha. I guess you'll find out tomorrow."

"Insh'allah," Tim says.

"Insh'allah or not, bro. You're done."

"Yeah. I guess I am."

"That's gotta feel pretty good."

"Yeah. I guess. Julie caught on really fast so today I had nothing to do. I packed, had a nap, read for the first time in . . . I don't know, forever? Then I just wandered around. No destination in mind. Went to compound 2, through the market. Can't remember when I did that last."

"So, you excited to get on the plane?"

"I can't really imagine it."

Laurence sets a beer down in front of each of us, winks, and sits back beside Marco.

"Cool."

Tim lights a cigarette, gives one to me, throws me the lighter.

"So what's next?" I ask.

"I don't know. I don't have any plans. I guess I'll have to look for a job."

"What about another mission?"

"I don't think so. We'll see."

"Well, Tim, after you leave, I'm the veteran."

"Yeah. Like Jean said."

"It's crazy, eh? That it has only been six months? So much has happened, the measles epidemic, Bev was here, the emergency team stealing all our water. It's like, forever."

"For those who think life is too short, come to Abyei!"

I laugh. "Yeah. We could put it on a poster with a picture of a fan, but with one of those 'no smoking' things drawn through it."

"And a picture of the Abyei jazz band," he says.

"Talk about lasting forever."

We smile at each other.

"What's the first thing you're going to do?"

"Don't know. Sleep. Eat."

"Your mom's going to freak with how skinny you are."

"For sure."

"I was going to get you a djellaba and a walking stick for a going-away present, but couldn't find one."

"I appreciate the thought."

David and Julie have finished with Saturn and are talking in the kitchen with Marco. I can hear the splash of the shower.

"Where's Angela?" Tim asks.

"I think she's still at the hospital."

"No way. She was there early this morning too. She's going pretty hard."

"I'll talk to her."

We're both quiet. In the background the generator clacks.

"Looks like they moved those bags finally," Tim says.

"Our security area? Yeah. It only took four months. I'm going to plant a garden. David has some seeds."

"It's different than when we came here, hey?"

"I was thinking about that. Laurence and Julie will only have seen it like this. The team is tighter, we've sorted out some of the problems with the compound, there's not a hundred people in compound 2."

"Yup. And soon there'll be a garden, an office, borehole," Tim says.

"Disco," I reply.

"Drive-in theater."

"Waterslide."

"Proper doctor."

"Your girlfriend."

He laughs. I take a sip from my beer.

"Well, bro, I gotta say. It's not going to be the same without you. You were a good, steady influence."

"Yeah, you too."

"No, I mean, you were calm. And I could laugh with you."

"Mmm." He draws on a cigarette.

"I wasn't having a very good time for a while, you know," I say. "I mean, a bad time. Like I wasn't myself. Not with anyone, you know? I just spent all my time inside."

"I know. I could tell."

"But it was easier with you. The past few months, the mission, was easier because of you. It's kinda been one of the best parts of it."

"You too."

"I don't know who I'm going to talk to when you're gone."

Laurence comes out of his tukul and sits down beside us.

"How was the shower?" I ask.

"Like heaven," he says.

The rest of the team comes from the kitchen. David says something to Julie in French, and she laughs. They sit down around our low table.

"Well," Marco says, "tomorrow the team changes. The person who has been here longest is going home."

We all turn to Tim and smile.

"So, Tim, you have been a very good person for us here in Abyei . . . mmm . . . and we are glad that you did a very good job . . . and we hope your journey is safe. And that you eat a lot of food." He raises his glass.

We do the same.

"To safe journeys."

Clink.

19/06: mirror.

each morning i wake to the sound of a bird pecking against the mirror that hangs on our shower wall. he cocks his head at his reflection for a second, then tactactac. i wonder if he is trying to set his image free, or if he wants to break through to the other world and its greener grass. it is dusk, but he is there now, tactactac.

just a few minutes ago, as i was leaving the hospital, i imagined myself back home. in the emergency room. leaning up against the nurse's desk to scribble down an order. the bright fluorescent light. the hum of electricity. an overhead announcement. a patient's call bell ringing. the intern behind me waiting to review a case. a porter saying, excuse me, pushing a patient past. just one live moment.

i understand why they call it shock. that's what it felt like. two left brains. or two right ones. a mirror image on top of a mirror image, turned upside down. it didn't match. if i changed places right now, in an instant, i wouldn't know where to begin. wouldn't know whether to sit down or stand up, where i finished and where everyone else started.

THE MAN EYES ME FROM the side, wary. I am talking to a friend of his, the one who brought him in. His friend is worried because the man has been acting bizarrely. Shouting, laughing, crying, starting fights with people.

"Has he ever been like this before?"

He has not.

"Did he do any drugs?"

Only alcohol, but none recently.

"How many days like this?"

Three.

"Is he sleeping?"

No.

"Eating?"

No.

"Is he talking about God a lot?"

Yes. Very much.

I look at the man. He is edging away, sliding down the veranda bench little by little, his wide eyes on me. I ask his friend to sit on the other side of him, and I turn to Alfred.

"Don't let him leave," I say quietly.

He nods.

The look in the man's eye is familiar. He is deeply paranoid, psychotic. Likely mania, given his age, but possibly schizophrenia. It could be something organic, medical, like an infection, but I doubt it. Something in the eyes. Too awake.

I go to the nursing room. A child lies on the blue bed, breathing quickly. I have not heard about her yet. A nurse in a white coat is bent over a patient's chart, squinting at an order. I unlock the metal drug cupboard and look for a vial of chlorpromazine, an injectable antipsychotic. Beside it sits the oral version, and I shake a tablet out and put it in my pocket, grab two oily ampoules of Valium. I fill two syringes with the chlorpromazine and put them in my pocket. I walk towards the guard.

I'll offer the patient the oral version of the chlorpromazine, but if he refuses, he will need to be restrained and sedated. It is not going to be easy. He looks strong. We'll need his friend, the nurses, the guard, maybe others. The cleaners. We'll put him in the front room. We'll get a bed ready, with restraints, in the front room, that room where the premature baby from the tubercular woman lay dead for three days, we'll take him in there, tie him down, sedate him, and then . . .

What? Keep sedating him? Start him on long-term antipsychotic therapy? Rally his social supports?

I'll sedate him, and keep on doing it until he stops being violent. Then I'll offer him oral therapy and ask that he come back to see me — Wait, I'll be gone . . . to see Mohamed every week. And then we'll let him go. And hope he doesn't start shooting police in the market.

I tap the guard on the shoulder. Follow me.

We'll get a bed, place it in the room, tie pieces of cloth or rope to it. I'll get some soft cotton padding from the pharmacy for his wrists and ankles. We'll ask him to follow us to the room. If he refuses, we'll tackle him, carry him, tie him, inject him, screen him for malaria, re-assess him in two hours, and again the next morning.

We turn towards the veranda and can see the bright smiles of a growing crowd. The man is gesturing and yelling. People think him hilarious. I can't understand what he is saying.

Bed, rope, cotton, more people.

I scan the crowd for Alfred and gesture him forward. He is laughing.

"What is he saying?" I ask.

"Only nonsense."

"The man is sick and if he leaves he will get sicker. I'm going to try and give him medicines, but if he says no, I will have to tie him down. Okay?"

"Okay."

"You need to tell this to his friends too, so they understand, all right?"

"All right."

"Also, I need you to get a bed from the container and put it in the front room, the one where the baby stayed. Ask Deng and Deng for some rope too. Once it's there, you and the guard and the Dengs meet me on the veranda."

He translates to the guard and they set off together. I hurry to the back of the hospital, squeeze myself past the coolers, and unlock the clinking lock from the pharmacy's metal door.

A cotton roll. Two. Wait. Tape. Better than rope. Two rolls. Three. One for each hand, bind the feet together.

I return to the front, and can see the man perched on the veranda bench like a bird. Roars of laughter.

The bed is in the front room. The Dengs are fumbling with pieces of yellow nylon rope. I stop them, hand them each a roll of tape, and point to the two corners at the head of the bed. I start wrapping the third roll around a bar at the foot.

The bed is ready. Chlorpromazine in my pocket.

I turn the veranda corner and the man knows. He slowly puts his feet on the floor, starts to stand. His friend puts a hand on his shoulder.

"It's okay, it's okay." I sit beside the man, put my hand on his other shoulder. He sits back down.

"Tell him that I think he is sick, and that he needs some medicines. I think these will make him better. Give him some sleep."

I take the pill from my pocket. He leans away, wrinkles his face.

"He says he feels fine," Alfred says.

"He's not fine. He needs help, or he is going to get sicker."

"He says no. He wants to leave."

I turn to face Alfred. "Tell him that I want to talk to him in a private place. There are too many people here. It's too crowded."

The man nods.

"Ask him to go towards the front room. I'll ask him to sit on the bed. If he does, I'll ask him to lie down. If he doesn't do those things, we will have to help him. And tie him with the tape."

I gesture the man forward. My translator stays behind and talks to the rest. They follow.

As we draw close to the front room, the man starts to run. I grab his arm. He stops. Miracle. The others catch up to us, and as they do he begins to struggle.

There are four of us on him. Now five. He is kicking, yelling.

"What is he saying?"

"Nonsense."

Two of us have his arms now, three his legs. Mohamed is here now too, back from lunch.

"Okay. In the room. Careful with his head."

With so many of us, the man has stopped resisting. He lets us lay him on the bed, flops his arms willingly to its corners. I wrap his wrists with the thick cotton pad, then his ankles. Only when I start to bind his legs with the tape does he begin to fight again. His friend sits on him.

He is now bound, with MSF tape, in a Y on the low cholera bed. I check his restraints. They are snug, but not too tight. Good.

I offer him the pills again. He refuses. I take the syringe out of my pocket, clean a spot on his thigh with an alcohol swab. He looks into my eyes, starts speaking softly, repeating something.

"What is he saying?"

"He is saying 'Why, why, why?'" my translator answers.

I inject the chlorpromazine into his thigh. The man winces.

Whywhywhy.

I throw the sharps into a cardboard container and stand up. His friend looks at me hopefully.

"Tell his friend that someone has to stay with this man all day, and all night. They need to wake him up to give him water every few hours. I'll remind the nurses."

I leave the room. A crowd of interested mothers and nurses has gathered, peeking around the corner to see the man tied up with tape.

"Difficult," Mohamed says, behind me.

"Yeah."

By the time I return with the malaria check, the man is snoring.

21/06: longest day of the year back home.

a woman in the single room at the back, a cursed room that no one leaves, is racked with tuberculosis. last week she delivered a baby prematurely. he was no bigger than a bird. i didn't even know she was pregnant. i showed up one morning and looked into the room and saw two stacks of breathing bones hanging onto each other, skin and angles.

i need to write about other things.

once, when i was walking through moma, i watched a man lead a woman around by her arm. he would stop at a painting and say, "this one . . . this one is . . . modern. abstract . . . it is a large canvas, perhaps ten feet wide and six tall . . . the background is yellow, and there are thick blue strokes carrying away from the center that fade to gray as they near the edge . . . in the bottom left is a thin circle of white . . ." she asked, "what is the color of the circle's center?" "gray," he answered. she paused, touched his elbow, and they moved to the next.

there are snakes in the hospital. every few days you can see a cleaner carrying one to the waste area, draped over a broom handle like a piece of rope, beaten flat. earlier in the week, we found one on the bottom tray of our delivery room trolley. our midwife nearly picked it up, thinking it was a piece of cloth. the next day, they found one in the single room at the back, beneath the bed. the baby died later that day. cursed room.

i used to sit by a river that ran through the small cambodian town near to where i worked. i often went there at the end of the day to read a book. children took turns sitting beside me. one night, as the light was fading, i looked up and saw a meteorite blaze across the sky, so close that i could see little pieces of it break off and flame out. the children beside me pointed at it, amazed.

today a boy came to the hospital from "far away," brought by his father. his leg was full of holes from an infection that had festered for two weeks. he was thin from it. i lifted his leg off the bed to look at the other side, and it came apart at the knee, his joint glistening brightly. we took a picture of it.

a high-energy physicist was describing her job of accelerating particles as fast as they would go, then smashing them together and watching what bits flew off. she was talking about what makes up quarks, what she considered the smallest building block of the universe. the hand of a woman beside me beat mine. "but, don't you think that if we keep on looking, things will just keep on getting smaller and smaller?" the physicist seemed puzzled, like she had never considered this inevitability, that no matter how much we pry into it, we'll never get to the bottom.

when i was in bolivia, in copacabana, i got lost. i was looking for a restaurant with a map i had drawn on a busy bumping bus. i could make no sense of it. i gave up. as i turned around, i caught the faint strains of a violin. i couldn't place where it was coming from. i turned down one street, then another, walking further and further, following the music. i finally arrived to the edge of a valley, outside of town. across it, on the other side, light poured out of a large house, and with it, the sound of an orchestra, strings, horns, piano, thick drums. the moon was fat and full. in its yellow light i sat at the top of stone stairs that led into the valley, and listened. an orchestra. here? a music lover. this late? here? the movement finished, and i stood, dusted myself off. i turned to walk back, full of thoughts, a witness to a beautiful mystery. i saw a man standing at the door of his small house, holding a baby in his arms. "que pasa?" i said, and gestured back to the valley.

"ella esta muerta," he said.

she has died. of course. a dirge.

last year i was working at st. mike's hospital in downtown toronto and walked into a room to tell a man he had a badly broken jaw. "what happened?" i asked. "if you don't mind telling me."

"well, i'm not from here, you see," he replied in a thick native-canadian accent, through clenched, broken teeth. "i came from the nort'. looking to get a job as a counselor. i don't got any money, eh, don't know anyone in the city, at least not yet, so i'm staying at a shelter. it's not very good. lots of drugs. so tonight i saw someone, a brother, selling. i walked up to him and said, 'what are you doing? you're poisoning us, your own brothers and sisters. don't you see that?'"

"they got angry and chased me, then i guess they broke my jaw. but i'm not done with them, doc. i'm just getting started."

he is the only real hero i have ever met.

I AM IN BED, TRYING NOT to think about guns. It is the only thing that seems to put me to sleep. I don't know why. I don't remember when I first used the trick, but I can remember my surprise that a character in Jonathan Franzen's *The Corrections* does the same. I think there is more war inside of me than I thought.

. . . the boy . . . did i use humidified oxygen . . . i did . . . what haven't i . . . no . . . tomorrow . . . figure it out tomorrow . . . (yawn) . . . oh, good . . . here i go . . . sleep . . . no . . . Thursday today . . . how many left . . . shhhhh . . . tired . . . quiet . . . a black hole . . . that's what i want . . . no thoughts . . . nothing in . . . nothing out . . . silent . . . black . . .

The other day, I was walking home in the rain. In the distance, I heard the whine of a siren. Oh, I thought, an ambulance. I guess they're on their way to the hospital. Wait. What? Ambulance? People arrive on donkeys.

The sound approached, and a white truck with an ambulance stencil on the door flew past, its siren informing only me and a frightened goat of the emergency it held. When you are considering becoming the driver of a new ambulance in a land of donkeys, the chance to use the siren is a firm pro.

It was new. From Agok. It was the first I had seen of it. The emergency it contained was a woman who had delivered a child eight days before. In an effort to clean her after, with some half knowledge of sterilization, her family doused her perineum with boiling water. She had thick burns around her vagina and on her buttocks. Three days ago, she developed diarrhea and the burns were deeply infected. The child had died because she was in no condition to feed it. She spent eight days in the bush, screaming.

. . . black . . . crow's nest . . . bet I could fall asleep in a crow's nest . . . wind . . . curled up on the wooden planks . . . listing back and forth . . . creaking . . . clouds above wind . . . starless . . . tilt . . . tilt . . .

Yesterday, I was administering medicines in the TB area. Developing the program has been a priority for me here. I was cutting foil pill pouches into smaller amounts to make sure taking the correct dose is as easy as possible. Dozens of patients walked in and out, some coughing, others not. I wasn't wearing a mask. I used to, but I stopped. I watched an inpatient, our newest and sickest, leave the former measles recubra where we placed her because of our bursting rooms. She was leaning on a long stick, which she would plant in front of her, then catch up to. In the morning sun, the two of them cut the thinnest of shadows.

She slowly picked her way across the field, leaned her back against the wall outside my door, and slid down until her head, hanging between her sharp shoulders, hung between her sharp knees. I finished with the patient in front of me, rose, and tapped her shoulder. She is deaf. She stood, shakily, and sat in the chair. I started to cut the foil.

As I did, shrill cries came through the window. I knew what they meant. I kept cutting. Angela came to the window, pressed her forehead up against its wire mesh.

"You know where *that's* from, don't you?" she said.

I nodded but did not look up. The baby she and I spent three days feeding from a syringe had died because, at some point, we went home to feed ourselves. His relatives were wailing. I finished cutting the pills, and explained through gestures as best I could how to take them. More wailing. I motioned for the next person, and when I looked up to the window again, Angela was gone.

. . . *tilting . . . a hard, blue iceberg . . . take an ice axe and chip out a chair . . . sit . . . watch the ocean float a fleet of ice . . . sun glancing, glinting through cracks . . . cold bright light . . .*

Angela and I walked home from the hospital together this morning. I told her that I see her going through a similar transition to the one I did. You feel that if you leave the hospital, let your guard down for one second, someone might die. For fear that it will not get done, you take the syringe and feed the child yourself, you hold it, fret over it. It becomes a symbol of your success, the reason why you came here in the first place. If you can't save them all, if you can't be there all of the time, at least you can save this one, at least you can be there this time. So, you try. You keep on looking after him, and even in your sleep, you hang on tightly.

. . . cold . . . statue . . . crawl into the middle . . . cold brass . . . dark . . . curved . . . echoes . . .

Several years ago I wrote a list of ten things I wanted to do before I die. Sleep inside a statue was one. I have a strong imagination of how deep the sleep would be there, the sharp smell of brass, only the most insistent rays of light bending around corners, muffled museum echoes. I have eyed the Henry Moore sculpture outside Toronto's Art Gallery of Ontario. It has the right curves, but it is not as deep as my dream.

. . . hold it in the right hand . . . heavier than it looks . . . steady . . . now the left . . . steady . . .

22/06: ballast.

it is friday, our day off. it is 8:30 and the sky is a disappointing blue. at this point, we crave clouds.

my plan for the day, after i finish this, is to break some ground beside my tukul and make a garden. i am going to plant carrots. i will leave before they are ready to eat, but i can watch them start. and it seems like honest work. like washing dishes. i am looking forward to it.

i admitted a boy with a blind mother the other day. i didn't notice at first, but later in the day saw her feeling along the edges of the room towards the door. i took the tube out of her son's nose this morning, and he is drinking. he is still so very thin, his skin stretched tight over his ribs, like paper over a wire frame, like if you turned your back, he could blow away. but not for long. if we have our say, he will be so fat he will be able to waddle through the eye of a hurricane. after him, the next one the same. in fifty years, people will be writing about abyei's epidemic of obesity, and the graph will start in 2007.

i wrote "in twenty years," erased it and wrote "thirty," and finally, "fifty."

maybe fifty. if i am alive, i will be an old man, eighty-three. i will walk down abyei's streets, shaking my head. i will stop for a rest in an otherwise empty nutrient shop. the man behind the counter will take off his computer glasses, and smile. he is in his 50s, fat, pleasant. we will start to talk. i will start to tell the story i have already told to five uninterested strangers, how when i was here last, fifty years ago, there was nothing. only a hospital. and now, all this.

he will shake his head with me. he was born in abyei and, except for a few years in juba, has lived here all his life. he too has seen it change.

he lived in a tukul, made from grass. there was no electricity, no trains. two of his brothers died from diarrhea. he nearly died too. when he was three.

"how old are you now?"

"fifty-three. more or less."

"was your mother blind?"

that is one version of the future. it already exists; it simply needs to be arrived at, uncovered, rolled into place. another is that this place remains forgotten, largely untouched by the best of the best things in the world. your attention, like mine, turns to other more personal matters. we read about abyei tipping once again into war, about thousands displaced. we shake our heads. in fifty years, if i'm alive, i will be an old man. i will look at abyei on google universe and all i will see are sticks and plastic bags fluttering in an empty field.

but for now, we are here. i meant to say this before, but i haven't. when i write "we," i don't just mean the team or msf, i mean in the larger, more collective sense. you and me, and everyone we know. i mean the "we" as a species that has, through culture and nature, manifested a system of humanitarianism. that supports the idea that we should put ourselves in the middle of places that threaten to tilt into war or be swallowed by disease.

i believe this sincerely. we are here, you, me, and everyone we know, because there is something inherently valuable to our presence. it is the concrete manifestation of a quality in all of us, one that when exercised feels entirely correct. the feeling of standing between two people who are angry enough to fight, or stopping to help someone stranded by the side of the road. once you do, you realize the perceived risk is less than the actual one. we all know that it is better than the feeling we have when we turn our heads and pretend not to see. so, that's why we are here. because of that part i share with you and everyone we know.

'M WATCHING MARCO hunt letters on a keyboard.

"I can type, if you want."

He shakes his head. It is midmorning. I left Mohamed in the hospital so I could come back to the compound and do my end-of-mission evaluation. I leave in two weeks, and Marco is leaving on his R&R next Wednesday. I won't see him again once he goes. Not in Sudan, anyway.

"So, James . . . mmm . . . what would you say you accomplished while you were here?"

The sky is cloudless. We are edged into the shadow that frames Marco's tukul. Each minute it grows smaller and we shuffle our chairs to find it again.

"Um. I think the part I liked most, and worked at the most, was probably the tuberculosis program." I liked watching people get better instead of watching them die.

The corners just outside our tukul used to hold scruffs of thin grass. They are now lush, dappled with flowers. As we speak, butterflies jag between them.

"And I think I did okay with the medical team. I think their morale is good." Thank god for them. They saved me. Especially Mohamed.

We skiff our chairs closer to Marco's tukul. A swallow dives out of his door and circles away. Marco smiles.

"She has a nest in there. We share."

The compound now has brick paths that take us from the gazebo to the kitchen, from our tukuls to the latrines. The floor of the office has been poured. This morning, I watched men spackle its walls. One would take a dustpan of thin cement and fling it onto the wall. The other would smooth it with a plastic blade, work it in larger and larger waves until it disappeared. Both of them were shirtless, spatters of cement on their strong backs. Once the office is built, we will take down the walls that divide compound 1. The tents too.

"And what did you find hard about the mission?"

Yesterday I took a shovel and pick from the bones of the new office and broke the ground beside my tukul. It was hard work, all clay. I have blisters on the first knuckle of both of my thumbs. This morning, after last night's rain, the ground is firm and smooth again, no sign of my work.

"I never felt like I could get away. I think we could have used some more support, too."

Marco told me that we are getting another midwife, one more nurse, and a nutritionist. A pharmacy assistant will be coming to straighten things out. No more bits of paper under a calculator.

"But the mission is better and better."

Once the fence beside the tukul goes, and the tent is moved, the compound will be wide open space. A volleyball net can be set up. Underneath the tamarind tree, we can stake a hammock. No more meetings in the gazebo. It can be a place to read, to play cards.

We have started to get occasional food from Khartoum now. With the last shipment of drugs, I received two kilograms of muesli. A nurse returning from R&R brought two containers of yogurt. I used these, and some skim milk powder, to make more. Though Helen's trip did not cause a food revolution, Ruth has proudly added potatoes au gratin to her repertoire and makes it at least three times a week.

"And what do you think you could have done better?"

The other day, Marco reluctantly gave us permission to visit the UN bar. He said that he would not attend, that he thought it wise to keep our distance, but that we were grown men and women who could make our own choices.

"I . . . I think I was too serious. I didn't relax. If I was done working, I would go to my tukul and write. I didn't take enough walks. I didn't visit compound 2 enough. I should have traveled more, spent less time in the hospital."

The ground where I slept, under the tree, is now mud. I tried to walk there the other day in my rubber boots to look for another foam bed. Mine in my tukul was too thin. As I walked past the tree that was once my leafless roof, I looked up into its deep green, and stepped out of my boot and into the thick black muck. I found a bed, one used during the measles mission. It was stained, but better. When Laurence saw me carrying it back, he said he was going to order some proper beds from Khartoum.

"Will you do another mission?" Marco asks.

There is no shadow left to slide into. The sun is straight above us, beating hot on our heads. Sweat beads on my forehead. Marco stifles a yawn with his hand. I need to go back to the hospital and help Mohamed.

"Yes."

Marco folds his computer shut.

"Halas."

Finished.

02/07: day.

now is the point in the story when the character begins to be pulled towards a future he thought would never come. the character, however, cannot appreciate any signs of movement. he still measures days in the same way: from dawn to dusk.

Julie sticks her head into the log tukul. I am typing on its computer.

"Coming, James?"

"Um . . . yep. Right now." I press "send," close the computer's plastic lid.

The team is standing just outside the gate. Save Marco. He is in his yellow housecoat, arms folded in silent disapproval. The rest of us are going to the UN bar tonight.

"Sure you don't want to come, Marco?" I ask.

"No. I stay here."

"All right."

Laurence sticks his head inside the gate.

"James, let's go. The driver's here."

"Hey, Laurence, since you will be acting field co when Marco is on R&R, can we have our morning meetings at the bar?"

"Well, we'll probably be there from the night before, so I guess it makes sense. We might as well take our lunch there too."

"What about dinner?"

"Only every second day."

"Okay."

"And are we still going to use Marco's tukul for our girlfriends?"

"Of course."

Marco shakes his head and turns around. I hop into the back of the Land Cruiser and slam the door. Laurence climbs into the front. Angela, Julie, and David are already inside, hunched on bench seats.

We turn onto Abyei's road. The UN compound is on the outskirts. We crawl through town, the driver honking at bicycles in his way. They swerve out of our cone of light, and we slowly pass.

"The gas is the skinny one on the right," Laurence says to the driver, who ignores him, his nose against the glass.

We approach Abyei's speed bump, formed by an attempt to bury the power cord of a generator that crossed the road. Tim and I called it Mount Abyei, the highest point for miles. I look around the cabin of the truck for someone to whom to tell my usual joke, that if I don't survive the ascent, to tell my family I loved them. Everyone's different. We bump across it.

The driver speeds up as we leave town. The gravel shakes us. We pass an SPLA checkpoint, the same one as on my morning run. From inside, a disembodied hand waves us through.

The road is empty. Coming up on our left is the storage compound for the World Food Programme. Its lights, lit by a generator, are strangely dim. As we draw closer, I can see why. A blur of bugs, thousands of thousands thick, whirl and loop around them. Tiny electron orbits of mosquitoes, an occasional parchment of moth wings. I imagine swiping my hand through their fast field, feeling them whap against my skin like sand.

Why the attraction to light? A remnant of their pupal stage, where they crawled towards an opened end? Or the right way to struggle from a bird's mouth or a sticky plant's. Maybe it's just something that is beyond their control. Maybe before humans brought light to the dark, moths used to fly all night towards the hollow moon.

We are soon at the UN compound. Four helmeted UN peacekeepers sit in a guardhouse, yawning. One gets to his feet and gestures our car forward. He takes a comically large dentist's mirror and reflects the underside of our car, looking for bombs. He waves us out, goes through our IDs one by one, and then lets us pass. Our driver backs the Land Cruiser away.

"Do you think he was drunk?" Laurence asks.

"Who? The driver?" I ask.

"Oui."

"Could explain why he was going so effing slow. I was too far away. I'll look on the way back."

"When you're drunk."

"Exactly."

We pass through the UN parking lot. Dozens of new Land Cruisers, their long CB antennas bent like mousetraps ready to spring. Containers full of soldiers, from Bangladesh, Zambia, Germany, and

Canada, sit humming and air-conditioned. Several hundred peace-keepers are stationed here in Abyei. Recently, both military groups, North and South, curtailed their movements. The UN soldiers are now forced to drive in smaller and smaller circles.

The bar lies just on the other side of a field flanking the parking lot.

"Watch for snakes," David says. We look at our feet as we walk through the thick grass.

In a courtyard between containers sits the bar. Its roof is a tukul's roof, its floor cement. Underneath harsh fluorescent lights are tables made from large, empty spools, and around these, a few plastic chairs. To one end is a counter. On it, a soldier sits, his shaved head resting in the crook of his elbow. Above him a fan slowly spins. It is quiet except for the calls of crickets and the hum of the large generators, different from the racket of our small one. The soldier sees us and sits up straight. Women have that effect in Abyei.

We each take a seat at one of the spools. There is no one else in the bar. Laurence starts to stand. I leap up.

"Let me. Pilsner, David?"

"Pilsner."

"Laurence?"

"Pilsner."

"Angela?"

"Yup."

"Julie?"

"Same."

I lean against the bar.

"Five pilsner, please."

The soldier reaches into the glass cooler behind him, pulls them out one at a time, and pops their tops off. There is no satisfying hiss.

"Sorry. They all got frozen yesterday. Cooler was too cold."

I shrug and hand him twenty-five dollars. He puts it in a tin box. I pass the bottles around.

"To beer," I say.

"To Abyei," Laurence says.

"To the UN," David says. "Just kidding."

We all take a sip. Flat. Cold. I reach for one of Laurence's cigarettes. He nods.

"So, James . . . you leave soon."

"Looks that way."

"Have you heard about your replacement?"

"A little bit. First mission. Tropical disease experience, which is good. Speaks French. That's the only bad thing, I guess."

"Careful. Marco's gone soon."

"She's not going to arrive before I leave, though."

"Oh?"

"Visa problems or something. And I can't stay. I start work in August." I told Brian, when I first went through Khartoum, that I had agreed with the hospital to return and help out in the summer. People are on vacations, want to get rid of shifts. It was a foot in the door to the hospital, the university. Now it is a good reason to leave. I'm exhausted.

Angela and Julie are chatting with the soldier behind the bar. He is thrilled. Laurence and David start talking in French. I finish my pilsner and order another. Also flat. Cold.

Laurence leaves to use the latrine. I turn to David.

"You are leaving too," I say to him.

"Yes. As soon as I can get a flight."

"Through the South?" I ask.

"Yes, to Juba. Juba-Loki, Loki-Nairobi, Nairobi-Geneva."

"Then what?"

"Not sure. Another mission, I guess. Whatever they tell me. Maybe back here. Still no borehole."

"I see . . ."

David starts flipping the lighter, tapping it on the table. Neither of us wants to talk about work. Tap. Tap.

"Well, David, I'll make you a deal." He stops tapping. "You know how I told you one of the things that would frighten me most would be being at sea, on a sailboat hundreds of kilometers from shore, in the middle of a storm?"

"Yes, I remember. Me too."

"And I don't know if I will ever do it, but because I'm afraid, I kinda want to. Know what I mean?"

"Yes. I'm the same."

"Okay. So, if in your life, in the next ten years or twenty years, whatever, if you decide you want to sail across the ocean and want someone to do it with, I'll do it."

He shakes his head. He doesn't follow. I try again.

"If I had to sail across the ocean, and I could choose someone I thought would make good company and who I could work to solve problems with, it would be you."

He doesn't understand my meaning.

"You know. We sorted out the recubra. And the gazebo. Remember? When it was raining."

"All right," he says, hesitantly. "I'll let you know."

"I mean . . . we don't have to . . . just . . ." He looks towards Julie and Angela. "Forget it."

He stands, goes to join them. I drain my second pilsner, pick up the red lighter. Tap. Tap. Tap.

I AM LOOKING FOR my clothes in the clothes cupboard in the corner of the gazebo. It is well after dinner. The generator kicks noisily in the corner. Ah. There they are, an unfolded bunch of them.

I close the wooden door and tie it shut from storms. I place my clothes on our dinner table and start to fold.

David is gone. He left yesterday. He drove for two hours to a flooded landstrip and waited as the plane buzzed it once, twice, then banked away. Desperate, he and the driver followed in the Land Cruiser and watched it land on a drier piece of earth a few kilometers away. They tried to reach it, but a river blocked their path. They drove back and forth, but could find no place for the truck to cross. Finally, the driver stopped, David hiked up his trousers, grabbed his bag from the back, and forded the river. He arrived just in time. The driver put the car in reverse to begin the drive back to Abyei, but he was hopelessly stuck. It took him hours to get out.

Where everyone else is, I don't know. Sleeping, listening to music, sending email. Oh, there's Marco, walking back from the log tukul. He is going on his R&R soon. To Jordan.

He stepped into the kitchen to pour himself a glass of water, and is now walking towards the gazebo. He takes a chair at the end of my folding table. Smiles.

"So."

I smile back.

"So."

"The great doctor goes home soon."

"Insh'allah."

He lights a cigarette, and exhales slowly.

"Soon, Abyei will be very small to you."

"Really?"

"Like . . . poof. All these problems become not yours."

"I would be surprised if it was that easy," I say.

He shrugs.

"I am going to be worried about you guys until the next doctor gets here. I can't stop thinking about that."

"Even that will disappear. Poof."

I shake my head and sit down.

"You glad to be going on your R&R? To another Muslim country in the desert?"

He nods. "Very much."

"Aren't you going to be worried about us?"

He laughs, thinks for a second. "No." He laughs again.

"Could I have a cigarette?"

"Of course." He offers me the package.

It is rare for Marco and me to be sitting like this, just the two of us, talking. We both like each other, but we are both quiet, busy watching. I prefer writing to talking; he prefers listening. I am always moving, full of plans. He told me, during my end-of-mission evaluation, that after he arrived, he watched me for a couple of days and thought, "It seems Abyei has two coordinators."

I remember those days. I learned from them.

"Did you read the book I gave to you?" he asks.

"Um. Some of it. It was good. I have to give it back to you before you leave."

"Just put it down in my tukul."

"Hey, let's sit outside?"

"Yes."

I pull two chairs off the gazebo floor and put them in the sand. Above us, a sky dusted with stars.

"So," I say.

"So."

"This is your first mission as field co, right?"

"First. Yes."

"You were a log before?"

"Yes. Three missions or so."

"Where again?"

"Sudan, Angola, Congo."

"So why field co?"

He shrugs. "I wanted a new . . . mmm . . . challenge? To make a project work, but not only by fixing machines. It's a bigger work. Much work with people, trying to understand them, their problems, how to help them do their job."

"Are you going to do it again?"

He pauses, shuffles his chair in the sand. "I don't know. I think about this. The part I like best is the medical activities, the hospitals, the mobiles. I don't like much sitting in security meetings, or meeting with military commanders. Maybe it would be good with HIV."

"I think you're good at it. You made things calm, at least with me. It was good to have you say, 'We just do what we are doing. We make no changes unless we have to.' It was important for me and Tim to have someone tell us that."

He laughs. "It is because I am slow. I need time to think, see the situation. Maybe it changes. I take long decisions."

"I think that's good. At least it worked for me."

"Well, then, we are lucky."

The generator winds down. I glance at my watch. Ten.

"What did you do before MSF?"

"I was in school for nuclear engineer. But I stop."

"Why?"

"The first few years were good, I like very much. Just learning about the atom. But in the last two years, it was about practical, and I knew that I would be then working in a power plant or something like. I enjoy very much the theory, but I think I wouldn't enjoy much the job."

"I always want to know more about that second, that one instant from when nothing went to everything," I say.

"For me too. That's why I study."

"I think I told you. When I was in Africa last, I came here as a writer. I traveled around from country to country, writing about HIV. A blog. I learned a lot."

"You told me," he says.

"Well, I traveled through Zambia with a photographer. She was great. We worked well together, and we talked about doing it again. She said she wanted to travel around the world and take photos of different cultures dancing. I said I wanted to go looking for magic."

"Oh?"

"Yeah. I don't know if 'magic' is the right word. I mean . . . like . . . the unexplainable."

"Okay."

"Just to see if it exists. I used to think it did, but I'm not so sure any more. You know?"

Marco shrugs and butts his cigarette out. I tip back on my chair. We sit there for a while, quiet. Above us the Milky Way is bright, a smear of a thousand suns.

From nothing, everything.

10/07: interspace.

the best way to get a hedgehog out of your room is to poke him with
something blunt, like a shoe or a book. then, when he curls into a ball,
you just roll him gently from behind your trunk and out the door.

a vine that i have been watching for a few days has now crept into my
tukul, and decided, for some reason, to turn left and follow the wall.
quietly, nature would reclaim this tukul if i let it. only bats and bugs
and vines and clicking crickets. it is one of the things that gives me
some solace. if we humans don't figure it out, if we use everything
until there is nothing more to use, and slowly or suddenly join the fossil record, it's ok. there are other things besides us.

friday the 13th. that is when i fly. three days. were these the ones i
have been waiting for all this time? they seem ordinary.

i spent an hour last night looking at flights, responding to emails. at
dusk, i folded my computer into my backpack, and started home. i
quickly encountered some acquaintances from another ngo out for a
walk. i tried to talk, but could not. the words that came were jumbled
and strange. i had spent an hour in an unfamiliar interspace, pulled
from this place to place to place to place at a hundred kilobytes per
second, and it had left me dizzy and uncertain. it didn't fit well with the
cows, and the water pumps, and the women balancing buckets. after
a short, stilted conversation, i returned slowly home. by the time i arrived, i found the ground beneath my feet.

and it is still there. here. abyei's brown ground. all dust when i came in
february, cracked and shifting with the wind. now, as i look out at a
black and heavy sky, soon to be thick mud. it has changed. completely.

this is the point where i begin to wonder what i have changed. this is when you start the questioning, only now, just as the days push up against one another. you don't have today and tomorrow any more; you have lost them. in their place, TODAY and TOMORROW, too swollen to change, and you live them like a race.

so i was in the tb office today thinking about what i will leave behind. as i was balancing in the interspace, the one between here and there, then and now, one of the young tb patients walked in. she is about eight years old, and has been on treatment for two months. after the first meeting, i have not seen her parents. she comes every week on her own and always wears the same torn, overlarge black dress. she peeks around the corner, then bashfully slides into the room barefoot, and steps onto the scale. she answers my questions shyly, only with nods. when i finally place the foil packages in her hand, she skips out of the room. i adore her. so brave.

when i saw her this time, for the last time, i had this overwhelming urge to give her everything. i didn't even know what everything was, i just wanted to give it.

and i knew then that i was thinking about things the wrong way. when the plane takes off and the abyei ground falls from beneath my feet for good, the best things i will have left behind are not the ones that can be summarized on my end-of-mission report. they are the bright, beautiful parts of the day that can only be lived here. there are many. i will miss them.

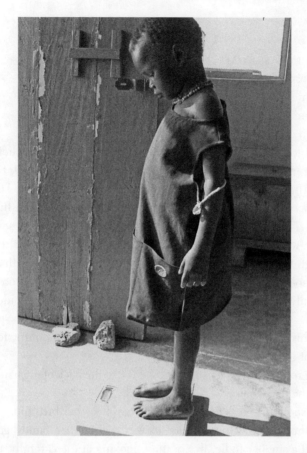

"Dr. James, hospital. channel 6."

"Hospital, go ahead."

I am on call, for the last time.

"The woman with burn is having heavy breathing, over."

"I'm coming. Over and out."

I reach to the chair beside me, feel for my headlamp, click it on, look at my watch, 00:12. I tangle through the mosquito net, take my scrubs from the rope, put them on, pick up the pharmacy keys, my stethoscope, walk to the driver, "Mustashfa," he rises from his chair sleepily blinking, gate opens rumblerumble, Land Cruiser starts gruffly, we roll past the military compound, I slam the door shut, walk through the front gates of the hospital, the nurse is there with a flashlight, no generator at night any more, too much power, gas too expensive, only candles and flashlights, mosquito nets hang like spiderwebs, spooky.

"This way," she says, shining the flashlight in front of my feet, not in front of hers.

We round the corner (the hospital is like the back of my hand), and enter the dark room.

As soon as I cross the threshold, I can hear her breathing. My instant thought, my first, before I even register her family gathered around a single candle, five of them looking at me carefully, is, she's dead.

I don't need to know any more, don't need to examine her. But I do. Maybe she can feel the bell of my stethoscope on her chest (her breathing . . . noisy . . . like marbles shaking in the hose of a vacuum cleaner . . .), or my fingers on her wrist (her pulse is fast . . . thready . . .), or my hand on her stomach (soft . . . no peritonitis . . .).

"Do you want oxygen monitor?" the nurse asks.

"No." Just her chart.

The nurse has it in her hands. I look back over this woman's hospital story, her fevers, her medicines. Oh. Here's where she came in, from days away, her perineum burned with boiling water. And here's the hemorrhage, her bed full of blood, took her to the operating room. Okay. Right. She arrested. Here's where, as I was getting my blood screened to donate, the young soldier in dark glasses who didn't know her came to the hospital and said, "I heard someone needs blood," and I saw Haj, his uncle, our oldest nurse, in Abyei for decades, beaming proudly, and the boy gave and saved her and she started to get better, and our talks of transfer grew less frequent and the antibiotics started to work and we were happy, Mohamed and I.

All that in scribbled notes, dots of vital signs, cross-hatched marks of delivered doses. There were no more medicines to try, nothing that could change the story at this point, no one who would read it after this.

I stand up, let her hand go. It lands limply by her side. I face the family.

"Malesh. She's very sick. I don't think she will live until morning."

Sepsis. I think she has sepsis. There are bacteria in her blood, dividing from one into two. The antibiotics killed millions on millions, but one became resistant and now there are simply too many.

"It's her breathing. It is too bad."

She has inhaled her own vomit, her own dinner, a glass of water. That, or she has acute respiratory distress syndrome. The bacteria make a waste, a toxic waste, and it causes capillaries to become weak, to leak. Her lungs are full of water, water mixed with proteins and salts. It will drown her.

"I'm sorry."

For her. For you. For me. Because as soon as I step off the plane, you all will collapse and I'm sorry I feel so much relief at that thought.

I leave her gasping in the room.

I walk to the nursing desk, and scribble an order on her chart.

"Furosemide," I say. Useless. "And oxygen." Useless.

"There's nothing more I can do."

Don't call me about her again.

I walk through the hospital gate. The driver is waiting, napping. I rap on the window and he starts the truck. We roll down the driveway, past the dark military compound, and home.

I walk into my tukul and look at my watch. 00:22.

WHAT TIME IS IT? Nine.

"Laurence, what time do I have to leave?"

"Eleven-thirty at the latest."

Gotta go to the hospital, say goodbye to Aweil. To the market, take some pictures, fuck the rules. Get my emails off the computer. Shit. That'll take a while. Say goodbye to Mohamed. Clean my tukul.

In a whirlwind rush, I grab my camera.

"Anthony, see you at eleven-thirty, right?"

I half jog to the hospital, 460 paces, this is it, the last time.

Stupid cannon.

"Hey, Majak . . . yeah, last day . . . nice to know you . . . okay."

Push past him. I've got all these toys Aleza sent me. Aweil.

"Hey, sweetheart. I like your new dress . . . Come here." She lurches towards me.

The spinning top. That's the best.

"Here, check it out. Pretty."

And the super bouncy ball. And the bubbles too. I sit her on my knee.

"Well, beauty. Be good. I hope you find your dad and he loves you and you go to school and have ten children and a hundred cows and you live forever. Okay? Complete survival. Don't forget." I don't want to put her down.

Oh, here are the brothers. I've got more toys. The parachute and this crooked airplane. Here.

"And this one's for your brother. No, not for you, your brother. Here, watch."

It flies crooked, too.

"Here's a little soccer ball. It rules. No, that's it. I've got to save some."

I set Aweil on the ground and spin the top. She shrieks in delight, and I hurry away, top still spinning. I do not look back.

The feeding center recubra. I've got all these glow-in-the-dark bracelets.

"Hey, moms. Hey, babies. Come here."

This little girl's my favorite. She has been in and out of here three times. So shy.

"Yeah, you. Hi, sweetie. Don't be afraid. Here. It can go on your wrist. Like this."

It looks like a piece of ordinary plastic.

"Sorry, hon. It'll make sense tonight."

What time is it? Ten. I don't know if I will see Mohamed.

"Bye, Majak. Say goodbye for me to everyone. Angela, here, take my pharmacy keys. I'll see you back at the compound."

All right. Got my camera. I should take a picture of that water pump. Been meaning to for months.

I jog to the start of the market, to the queue of girls hammering up and down on the pump handle, one-two-three, one-two-three, again.

"No, don't stop. Keep pumping . . . Oh, forget it. Come here. All of you. Yeah, see a camera. Look. That's you. See? Hey, let's all bend over it like this, look at the camera. One, two . . . Click.

"Look. It's all of us. See? You. And there's you. Look. Okay, gotta run."

I dash into the mud market. Click.

And the restaurant. Should show people that. Uh-oh.

"Oh. I'm sorry. I get it. No picture. Sorry."

Whoa. They were not happy. Must be military. Wonder which side. Lucky. Don't need trouble today. What time is it? Ten-thirty. Shit. Back to the compound.

"Anthony, we still on for eleven-thirty? All right."

Okay. I won't sweep my tukul. Gotta put my email messages on this data stick.

What time? Eleven. Shit.

"Angela. Here is my Swiss ball. Yeah, Swiss mission, Swiss ball. And here's the cement dumbbells. Yusuf says he wanted the barbell, but it's up to you. This protein powder I opened once. It's pretty awful, but not as awful as black and brown."

Eleven-fifteen.

"Anthony, you ready? I'll grab my things."

Eleven-thirty.

"Laurence, brother, goodbye. I am glad I got to know you. Good luck with the drivers and all those hard parts. I'll see you somewhere in the world.

"Julie, take care of Laurence for me. Make sure he gets the office finished. And the garden. So far it's only radishes, but you never know. If anything grows, let me know.

"Angela. Don't work so hard. Try to take a rest. You'll figure it out. If you need anything, anything, have any questions about anything or anyone, any patients or the TB program or . . . What? . . . Okay, we gotta go . . . You have my email . . . bye . . . bye . . . bye . . ."

11:35.

"Anthony, stop at compound 2."

I'll ask the guard. "Is Mohamed here?"

At the mosque.

"All right, let's go."

Mount Abyei. Tim. The market road, flooded. That's where I used to run. The road out of town. Here I am.

So green. Wow. That man, praying in the middle of a field. Beautiful.

"Shit! Anthony, give me the handset."

My travel permit. It's expired. Goddamn.

"Julie for James, Julie for James."

No fucking way.

"James, this is Laurence. Julie has gone to the market. Over."

"Laurence, I don't have a travel permit."

Silence.

"Do you copy?"

"I copy. Stand by."

"Anthony, stop the car."

I am flying south. They'll stop me at the airport.

"James, Julie is going to get one and deliver it to you at the airstrip. Do you copy?"

"I copy. Should I get on the plane without the travel permit?"

"Stand by at the airstrip. Over."

Twelve. Plane at one, forty-five minutes from Abyei. Checkstop. Waved through.

"James for Laurence."

"Go ahead."

"Julie is on her way."

Twelve-fifteen. Airstrip is quiet. A few other cars. Do I get on the plane if it comes? No. I'll bargain for more time.

People are standing up. There's the plane.

"James for Julie."

I see them. The plane lands.

"Here you go, James. Should work."

"Julie. Thank you so much. Good luck."

I board, the plane turns on its heel, and with one last look to the side, Abyei falls away.

(out)

17/07: soon, suddenly . . .

I am sitting in Khartoum's airport. For the moment, everything is life size. The crying kid next to me, the men walking to the airport mosque with prayer mats, the man smoking under the "no smoking" sign. Soon, the hatch on the KLM flight will close, the announcements will begin overhead, and the telescope will start to swivel. By the time I arrive in Europe, it will have turned completely and everything in Sudan will seem far away.

I tried to have a simple conversation with the driver on the ride here, but I couldn't manage. Every thought was short-circuited before I verbalized it, my neurons a crossed jumble of sparking wires.

So much left unwritten. There are a million things. I wanted to write about the Casio F91-W, how it is the watch for all developing world traveling needs, reliable and unglamorous.

I wanted to tell you how some of the women in the hospital, the mothers of the children in the TFC, wrote and sang a song to Laurence and Angela when I was on my R&R, wishing them strength. I wanted to describe better the team, Laurence the logistician who I would trust with my life, Marco and his calm, wise ways. All these things, untold. And many more. Alas.

In some cruel twist of fate, I already miss Abyei. How can that be? It is already strange to feel untethered, to not have responsibility in something so worthwhile.

I will write some more posts, perhaps with a different frequency, as I see how well the next places fit.

Oh, the flight boards. I just looked back over the post, and I capitalized everything for the first time. Huh.

Soon, suddenly, not Sudan.

CHAPTER IV

Wow. EVERYTHING IS FOOD.

The bus from the airport is slipping quietly down Geneva's summer streets. I am sitting in the back, dirty and unshaven, marveling. I can't take my eyes off the stores we pass.

All this stuff.

The bus angles around the corner, bending in the middle. The corrugated rubber at its swivel point bunches.

Bakery next to bakery next to convenience store.

The bus slows to a stop. The street name is called out in French, then flashed in bright electronic letters on a small billboard near me. A woman waits at the rear door. She has a walker. A young man wearing iPod earbuds helps her board, lifts her walker with one strong arm and puts it beside her.

Everything is straight, right angles.

I try to think of Abyei, and I bounce back to here, my dirty nails curled around the back of the seat in front of me, staring. My stomach turns. I need a bathroom.

An announcement in French.

This is my stop.

I pick up my two bags, red with Abyei's dust, and step past the woman with the walker, nearly knocking her with my swinging duffel. The doors hiss shut and the bus pulls away.

I'm standing on the edge of a sidewalk in the morning sun. The air is sweet and full. I am two blocks from the MSF office. I've never felt less anywhere.

I walk the final distance and pass through the sliding doors. The same woman is at the front desk, bright and cheerful. I put my bags at her feet and she looks at me and smiles. Halfway home. Halfway gone.

I point to my name on the arrivals board.

"That's me."

She hands me a stapled piece of paper. I tear it open. Times and dates.

"You are scheduled to meet with Diana at one, but Alex wants to meet with you at some point."

"Alex?" I ask.

"He's the director of communications."

"Oh. Sure. What time is it?"

Twelve.

"I can do it now. Can he?"

She calls. He can.

"I'm going to go downstairs and get a coffee. Can I have a key to the storage room?"

Bags, gray boxes. I look in North Sudan's. A package for me. From Jack. I open it. Music. A false thumb for magic tricks. I can't wait to see that guy. I shut the door and walk downstairs.

Coffee machine. I fumble in my pocket for change, plug it in. The machine whirs hot coffee. Can you fucking believe it.

I sit at a round table. To my left is someone halfway to the field getting briefed. Burma.

A tall man with a beard approaches me. I stand.

"Alex?"

"Yes. James, right?"

"That's me. Glad to meet you."

"Let me grab a coffee. We've got a lot to talk about."

"Sure."

I sit down. He turns to the machine.

Whirrr.

He returns to the table, sits, crosses his legs, crosses his arms. Frowns.

What?

"I have some concerns about your blog."

What?

"I came across it the other day."

The other day?

"And I was surprised at what I found there."

But I sent the posts before they went. I followed the rules. I thought about security. The videos were big, so I just . . . I thought I was . . . I thought you would have . . .

"It made me upset."

But MSF . . . the feedback . . . from Canada. And the U.K. You used it for fundraising.

"The video of the hospital. Shot from the hip."

It wasn't.

"The video of your last day . . . staged."

No.

"And your readers . . . a couple of medical students."

People from everywhere. Jamaica, the Philippines. People in this office. My parents, my friends.

"If we wanted an article about Abyei, or videos, we would have sent professionals."

But you didn't.

"I want you to take it down."

It was so important to me. It helped me through.

I stop him.

"Listen. I just got back. I'm sick, and I'm tired, and you're the first person I've seen, so . . . no, wait. . . . I worked hard, and if I had an hour, I sat with . . . goddamn . . . tissues under my wrists and told the story because I thought that was part of it. But now I'm done. My contract is over. So if you want to talk as two colleagues, I'm happy to do that. If not, well, I think I would rather just be alone."

He starts again. No concerns with my medical work. TB, great. Geneva. Canada. Blogs.

I sit back. My attention turns again to the table beside me. The woman who is going to Burma is leaning forward, scratching important details into her small notebook. She glances over at me once, and smiles.

Her face is open and ready.

23/07: corner.

so. it was like marco said. the sights, the noises, the days that surrounded me so completely, they collapse. they collapse, but they don't
disappear. it is as if you have shut off an old tv and all the images and
sounds are compressed into that one bright point in the middle of the
screen. incandescent, it lasts and lasts, too bright to forget.

since i last wrote you, i have left sudan and passed through geneva for
my debriefing. i am now in amsterdam, about to end my relationship
with some parasites. you have to understand, it is not them, it's me.
i'm better on my own.

the debriefing in geneva was interesting. aside from the usual talk
about objectives, accomplishments, and future plans, there was considerable discussion about my blog, and about blogs in general. there
are some who feel that they hide the slipperiest of slopes, that they
are akin to voyeurism, a commodification of the msf experience. others, like myself, are convinced that its immediacy and combinations of
media allow a story to be told in a new, powerful way and that there is
a benefit in their telling. the more first-time volunteers who understand what it is truly like in the field, the better. the more people who
know about abyei the better. perhaps what jane jacobs said of city
streets is true of dusty border towns; it is the numbers of eyes on them
that makes them safe.

i can't speak to all the merits and demerits of blogs, but i think i know
why they work well; they are personal, immediate, and available. they
make a window in the world, and when they are at their best, it is almost clean. i haven't looked back through mine yet. not quite ready.
too many little mines, memories that need to lose some of their color
before they are recalled.

I AM STANDING NEXT to another luggage carousel, sleepless, blinking. I am holding a newspaper under my arm, and am fumbling to put my SIM card into my mobile. I drop it on the floor.

Fuck.

The belt starts to turn. I click the cover back in place and turn my phone on.

I have pared my things down. They all fit in one bag. I left all my books behind, most of my clothes.

I grab my backpack from the circular parade and lean it against a white cement column. I take my phone from my pocket and call Greg. He's coming to pick me up.

"Hello."

"Bro."

"James? Holy shit. Man. Good to hear your voice. Where are you?"

"Um. At the airport. Just got in from Frankfurt. I thought . . ."

"You're here already? Really? I . . . shit . . . I'll tell you what. Let me finish this beer, and I can be there in . . . like an hour?"

An hour? Bro. I thought. You're my best. Huh.

"Um. Forget it, dude. Driving here is a hassle. I'll figure it out. I'll take the bus. I've still got some traveling left in me. It'll be cool. You know, a gentle . . . unveiling or whatever. I'll call you when I hit the market."

"You sure?"

"Definitely. No sweat."

"All right. Call me when you get downtown."

"Cool. Bye."

I put my bag flat on the floor, sit on it.

What is this place? Home? I don't know. Maybe I should have kept going. Just hung out in Europe or something, did another mission.

I stand up, grab my dusty backpack, and heft it on. I walk towards the customs office and hand the official my form: nothing to declare. He waves me through. I approach the exit, and the gray doors slide open as I draw near.

Greg is standing in a crowd of strangers wearing a mullet wig, a tight white tank top, and powder blue pants, three inches too short.

"Man, I can't believe you fell for that," he says. "I thought I blew it for sure when I said 'after I finish my beer.'"

I don't know what to say, I'm so happy. I give him a hug.

"You all right?" he asks.

"Yeah, dude. Just got all right."

"Yo, let's get out of here. People have been staring at me for like . . . an hour."

"I wonder why."

"Can I take that?" he says, pointing at my satchel.

"Hell yeah."

We walk through the airport's sliding doors.

"You sure you want a ride? Will it be enough of a slow unveiling? 'Slow unveiling.' So, you spent six months in Sudan and it turned you into an Elizabethan poet? That's what happened?"

"Fuck off."

We find his car in a row of others.

"Okay. I'm not going to ask you how it was. What I will ask you is this: wanna go to a pool party? Everyone's at the Radisson waiting for you. I've got an extra pair of trunks here, and a towel. Whaddaya say?"

I want to go back to my apartment. Sit in the dark.

"Sure."

"Cool."

We drive on the highway, watch traffic whir smoothly into traffic, then out again. Seems the same. Easy.

"Who's all gonna be there?" I ask.

"Lots of people."

"How many?"

"Dunno. It's also Jay's birthday or something."

That's better. I don't want to talk.

"Cool."

We park downstairs at the Radisson and sneak in the side door, stop to buy some cigarettes. We change in the bathroom on the main floor, then walk up to the pool deck, trying to look like guests so we don't have to pay.

I pull open the glass door and step onto the deck. My friends.

Jeff. He moves towards me.

"Bro."

Hug.

"James!"

Cooper. He dives into the pool, swims towards me, clambers out, dripping.

"Buddy."

Wet hug.

More people. Fast face. Flash. Flash. Hug. Welcome back. Flash.

"Want some of my hamburger?"

"Here, have some of this. It's a margarita or something."

"When did you get back?"

Flash. Flash. Flash. My brain is attached to an electrical wire.

I move away from the table. Jeff's still looking at me. I move to the railing that lines the pool deck, lean against it. I take out a cigarette and light it, turn around and look at the water of Lake Ontario.

Everything is in its right place, but it doesn't fit. Whatever it was before, this round thing that I was a part of, seems broken now.

Leaning against the railing doesn't get me far enough. I want to dangle.

Sailboats dot the lake, their sails puffed fat in the wind. Someone taps me on the shoulder and I turn around. Jay.

"So, dude. How was your trip?"

"Yeah. Uh. It was good. Happy birthday."

"HELLO?"

"Hello."

"Hey, Sarah."

"Welcome home."

"Thanks."

"Where are you?"

"In the market. Walking Greg's hound."

"I see. It's good to hear your voice."

"Yeah, you too."

"So . . ."

" . . ."

"I thought I would leave you to visit with everyone at the pool party. Thought it might be a bit much."

"Yeah. Thanks. It was."

"So. Glad to be back?"

"Yeah, I think so. I don't know."

"Are you sleeping?"

"No. Not really . . . Parker! Come here!"

"Sounds like you've got your hands full."

"I think he just ate a pigeon skeleton."

"Gross."

"Definitely. Except, well, at least it's a pigeon."

"Still a pigeon hater."

"Completely."

"Were there pigeons in Sudan?"

"Yup. And they look exactly the fucking same. One day the last person on earth is going to look around and say, 'Hey. It's all pigeons.' And then they'll peck his eyes out."

"That's funny."

"Yeah."

" . . ."

" . . ."

"I missed you."

"Yeah. Missed you too. Hey, thanks for the packages."

"You're welcome. I'm glad you're home."

"Glad to be home."

"I haven't heard from you for a while. Not since you were coming back from Ethiopia."

"Yeah. Sorry for that. I was kinda . . . suffering, you know? Confused. A moment of weakness, I guess."

"I told you it was okay. You could have called any time."

"Cool. Thanks."

"What are you doing after you walk the hound?"

"I'll think I'll— Parker! Come here! Can you hold on a second?"

"Sure."

" . . . "

" . . . "

"Sarah? Sorry. Um . . . I've got some stuff to do. Work tomorrow."

"Well, I was supposed to leave yesterday. I'm going to the coast for a while, but I had to delay my flight to take care of some things. I leave tomorrow."

"Oh yeah?"

"You want to get together?"

"You know what? I don't think I can. I said I would meet Scott. You know he's driving across Canada in a sno-cone truck, right? He's in town tonight and I haven't seen him for a year or so. Plus I'm kinda tired."

"I see."

"Yeah."

"Okay, James, I'll let you go."

"All right. Good to hear your voice."

"Mmm-hmm. You too."

"Enjoy the coast."

"I will."

"Bye."

"Bye."

31/08: last.

i am on another airplane, packaged into a tiny seat watching a stewardess deliver tiny packages of food. underneath us, blueblue lake superior. after an evening emergency shift, i was up early unpacking from my last trip and repacking for this one to edmonton, to see my family. i haven't been home to alberta for a long time. i miss its wide skies and flat stretching land. i find there some of the breathing room i lack in toronto. most of all, i miss my family.

this morning i left my apartment in kensington market in a flurry of jangling keys and last-minute grabs, the chaos of my hasty departure tempered by the cool certainty that neither my clothes iron nor the burner of the stove were on. in the four weeks since i have been home, i have used neither. not once.

the contrast between my life in sudan and the one here is complete. it is like someone took the grand tape loop of my life and cut out six sudan months, then glued it together again. the coming home jubilee is like the going away one was, just in the summer. my friends are the same, my job the same, my apartment the same.

am i? i can't tell. i would suspect my friends would answer yes. overbusy, always packing or unpacking, an overarching interest in frisbee. my outside is ok. inside, i don't know. i haven't taken the proper pause. there is a hard spot right here, right where paola pointed when i stood in the kitchen leaning against the dirty counter trying to neither think nor feel, and it sits there like a stone.

most of the time i think i am ok, but then i write a line or two about standing in the compound kitchen, and i can feel the trickles of sweat on the back of my neck.

i haven't been able to go back through the blog yet. i haven't looked at it, except to read the latest comments. i'm not ready to live the technicolor reality of it. but i have to. i've been given a chance to turn this into a book, and need to get started, need to find out what i have left behind.

so that's my latest and last news. i haven't told many people, and do not plan to. i don't want everyone to know. posting the news seems different.

the book will not be the blog. it will be different. the blog was a living thing, kept alive by all of us. if i took it, printed it out, and bound it, it wouldn't be the same. it would be an inanimate version: still, frustrated, lifeless.

the book will be more careful, i will have more time to write about things i had only seconds for in abyei. i am excited for it. not just for the chance to write, not just because i look forward to distilling my thoughts until they are clear, not just for the chance to unclench the spot paola pointed to in the kitchen, but also for the life that i will need for the book to happen. it will mean fewer last-minute grabs, more slowness. for now, i need to rely on this blue-seated airborne prison in order for me to pen you a letter. may this pass.

30,000 feet below, manitoba's land is bound by white gravel roads and green looping belts of rivers. i will be in alberta soon. i haven't seen my brother in forever. his wife is about to have a baby. we will play frisbee and talk about that. later, i will travel north to where my grandparents live. i have heard that my grandfather has made a map detailing every moose my family has hunted over the past 60 years. i hope to go walking with him and learn more about where i am from, so i can know better my home. and maybe for the first time since abyei, i can find some slowness. may it last.

M Y KEYS FALL OUT OF MY pocket and jangle onto the floor. I pick them up, put them into the lock. The door is already open.

"Oh yeah. My housekeeper is here. She's going to love this."

"What?" Jack asks.

"Tearing apart my stereo and throwing my records all over the floor."

"But that table is perfect for the DJ booth," Ryan says.

"Perfect," Jack says.

"Yeah. It is," I agree.

"I promise, tomorrow, after we're done cleaning up from the party, I'll help you put it all back together," Mike adds.

"Yeah, right."

We start down the hallway.

"Hey, shoes, shoes. Show some respect."

We climb the stairs.

"Helloooo. Merl? It's Dr. James."

I pass my room. Merl looks up in surprise.

"Oh, Dr. James! You startled me. I didn't expect you home," she says, holding her hand over her chest.

"Sorry. Didn't mean to. We've come to undo all of the work you've done in the spare room and leave a terrible mess behind."

"Oh, that's okay."

I look around my bedroom. The bed has been moved. My dresser too. The suitcases, once under my boxspring, are now stacked in the corner.

"I wanted this to be a surprise. I hope you're not angry," she says.

"No. It's good. I'll let you get back to it."

Weird.

I enter my other room. Someone has already moved my stereo to the floor. Thump. I watch my records slide out into a fan. We unplug the RCA cables, the power cords, leave them in a bunch.

"One, two, three." Jack and Mike lift the broad wooden table and start to carry it downstairs. As they turn the corner, a rear leg catches the wall and draws a long scratch.

"Sorry."

"Sorry."

I go back to my bedroom.

"Merl, don't worry about the spare room. I'll clean it up when I get back. It's a mess."

"Okay, Dr. James," she says sheepishly.

I haven't met her before. Only left checks. And notes. She has been helping me out since I got back, more than a month ago. She is in her forties, with peppered gray hair and long trailing earrings. She speaks with a soft Caribbean lilt. I sit down on the wooden chair in my room.

"You mentioned in one of your notes that you weren't sleeping very well, and I keep on hearing the pipes bang behin' this wall, and thought that it would be better if your head was against this one."

I nod.

"And then when I moved it, I saw all these bags under your bed. Now, Dr. James, a body can't breathe good if his bags are where he is sleeping. They make him dream about leaving."

I nod again.

"You need to make your home a sanctuary. I know where you just came back from; you were helping my people. The other James told me. He's my client too, you know."

She puts a book she had in her hand on my bed.

"Now there's something you should know about me, Dr. James. I don't just clean people's houses. I help them take care of themselves."

I don't know what to say. I haven't given myself a minute since I came back. Not one. Running, running, running. I wanted to run so much that I am worn out, huffing, exhausted, dreamless. Then this kindness, my bed from one wall to the other. For a minute, I can't really speak.

"Merl. I don't . . . um . . . I guess it's . . . uh . . . I mean, thank you."

She stands in the middle of the room, resting one arm on my frayed broom, and looking right at me. Right at me. I tell her everything.

EPILOGUE

I'M IN ABYEI. IN THE HOSPITAL.

Mohamed walks across the small hall to the operating theater and I follow him. He is trying to get the key into the lock. It always sticks.

I tap him on the shoulder. He turns around.

"Mohamed. Have you ever intubated someone before? No? Sometimes it is best to look in a dead person's mouth, to see the anatomy. In case you need to do it one day and I'm not around. Do you want . . . I mean . . . we could . . . with her . . ."

His eyes widen. He is shaking his head no. No. Of course not.

Mohamed unhooks the lock and steps inside the operating theater, a tangle of intravenous tubing in his hand. I stand there for a second, then turn around to help Antonia clean the woman's body.

The curtain that hangs in the door frame gusts with the wind, and I can see the bent legs of a man on the bed just outside.

The room is blurring.

I should make some dinner.

I'M IN A HOUSE on a northern lake. I drove up this afternoon. Today is the first day of the book. On the table beside me is everything I have brought for my weeks up here. Dried food, vegetables, coffee. A bottle of wine. A box of books. My printed blog. Snowshoes.

This morning, I packed my things into my pickup, scraped my windshield, then sat in the cab, blowing on my red hands, thinking about what Jeff had said the night before. I told him that I was nervous about this, about going through it all again.

"I mean, I've been writing a bit but . . . here and there, you know? And when I want to think about something else, I leave it. Now I've got to be alone with it."

"But that's what you said you wanted, right?"

"Yeah. It just feels big. Like I'm finally going to sit down with the elephant in the room and be, like . . . . 'Hey.'"

"That's good, though, James."

"I guess. I came back, and from the minute I did, I just filled all my time up. I'm sure everyone does the same. Things that are tough, you just put behind you. But now that I have to slow down and look around, and back, I realize that things aren't the same."

"That's interesting."

"Remember the other day? When we all went for brunch? Scott, Cooper, Ian, Simon, me, and you? I was sitting there just listening to all you guys talk shit and laugh, and I was like, wait a minute . . . what's this clear, sweet feeling . . . it feels like . . . joy. I hadn't really felt that for a long time."

"Dude. Half your book should be about coming home."

So that's what I was thinking about. The truck was warming up. I turned on the radio and put my coffee cup in its holder. I straightened up, and felt something else. A deep, quiet well. It came up from the bottom of me. The cracks in my windshield started to blur.

What?

I shook my head. Where was that from? I turned the music up. No tears in Sudan, none since. Why now? What, was I feeling sorry for myself all of a sudden? There was no reason. I shifted the truck into gear.

I drove past Toronto's fading sprawl and watched the spaces between buildings grow. Soon I was far from the city, the hills round shadows. I drove the last kilometers with a map on my steering wheel, making lefts and rights on an unbroken white palette.

It was freezing in the house. I found some firewood and stacked thin sticks on top of crushed pieces of paper, and struck a match. Soon, the fire was flapping fast, sparking. I sat down on the couch and twisted open a beer. My computer screen sat blank beside me, its cursor blinking. I looked away.

Books. A whole shelf of them. Perfect.

I took one down. Romeo Dallaire's book, *Shake Hands with the Devil*. I thumbed through it. I hadn't read the whole thing. I started, then stopped. Couldn't. Maybe while I'm up here. What was I feeling so sorry about earlier? This man . . . he saw crowds of people die. His ghostwriter. She killed herself. I think that's right. Who told me that?

I turned the book and looked at its cover. There he was, squinting under a blue beret, his face flat. I tried to imagine what it was like for him in the hot sun, sweat trickling down the back of his neck, one hand on his pistol, looking at a world beyond both his control and his imagination.

Jeff's right. It's good to be alone with this, these big feelings. The lady. The one with the umbilical cord hanging out and no IV no IV no IV. Her arm was stretched like a balloon, like a thin shiny balloon.

I put the book back on the shelf, sat down at my computer, and started to write.

Oh man. Mohamed. Did I say that to him? Really? That was me?

I leaned back in my chair.

And her husband. I pushed through the curtain and he looked at me with wide, sad eyes. The baby, his new son, crying on the bed beside us. He asked me for help. Me. Could I help him take his wife to be buried?

No. I said no, I am here on behalf of humanity, and though we have the means, most of the world feels you're too black, or too far away, or there are too many invisible borders or something, and all we have is one Land Cruiser, and we can't be a hearse and an ambulance, and I'm tired and sick and sad and her arm was like a shiny balloon and no.

When I saw him two weeks later, he smiled me a sad smile. He was sitting at the entrance to the hospital, black chunky handset in front of him. He was our guard. Our hospital guard. I didn't recognize him that night, with his new baby crying beside him. It was too dark, or I couldn't look him square in the face. I didn't know. I would have driven him myself.

Would you have? Are you sure you didn't recognize him?

The room starts to blur.

I close my computer and walk to the kitchen, take some onions and garlic from the box on the floor, chop them, then fry them on the stove. I add some peppers, some tomatoes, and leave them to cook. The house is filled with their warm smell. I put on water to boil, pour myself a glass of wine, and walk back to the living room. I shuffle through the stack of CDs next to the small stereo. Beethoven piano sonatas. Perfect. I put it on, turn towards the window.

It faces the frozen lake but it's dark and I can only see shadows. I touch the back of my hand to the clear plastic stretched across the frame. It is cold, slick with moisture. Through it, I can see the room behind and my dim reflection.

My flat face. And I'm sitting in the TB room, cutting foil pill packages.

Two. Four. Six.

I hear wailing. A chorus of it. From just around the corner.

Eight. Ten.

Angela's face appears in my peripheral vision, pressed up against the mesh window.

Fourteen.

I put the pills in a plastic bag.

"You know where *that's* from, don't you?" Her forehead is dimpled into hexagons by the wire.

I nod. I don't look up.

I know, I know. Go away.

She waits a full beat, two, then pulls away.

And I'm back here, onions in the air. The reflected room starts to blur. This time, I know what I'm sorry for. I'm sorry I didn't nod and say:

I know. I know. Come here.

I AM LYING IN BED thinking about circles. A strange winter storm has blown through and a nearby town is flooded with rain. When I went to make coffee this morning, there was no power. I stoked a fire, boiled the water there, then spent the morning writing on the remaining bars of my battery until my screen blinked black.

I left Tim in the market. We were just about to have tea, and talk about love. I was glad to see him again.

The book is a heavy, weighing thing. Up so close, it feels as big as a blue whale. I have to stand up every so often, and walk around the table thinking about how I can make it real. I want only its truth. I want to make up nothing.

I think about what I should include, and what I should leave out. Right now I am trying to see how I can bring back the little boy who had cut the tip of his finger off. I sewed it back on as best I could and he and his father came back to see me every few days for a month. After the stitches were taken out, something I did after a week, the visits were unnecessary. Still, when they asked me if they should come back, I said yes. Every three or four days, in a crowd of feverish waiting patients, I would see the boy with his wrapped finger, its gauze now black with dirt, and I would catch his father's eye. He would smile at me and I would stop whatever I was doing and wave them towards the emergency room where I would unwrap the long strip of cotton and replace it with a new one. The father would ask me, for the tenth time, how best to care for the healing wound, and I would sit down beside him and explain.

I don't know how to return to him, can't properly enunciate why this small act was among the most memorable of my encounters. The only thing I can come up with is that it held a reliable bit of kindness.

I leave him out. It's a circle. A friend of mine talked to me, after I was back, about what I had written when I was away.

"You wrote in circles. Everything looped. You need to make a straight line."

But, I said, my life was a circle there. Like here. Straight lines don't fit.

Now I'm lying in the loft of the house on the frozen lake and thinking about that. I set down the book I'm reading. It's about "time."

Maybe it's all circles. Start to finish, back at the start. Customs officer in Sudan, customs officer in Toronto. Our lives, from dust to dust.

I turn over on my side and blow the candle out. Things go black. I listen to the wet snow slide from the tin roof.

Thump.

From the beginning, to the end, then back. Big bang, big crunch. Away from that first instant, then towards it again.

I start to dream.

Or not.

I wake up. The smell of candle hangs in the air.

Or not. Maybe life is a lightning flash, where things are close enough together to allow planets to turn around suns, but it won't last. From that one thing that was everything, the universe is on a trajectory where the space between things, even specks of dust, will be so infinite that we might as well just call it nothing. From everything, nothing.

I kick my feet loose from the covers of the bed. I can feel a chill settling into the house.

Time, and the world, and life, and circles, and space, and me here, in the cold dark. So what if this tiny town gets torn apart, and with it Sudan, and with it another part of our wide world. So what.

Another lump of snow thumps loosely outside.

I can hear my heart in my ears. Past the foot of the bed I see only blackness.

Thump.

I lie for a long while. I start to think about guns. I stop. I think about things getting smaller and smaller, dividing, subdividing, cubes collapsing into themselves, and sleep starts to softly pull from the edges.

I AM STANDING in front of an audience of medical and nursing students at McGill University. Seventy or so of them are sitting in the lecture theater, and in the front row are several of my friends. I haven't had a chance to talk to them about what I saw in Abyei yet. It took me three months to mention it to the people closest to me, and when I did, I didn't know what to say. Neither did they. We talked about other things.

The people in the audience are looking away, starting to talk about other things. I am having problems with the computer. A slide has stuck. A few helpful observers are standing in front of me, pushing keys.

The topic I was asked to speak on is "Thinking outside the box," about how the practice of medicine changes in lower-resource settings, particularly that, in the absence of diagnostic and therapeutic tools, one must rely more on his clinical skills.

My intent is to dispel the notion. I want to show them that with an absence of resources, one is only more likely to get it wrong.

The slide that is stuck is the video I took as my plane touched down in Sudan for the first time. People are beginning to fidget. I wince.

I had showed them the top of the building we were sitting in, as viewed from Google Earth. I panned away, and we could see our street. Then Montreal's mountain. Then the whole city, the estuary of the St. Lawrence, the country, North America. We were so high it was dizzying. As we flew farther, I cut to a picture of the world stretched flat on a map. It was cut into pieces with yellow borders, boxes of countries. Then I showed a picture of the earth at night, taken from space, our lights scattered throughout the blackness like bright bits of mold.

"It's easier to understand without all the boxes. We can see better who we are. Where our resources lie."

We hovered over Africa's darkness for a second, then we fell, hurtling towards Sudan. A hazy shadow of a river approached, and beside it, white letters spelled "Abyei." As the satellite photos blurred, I announced:

"Welcome home."

Click.

Nothing.

Shit.

"Um. Well. You're supposed to be seeing the ground approach, like you were arriving on a plane. I . . . uh . . . took it when I was there about six months ago . . . and . . . uh . . . let's see . . ."

People are still in front of me, fiddling with the program. One by one, they shrug and go back to their seats.

I try to pick up where I left off, showing them the flat frozen pictures of Abyei's brown ground. I ask them to think about the thousand words that the half-built homes, the absence of electrical wires, cell-phone towers, and latrines tell them.

"And this is your hospital."

Click.

Nothing.

Shit.

It was the tour I took of the hospital, the one I posted on my blog, the one that garnered so much criticism from Alex in Geneva, who said it was staged, or shot from the hip, when it was neither.

It doesn't work anyway.

I want it to. I need the students to buy it. I want to bring them to that place. I want them to understand that even if we don't share space with these people, we share a time.

I have other videos I want to show them, ones I haven't shown anyone, ones that I haven't been able to look at before today.

They are of two children. One is starving and about to die. She fixes the camera lens once with her wide dull eyes, then turns away. The other is of a three-year-old boy who is breathing too fast, about fifty times per minute. With each breath, his skin sucks in and his ribs look like a Chinese lantern.

I want to ask them, "What is wrong with these pictures? Mmm-hmm. Yup. Accessory muscle use. What else? Sure. The little girl appears listless."

But then I want to ask them, "Have you ever seen a child so sick? Ever? Really? Where?"

You shared the exact same time as these ones.

I want to bring them there, to erase the distance until it is invisible and only the moment remains. If I can get them close, as near as I can without taking them there, in the hushed and conspiratorial silence that follows their arrival, I have one last question.

So what?

So what.

Tell me. What does it matter that fifteen minutes after this, the mother wrapped the body that once held her daughter and walked slowly down the hospital road, across the football field, and disappeared with her bundle into the market?

She did.

So what to you, so what to us as humans. It's possible that because you were too far to feel its ripples, it doesn't matter at all. But if I can make it seem closer, maybe you can sense that it does. Decide for yourselves what we are. Decide for me.

I never get to ask. I connect at times, and at others the eyes in the audience seem far away. I wish I had had more time to practice, I wish I had written this down. I wish I could take them, them and everyone I know, and show them that it's not what I thought, that the swiveling telescope, the mirror images upside down, the sparking wires, that disappearing bright spot, it's not about trying to reconcile two different worlds, it's about understanding that there's only one.

POSTSCRIPT

16/05:

Hi lastly,Abyei became ashes!!! yes,since Wed until now. the fighting continue between the SAF and the militia in one side,and the SPLA in the other side,the JIU are divided into SAF and the SPLA. .

in Wednesday,since 12:30 pm up to 2:00 pm,then from 2:20 pm untill the dark,we are evacuated from compound 1 in arround 7:00pm,via UN Tanker,yes,only through the tankers,they came up to CMPD1 then all inside,then to UNMIS,but the shooting never stoped. .

we slept over the night in UNMIS,then Thursday morning we evacuated from there by their helecopters to Kadugli,then this afternoon to Khartoum and Juba . . .

all the staff are physical intact,but emossionally unstable. .

nothing left from Abyei,except the mosque,which is concrete . . .

we could not take all our lagages,about half of the staff just evacuated with the clothes that they were wearing it. .

most of our computers in the office are looted,then CMPD1 and 2 are completely burnt . . .

out of 26000 inhabitant of Abyei,left less than 10 person in civilian clothes,the rest either in the bouche/forest,or wearing uniforms fighting with machine guns . . .

I will give more updates later on.

Alfred

ABYEI IS ON FIRE. War finally found that place. The people in the town have fled in the rain. I've heard since that one of our local nurses was killed.

A few civilians were left in town, trapped by the fighting. Unable to find food, they broke into the hospital pharmacy and ate the BP-5. I wish I hadn't eaten even one.

The town is on fire, and its people, some of my patients . . . Aweil. Where is she? In the rain. No.

It wasn't supposed to happen like this. We were supposed to save that place, all of us, me, you, everyone we know. We were at least going to try.

The thing you don't know is how happy she was. Once she started to smile, that day I was in Ethiopia, she rarely stopped. Now I wonder if she is tied to Rebecca's thin back, marching through the mud, or if instead of her, it's another of Rebecca's children and Aweil is sitting in the middle of a puddle, crying, people pushing past.

I look hungrily on the computer for news, to see familiar faces, to try to identify the cinders of our compound, or in the background, the hospital.

I can't.

I can't write about this any more. My thoughts are with the people huddled under tarps in the rain, with Sylvester in the hospital again, overwhelmed by war and the dead bodies and the dwindling supplies. It's time to stop writing about the world and return to it.

Good luck to you.

The beginning.

ACKNOWLEDGMENTS

THIS BOOK OWES A DEBT to many people. First, I would like to thank the dozens who commented on my blog; you not only offered me support when I needed it most but convinced my publishers that Abyei's story was one worth telling.

I would like to offer the highest arc of my gratitude to Avril Benoît and Ken Tong, both with Canada's MSF office. Their encouragement and support were unflagging, their advice golden. They are sincere champions of both humanitarianism and telling the story.

My thanks to Médecins Sans Frontières. It is an organization, of course, made of individuals. Some of them are my friends and colleagues, others my critics, but we all gather around the belief that all humans deserve to be treated humanely, no matter where they are. It is my sincere honor to be in your company. You deserve the widest support.

I am grateful to the University of Toronto, and its Division of Emergency Medicine, for allowing me the room in my career to do this important work. Thanks to Massey College for allowing me room in your basement, and to those of you who opened your doors so I could find the quiet space this book needed. To Westwood Creative Artists, my gratitude for opening the first and most important one.

To the people in my mission, thanks for being such compelling, easy characters to write about and worthwhile people to work beside.

To my family, your love and kindness have been mine for years, so too my appreciation of it.

To my friends, thank you for not asking "so how was it?" or "how is the book going?"

Lastly, to my editor, Martha Kanya-Forstner. This would not have been possible without your guidance. Thank you for understanding the book, and its author, so completely.

ABOUT THE AUTHOR

DR. JAMES MASKALYK is an assistant professor in the University of Toronto's Faculty of Medicine and a founding editor of the medical journal *Open Medicine*. He lives in Toronto.

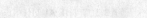

ABOUT THE TYPE

This book was set in Electra, a typeface designed for Linotype by W. A. Dwiggins, the renowned type designer (1880–1956). Electra is a fluid typeface, avoiding the contrasts of thick and thin strokes that are prevalent in most modern typefaces.